Mountain Bike Trails

North Carolina Mountains • South Carolina Upstate

Jim Parham

almond, nc

Milestone Press, P.O. Box 158, Almond, NC 28702
www.milestonepress.com

Book design by Jim Parham

All photographs by the author except as follows.
Mary Ellen Hammond: p. 1, 20, 36, 211.

Library of Congress Cataloging-in-Publication Data

Names: Parham, Jim, author
Title: Mountain bike trails : North Carolina mountains South Carolina upstate / Jim Parham.
Description: Almond, NC : Milestone Press, [2016]
Identifiers: LCCN 2016000047 | ISBN 9781889596327 (pbk. : alk. paper)
Subjects: LCSH: Mountain biking–North Carolina–Guidebooks. | Trails–North Carolina–Guidebooks. | Mountain biking–South Carolina–Guidebooks. | Trails–South–Guidebooks. | North Carolina–Guidebooks. | South Carolina–Guidebooks.
Classification: LCC GV1045.5.N752 P37 2016 | DDC 796.630975–dc23
LC record available at http://lccn.loc.gov/2016000047

Printed in Canada

This book is sold with the understanding that the author and publisher assume no legal responsibility for the completeness or accuracy of the contents of this book, nor for any damages, including injury or loss of life, incurred while attempting any of the activities or visiting any of the destinations described within it. The text is based on information available at the time of publication.

Riders in North Carolina's DuPont State Forest enjoy beautiful, well-designed trails through a lush green forest.

Table of Contents

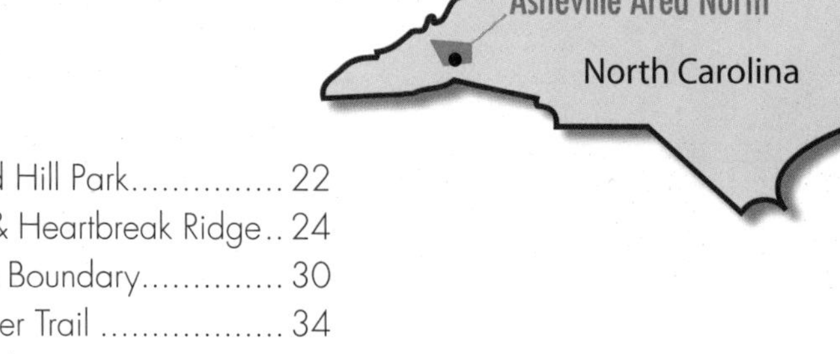

Pisgah District

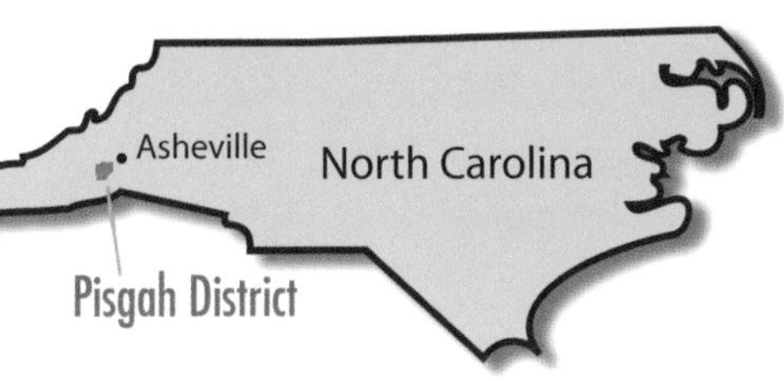

DuPont State Forest

Table of Contents (continued)

Nantahala & The Far West

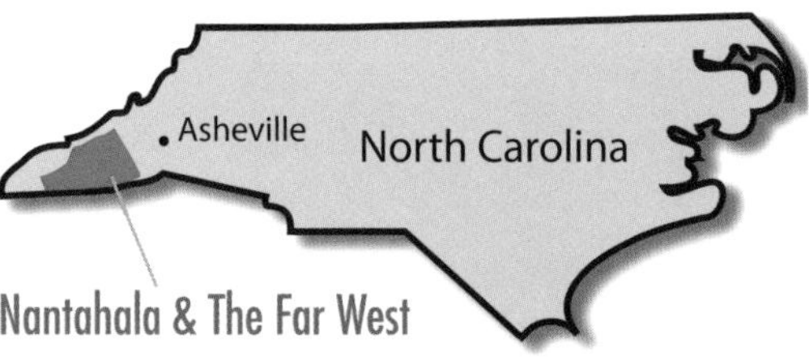

Greenville–Spartanburg

Greenville–Spartanburg

South Carolina

The Western Upstate

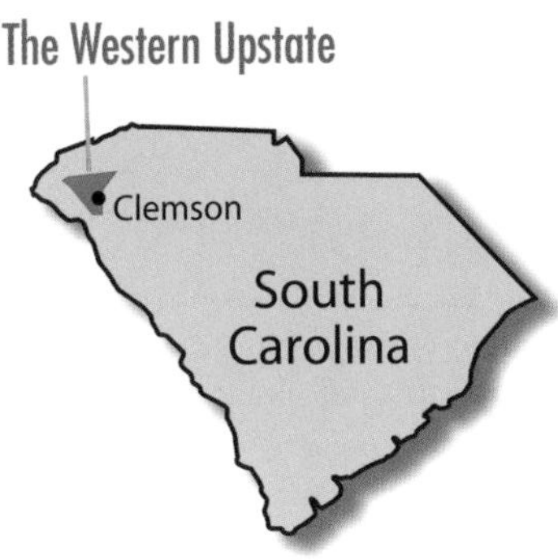

Appendices

Introduction

Welcome to mountain biking in the Carolina mountains, where rugged mountains rise to over 6,000 feet; rivers and streams are clear, cold, and sparkling; old forests are green, cool, and go on forever; and the mountain bike trails are fabulous. This huge variety of terrain and trails is exactly what your bike was made for. You'll find routes that take you to hidden waterfalls with plungepools so cold they'll take your breath away. You'll ride under canopies of giant trees and through bright coves filled with ferns and wildflowers. At clifftop views you can lose yourself in the waves of ridges that stretch to the horizon. You can then hop on your bike and roll down a mountain trail that swoops and curves all the way to the valley far below. From that very first trail experience, you may love riding here so much you'll employ nearly any means to do it more and often. That's certainly what happened to me.

Way back in the early 1990s I wrote the first guidebooks for mountain biking in the Southeast. Those original books in the *Off the Beaten Track* series covered the trails and routes for what was then a sport in its infancy. At the time, front shocks meant lowering the air pressure in your tire; toe clips were something you slid your shoes into and tightened with a strap. Though many of the trails—especially in Pisgah National Forest and at Tsali Recreation Area—have remained the same over the years, the sport itself has evolved dramatically. Ever-changing bicycles have improved in leaps and bounds, and mountain bikers are no longer considered the ugly stepchild when it comes to forest users. Today there are more riding opportunities than ever before.

This book covers the area of western North Carolina generally from Asheville to Murphy, and the Upstate of South Carolina from Spartanburg to Walhalla. Most folks refer to this region as the Carolina Mountains. From almost anywhere in the area you are never more than three hours by car from anywhere else, and it's excellent for mountain biking with lots of destinations to choose from. Many of the North Carolina trails are in the Pisgah and Nantahala National Forests. Also included is the huge trail network in DuPont State Forest and a couple of routes within Great Smoky Mountains National Park. In Upstate South Carolina, trails are found in a number of state parks, while others are within county parks and city limits. Clemson University's Experimental Forest is also home to two big networks of trails. All of the trails listed in this book are on public lands.

Off-road biking in the Carolina mountains means you're not hemmed in by the seasons. It's a rare day at any time of the year when you can't find someplace to ride your bike. Summers are typically warm, but not nearly so hot as in the hinterlands. If you're looking to cool off, head to the higher elevations found in Pisgah. Fall and spring in the mountains are ideal times to get out and ride your bike. Temperatures are pleasant and it is exciting to be in the woods when spring arrives with its abundance of wildflowers, or in the fall when the leaves put on a blazing show of color. Winter days can be the iffy-est of all, but rarely does it get so cold you can't ride. Snowfalls are sporadic, and typically when it's freezing in the North Carolina mountains it's at least ten degrees warmer down the hill in South Carolina.

The trails in this book are organized first by region and then by trailhead. Many trailheads offer access to multiple routes. Every trailhead description has a topographic map showing all the trails you'd reasonably want to ride, along with some suggested routes you might like to try. Give them all a spin or make up some new combinations. The idea is for you to have as much information at your fingertips as possible so you can go out and have a rewarding experience of your own. Most of the routes in the trailhead sections can be done in half a day or less. If you are looking for that epic all-day ride, turn to Appendix A for ideas to get you started. Alternatively, if you're new to the sport and want to be sure you begin with the easier rides, you can look to Appendix B. Finally, in the Appendix C you'll find elevation profiles for every route described in the book. They're all lined up side by side, so you can compare and contrast and further determine which might be best for you.

No matter what, make sure you do more than just flip through these pages and daydream of mountain biking adventures to come. You *can* do that, but what you really want to do is grab your bike and roll on out to the nearest trailhead—it's not far away.

Mountain Biking Guidelines

Gear Checklist

Nothing can ruin a mountain bike ride quicker than leaving something essential behind. Remember the Scout motto? Be prepared. Here's a checklist of items for most any route you choose.

Footwear

- comfortable bike shoes that fit your pedals
- woolen or synthetic socks that fit well (no cotton)

Outerwear (be prepared to add layers; no cotton anything)

- bike shorts and/or bike tights and quick-dry bike jersey
- appropriate ANSI-approved helmet
- bike gloves
- eye protection

In Your Hydration Pack

- lunch/high-energy snacks
- water (2+ liters per person); consider a water filter for epic rides
- insect repellent
- personal first-aid kit
- sunscreen and lip balm
- rain jacket (regardless of the weather)
- map and/or guidebook
- small plastic trash bag
- bike tire pump that fits your tubes
- tube patch kit
- bike repair multi-tool
- spare tubes that fit your wheels

Clothing & Fitness

Dress for comfort and the weather. Those impossibly small-looking, super-stretchy bicycling clothes hanging on the shop racks actually serve a good purpose—on a mountain bike, they are much more comfortable than regular clothing, so go ahead and splurge. They're a good investment. When heading out on a ride, the key word to remember is layers. The weather in the Carolina mountains can be fickle. A day that starts out with abundant sunshine and warm temperatures can quickly turn to cold fog or a sudden thunderstorm. No matter what the forecast, be prepared with multiple layers. A rain jacket over a long-sleeved jersey over a woolen or synthetic t-shirt, with a helmet liner or beanie to top it off, will keep you warm on the coldest riding day. If you're hot, take something off. If you're cold, put more on. You should have room in your hydration pack for everything. Usually it's your feet and hands that suffer the most when it's cold out. Beware of tight shoes, cover those fingers, and you should be fine. Remember, leave your cotton at home.

What about footwear? Mountain biking-specific shoes are not absolutely essential, but they are a very good idea. Pick a shoe you are comfortable with both on the bike *and* walking around. Unless you're a hard-core, never-get-off-the-bike racer type, you're going to want to explore on foot occasionally. Go for good traction on rocks as well as on the dirt. If the shoe fits well and feels good on the sidewalk outside the bike shop, chances are it will feel good when you're walking up to that waterfall in DuPont State Forest.

Why do I need bike gloves? Gloves serve several purposes. They give you a little extra padding while gripping your handle bars and help avoid blisters. They save your palms in the event of a crash. They keep your hands warm in colder weather. And they look good—everybody wears them.

Assess your fitness level. All the bike rides suggested in this book can be accomplished in a day or less—and sometimes much less—assuming you have an average level of mountain biking fitness. Attempting an epic ride "right off the couch" is not recommended. Before heading into the woods, assess your fitness level and choose a route that matches what you honestly think you can accomplish in the time you have available.

Safety

Getting to the Trailhead

For many of the rides in this book, getting to the trailhead is no big deal. Most parks and recreation areas have well-maintained roads and parking lots. However, there are also quite a few trailheads that can be reached only by traveling on unimproved roads. Driving a vehicle on a winding, rocky, steep mountain road is significantly different from traveling on smooth asphalt. Even if you are accustomed to gravel roads, it's a good idea to take things slowly and be extra careful. Here are some driving tips to ensure a safe and enjoyable experience.

- First of all, slow down—*really* slow down. A vehicle does not respond the same way on loose stones and dirt as it does on a paved surface. Too much speed and you'll drift dangerously to the outside of curves, where safe braking becomes impossible. Remember, the idea is to enjoy the scenery, not make time.
- Keep your eyes on the road. If you want to look at a view, stop the car in the middle of the road if you need to (as long as you're not on a blind curve) and take a look. Chances are no one is behind you, and you can move on or pull over if another vehicle comes along.
- Be prepared for washboards. Without constant grading, even the slightest uphill will eventually develop a washboard of corrugated bumps. You're most likely to encounter them on the inside of uphill curves, but they can crop up almost anywhere. Hit these with any speed at all and they can bounce you right off the road, not to mention rattling your car—and your teeth.
- Approach blind curves with caution. Some forest roads are single lanes with turnouts for passing. On a curve, keep to your side of the road and take it slow. You could meet an oncoming vehicle—and it may be a big logging truck taking up the entire road.

- Use extra caution at stream fords. Sometimes getting to the trailhead or a camping spot requires that you ford a stream. Before crossing, take a good look at what you'll be driving through. Does your vehicle have enough clearance that the undercarriage won't drag in the water? Is one side of the ford shallower than the other? Are there any obstacles in the water? Once you start across, take it slow. If the stream is in flood, don't try to cross it. This may be hillbilly country, but it's not the place to play Dukes of Hazzard. On the other side, be sure to tap your brakes a few times while you're rolling to dry them out.
- Avoid these roads altogether during inclement weather. Winter snows can turn a mountain road into a toboggan course, and day after day of heavy rains or freezing and thawing temperatures can turn a hard-packed surface into mush.
- Always fill your gas tank before heading out.

On the Trail

Safety on the trail is as much about using good common sense as it is about anything else. Basically it boils down to so many dos and don'ts, plus things to look out for. Here's a short list.

- Do let someone know your plans for the day before you go.
- Don't bike alone.
- Do dress appropriately and pack the items listed on p. 10.
- Don't start a long bike ride late in the day.
- Do keep your speed in check on steep descents.
- Don't cross a waterway in flood.
- Do carry plenty of drinking water.
- Don't drink water straight from the creek.

Things To Look Out For

It's rare to see a bear, but if you do, stand your ground.

Bears. Bears seem to be the number one thing people are afraid of encountering in the woods. In reality, the chances of meeting a bear on the trail are slim. When you do, the bear usually high-tails it for the nearest laurel thicket. Should you meet up with an aggressive bear, stand your ground. These animals can run much faster than you and they can climb trees. Make yourself look and sound as big as possible—wave your arms, shout, bang on something loud. This usually is enough to scare a bear away.

Snakes. Snakes are the second most feared thing in the woods. The chances of seeing a snake are good if you spend enough time outside. In the Carolina mountains there are two types of venomous snakes be concerned about—copperheads and rattlers (timber, pygmy, and eastern diamondback). Here again, use common sense. If you see or hear a snake on the trail, stop, assess the situation, and wait for the snake to move on or choose an alternate path around it. And no, this is not what is referred to when you hear someone say their tire was "snake-bitten." They are referring to a pinch flat.

Timber rattler. You can recognize a venomous snake by the triangular shape of its head.

Stinging Insects. There's nothing worse than bumping into a nest of angry hornets or disturbing a colony of yellow jackets or ground wasps. Such an encounter can quickly turn a peaceful ride in the mountains into a complete panic, with people jumping off their bikes and running pell-mell through the woods screaming and tearing their clothes off. Those stings can hurt like the dickens, and for anyone who is severely allergic, they can be deadly. If you have such an allergy, never ride without your epi-pen. And everyone should always be on the lookout; hornets like to build their gray, football-shaped nests over water, so be especially careful around creeks and streams.

Poison Ivy. Of all the plants in the mountains, this one seems to be the most prolific. It grows just about everywhere, but especially loves moist woodlands and areas around moving water. Basically it grows in two ways—as a vine that climbs trees, and as individual plants living in vast colonies on the ground. Wading into a patch or grabbing hold of a hairy vine poses no immediate threat, but wait about 24 hours and if you're allergic (as many people are), you'll develop a rash of intensely itchy red blisters wherever the plant touched your skin. If you've had more exposure than that, be prepared to suffer. The rash can take weeks to dry up and go away, often progressing to an oozy mess before it's gone. Should you inadvertently make contact, wash thoroughly with cold water in the nearest stream and hope for the best.

Poison ivy grows on the ground and on hairy vines that climb trees.

Crossing Streams

If the water is deep, you'll need to shoulder your bike.

When you approach a stream crossing, size it up. Is it small enough to ride across? Are there stepping-stones, and do they seem stable? How deep is the water? Can you move upstream or downstream to find a better place to cross?

If you can ride across or use stepping-stones, by all means do. Beware of crossing on logs. Sometimes a log can make for a good bridge, but it can also roll with you or break halfway across. If the rocks are super slippery, try taking off your shoes and leaving your socks on. They'll give you pretty good traction on the slippery surface. If the water is lower than your hubs, roll your bike and use it to help stabilize you. When it gets deep, you'll want to hoist your bike on your shoulder and step carefully. Finally, if the stream is in flood, don't try to cross at all.

Waterfalls

Every year people die at waterfalls, and some have died at waterfalls listed in this book. Here's what usually happens. They try to climb up the cliff or steep slope beside a waterfall to get a better view or take a picture or attempt to reach the top, and then they slip and fall. They try to peer over the edge at the top, and then they slip and fall. They try to climb the waterfall itself, and then they slip and fall. Everything near a waterfall—rocks, roots, fallen

Not all waterfalls have signs nearby to remind you of danger.

trees—is wet and slippery. If you do any of these things, it's only a matter of time before you slip and fall, too. At best you'll twist an ankle or break an arm; at worst it could be fatal. Certainly your mistake will ruin what could have been a nice bike ride for you and everyone else. Always exercise extreme caution and common sense around waterfalls.

Rules of the Trail

- Ride on open trails only
- Leave no trace
- Control your bicycle
- Always yield trail
- Never spook animals
- Plan ahead

Hunting Season

During the fall and on select dates during the spring, if you're biking in the forest there's a chance you'll run into game hunters. Most of the time, especially in small game season, this is not a problem. However, on opening day of rifle deer hunting season, around major holidays, and during bear season, it can be a big deal. On these days, in some places, it can seem that the woods are full of hunters—and you might not be comfortable with that. Regardless of whether you are or not, it's a good idea to wear bright colors in the woods during hunting seasons. For specific hunting dates in North Carolina, check the website at ncwildlife.org, or for South Carolina at dnr.sc.gov. Hunting is never allowed in state parks, county and city parks, or in Great Smoky Mountains National Park, so they are a safe bet all year long.

How To Use This Guide

Trails and routes are organized first by riding areas and then by trailhead. Within the trailhead section, information for each is subsequently broken down into different categories. You'll find a map legend on the very last page of this book, and elevation profiles for each ride in Appendix C.

- Trailhead Name
  The trailhead name appears at the top left side of the opening spread. Sometimes this is also the name of the trail you will bike on.
- Trailhead and Bike Route Data
  To the right of the photo you'll find the trailhead data. The data for individual routes is also found here when there is only one ride from the trailhead. Otherwise it is located at the beginning of each route description

  Type refers to the type of ride or rides found at this trailhead: backcountry, urban, or bike park. Backcountry rides lead you far from "civilization," usually with a destination in mind. Urban routes tend to stay in one particular area or close to town, and loop back on themselves time and time again to add mileage. Bike parks are tightly contained with jumps, banked wall turns, and many other skill-related elements.

  Parking lets you know if it's just a pulloff beside the road or a major parking lot. Limited means space for 1 to 3 cars, moderate means approximately 4 to 10 cars, and plentiful means there's lots of room for many more cars.

  Toilets tells you whether there are any at all to be expected. Yes means they are present and they flush. Portable means, well, there are some—but they might be smelly.

  Land Manager refers to the managing agency that controls the lands through which the trails cross. You can find more specifics on the land manager in Appendix F.

  Fee tells whether or not you'll have to pay a use fee or parking fee. For example, $5 means per vehicle and $3 pp means per person.

Access indicates the type of road you'll drive on to get to the trailhead.

Special Rules apply to some areas. Any such rules are listed here.

Distance is specific to the suggested route.

Surface refers to the various trails and/or roads you'll be riding on—single track, double track, forest road, pavement.

Difficulty is always subjective, depending on the area terrain and your self-assessed ability level. An trail rated easy in Pisgah is probably more difficult than one rated easy in the Greenville–Spartanburg section.

- General Information and Route Descriptions

  Following the photo and route data is a description of the various riding opportunities you'll find at this trailhead. When there are multiple route variations from a particular trailhead, this section does not contain any route directions. However, when there is only one route choice at a trailhead, general directions are given.

- Directions to the Trailhead

  Specific driving directions to the trailhead are given, usually from the closest town, along with GPS coordinates. Sometimes more than one trailhead serves the same routes. When this is the case, directions and coordinates are listed for all.

- Trailhead Locater Map

  Placed next to the trailhead directions, this gives you a clear idea of where the trailhead is and shows the route given in the text.

- Suggested Routes

  For many trailheads there are multiple routes you can put together using a variety of trails and forest roads. When this is the case, you'll find a few suggested routes to get you started. Often these are the traditional or more popular routes, but the list is by no means exhaustive. Each route has a short description of its highlights and then general directions to help you on your way.

- Route Maps

  In some cases a simple map showing the suggested route is given. You can use this in conjunction with the topographical map to help negotiate the terrain. Sometimes, when it makes sense, more than one route is shown on the simple route map. The routes are differentiated by color. Other times routes are so obvious that a simple map is not needed; you can just refer to the topo map.

- Topographical Maps

  These maps show all the trails, roads, and essential details for a particular trailhead. Often they are all you need to find a suitable ride from a trailhead.

Asheville Area North

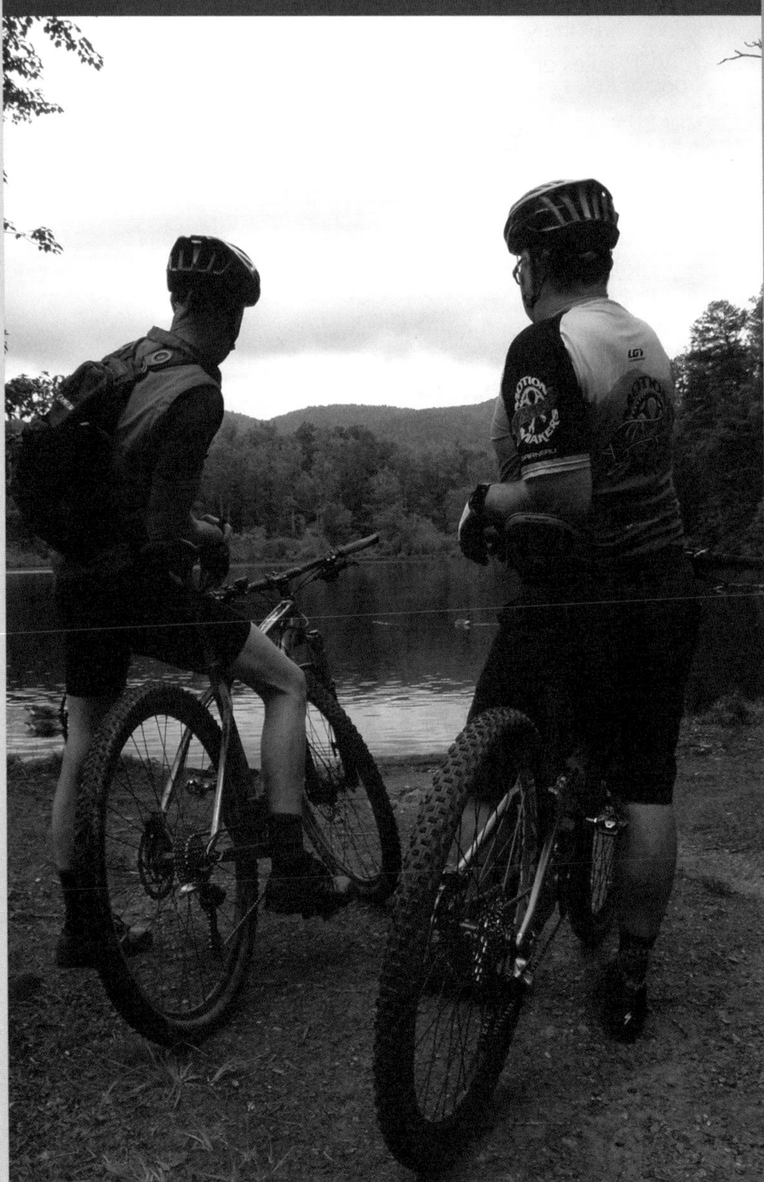

Lake Powhatan is a great place to take a break while circling many of the trails in Bent Creek just south of Asheville.

Asheville has always been a big draw for visitors to the North Carolina mountains. George Washington Vanderbilt didn't build his 1895 Biltmore Estate here for nothing. Over the years the city has transformed into an outdoor lover's dream town. With miles and miles of nearby hiking and biking trails in the Pisgah National Forest, whitewater rivers to explore, and immediate access to the Blue Ridge Parkway to name just a few, it is no wonder.

Mountain bicyclists in the area have a multitude of options for trail riding. Right downtown, above the French Broad, the local bike community has created a network of urban trails in Richmond Hill Park. Just to the east, outside Black Mountain, are the famed Kitsuma and Heartbreak Ridge trails. This is a place where epic stories are born. A half hour or so to the northeast, the downhill crowd can head to the Coleman Boundary for heart-stopping, frame-rattling fun. And about the same distance to the northwest is Laurel River Trail, where you can find a quiet spot for a summer swim. Everyone, though, will eventually head to Bent Creek. This is Asheville's trail playground and on any given day you'll find the trailheads loaded with cars. People come to hike, to run, and especially to bike. It's awesome.

If you're looking for a bike shop, you have plenty to choose from in Asheville. Everyone has his or her favorite and all are easy to get to from anywhere in town. Closest to Bent Creek are Motion Makers and Carolina Fatz, while a good number more are sprinkled around the city. Black Mountain has one shop near Kitsuma, and if you are up on Laurel River Trail you'll find a shop in Marshall. For more specific bike shop information see Appendix D.

Want to camp? There's a huge campground at Lake Powhatan in Bent Creek and free camping up at the Coleman Boundary. Looking for lodging or a restaurant? In this "Land of Sky," the sky is the limit.

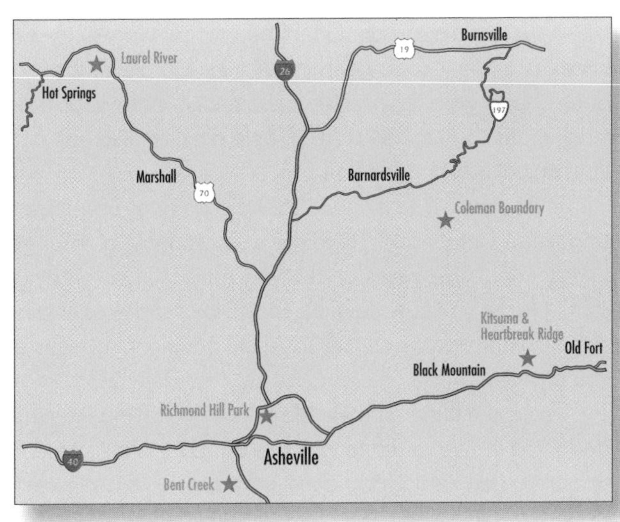

Richmond Hill Park

At Richmond Hill Park, you're either going down or grinding up.

Type	Urban
Parking	Moderate
Toilets	Portable
Land Manager	City of Asheville
Fee	None
Access	Paved road
Special Rules	None
Distance	2 to 5 miles
Surface	Single track
Difficulty	Easy/Moderate

You may be wondering why anyone would want to ride in downtown Asheville when there is such great riding in the national forest so close by, surrounding the city. It's a good question! Could be you just want to try somewhere new—or Bent Creek is a little too crowded to suit you. Whatever the reason, Richmond Hill Park does offer a good alternative for someone looking for a quick workout. You are much more likely to see more people playing disc golf on the adjacent course than actual users on the trail.

In this Asheville city park, the trails are well constructed, alternating between smooth and very rooty. There are also a couple of small boulder sections. Don't expect impressive views or anything particularly interesting to look at (though in some places you can view the French Broad across a set of railroad tracks). But since the trails twist and turn so much, you need to focus on the route in front of you anyway.

There are three different blaze colors marking the various trails. Blue blazes designate the easier route which is basically a lollipop configuration; it's least difficult to ride the lollipop counterclockwise. To do the entire outside loop, follow the yellow blazes all the way around. Red marks the connector trails.

All the trails are on the side of the hill leading down to the river. One fun way to do a ride here is to point your bike downhill and just follow your front wheel, taking whatever turn suits your fancy. As a rule, if you're rolling downhill you are heading away from the trailhead. If you're pumping hard going up, you're heading generally back to the trailhead. Connect all the trails and you'll ride close to 5 miles.

Getting to the Trailhead

Take UNC-Asheville exit 25 off I-26. Northbounders will turn left at the bottom of the exit ramp and then left at the first light. Southbounders will go straight at the traffic light at the bottom of the ramp. Either way, you end up on Riverside Drive. Go 0.5 mile and turn right, across the river on Pearson Bridge Road. After 0.3 mile take the first right onto Richmond Hill Drive. Stay on this road by turning right at the top of the hill and continuing through the neighborhood to a roundabout. Here you swing right into the Richmond Hill Park parking lot. There is a disc golf course here.

GPS Coordinates

35.618, -82.589

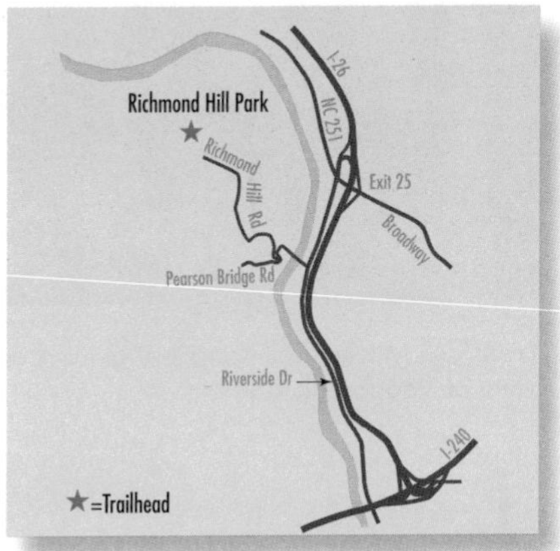

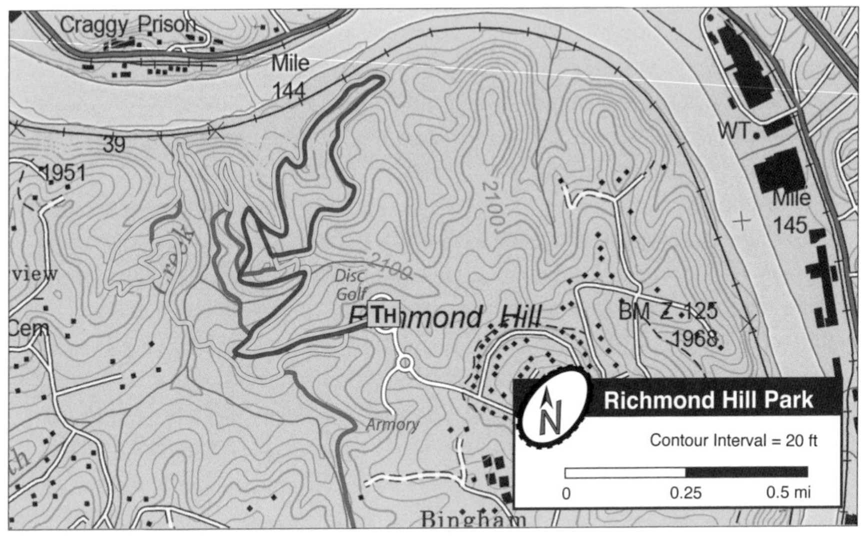

Kitsuma & Heartbreak Ridge

From Old Mitchell Toll Road you get a great view of Heartbreak Ridge.

Type	Backcountry
Parking	Limited/Plenty
Toilets	No/Yes
Land Manager	USFS
Fee	None
Access	Paved road
Special Rules	*Yes

* Check in at entrance before riding the trails on Ridgecrest property. Old Mitchell Toll Road is closed to bikes October 1 to January 1.

Just to the east of Asheville, along I-40 as it drops down the Blue Ridge Escarpment, you'll find a challenging network of trails with a reputation to match. This is the region of the famed Kitsuma and Heartbreak Ridge—both renowned for their incredible downhill runs. For local cyclists these trails are something of a rite of passage—"Have you ridden Kitsuma?" Answer yes and the next question will be "Well, what about Heartbreak Ridge?" Answer yes again and you'll get a knowing nod. You've passed the test. You are a member of the club.

Riders here have a number of options. Just off I-40 are two trailheads, one at the top of the escarpment and one at the bottom. The one up top is smallish and just down the road from Ridgecrest Conference Center. Use this one if you're short on time and don't want to continue driving down the mountain on I-40. Realize that by choosing it you are committing to finish whichever loop you ride with an uphill climb. The lower trailhead is much larger, located at the USFS Old Fort picnic area. Here you'll find pit toilets, water, picnic tables, and plenty of parking. Choose this one and you'll end whatever loop you ride with a downhill. Shuttles are also a good option if you are not into climbing. Shuttling Kitsuma is easy; drop a vehicle at Old Fort and cruise back up I-40 to Ridgecrest. Shuttling Heartbreak is a little more of a challenge. First drop a car at Old Fort and then circle up onto the Blue Ridge Parkway via NC 80. You'll find the far end of Old Mitchell Toll Road located at BRP milepost 354.7. Look for a white gate on the south side of the road.

Getting to the Trailhead

Choose from two different trailheads, one just out of Old Fort and one atop the ridge at Ridgecrest. For Ridgecrest, take I-40 exit 66 to the north side of the interstate. Turn right on Old US 70 and continue up past Ridgecrest Conference Center. At the stop sign, cross Mill Creek Road onto Royal Gorge Road and then follow it a short distance to the upper trailhead. For the lower trailhead, take exit 72 or 73 into Old Fort. Go west on US 70 and then turn right onto Mill Creek Road. After 2.5 miles, turn left into the Old Fort Picnic Area, where there is a much larger trailhead.

GPS Coordinates

Old Fort TH 35.635, -82.220
Ridgecrest TH 35.621, -82.268
Blue Ridge Parkway/Old Mitchell Toll Road 35.712, -82.275

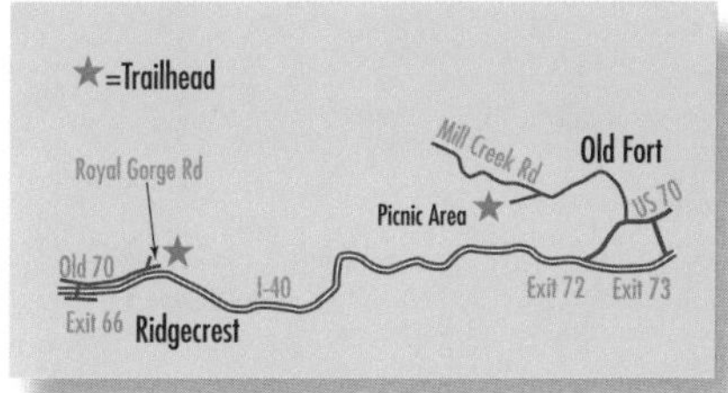

Kitsuma & Heartbreak Routes

Kitsuma

Distance 9.6 miles
Difficulty Moderate
Surface Single track, paved roads
Trailhead Ridgecrest or Old Fort

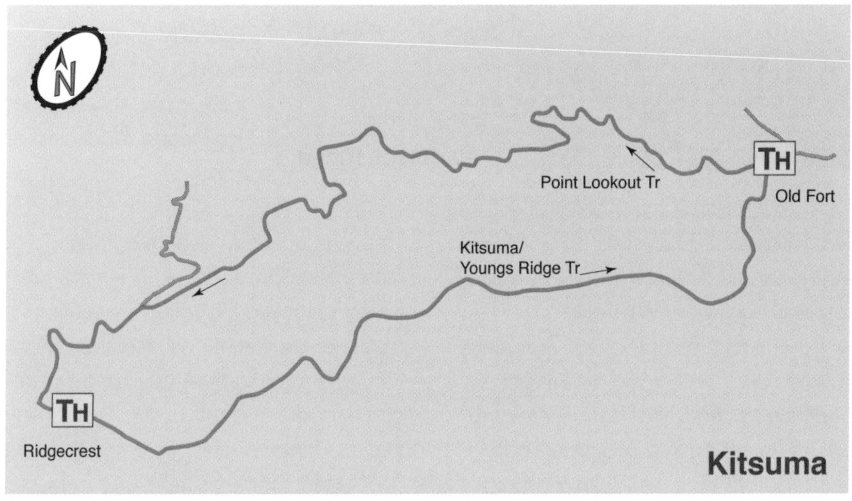

This route encompasses three trails and a road and is very straightforward. If you start at the bottom of the mountain (Old Fort), you'll begin with a climb on the paved but gated Point Lookout Trail. This road is the route US 70 took up the escarpment before I-40 was constructed. Cyclists discovered it years ago and now it is a designated bikeway, gated at both ends.

Eventually Point Lookout Trail merges into Mill Creek Road where you'll continue to climb. Just before crossing I-40, turn left on Royal Gorge Road and ride out past that trailhead onto Youngs Ridge/Kitsuma Trail. You're still climbing, and now it gets pretty steep for the next mile or so. There's a great spot with a view on the way up that you don't want to miss.

Just when you're pretty sick of all the uphill, the downhill begins. This is what you've been sweating your buns off for. From here the trail alternates between smooth and rooty and rocky. Watch for root drops, washouts, bumps, and banked turns. It's a blast—and your triceps are sure to be burning from all the braking before it's over. Until then, just hang on and enjoy the ride.

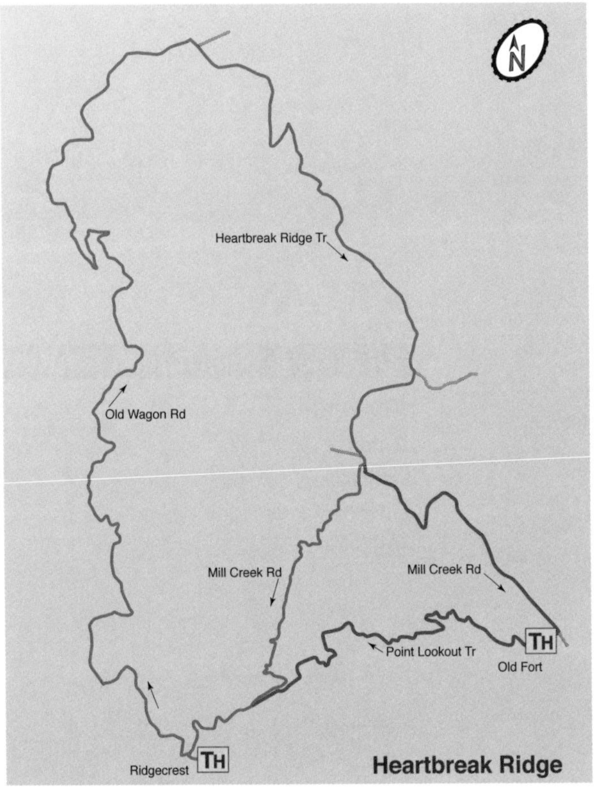

Heartbreak Ridge

Distance 21+ miles
Difficulty Extreme
Surface Single/double track, gravel/paved roads
Trailheads Ridgecrest or Old Fort

This is an epic ride and one of the more difficult in this book. A number of things factor into this rating—elevation, distance, remoteness, wilderness navigation, and route surface. The lowest point of the route is a good 3,000 feet lower than the highest, with an overall gain of 4,300 feet for the entire circuit. In fact, elevation may be the biggest factor in the difficulty. That's a lot of climbing and a lot of descending. And some of the downhills are pretty darn steep.

Much of the first half of the ride is on the abandoned and dirt Old Mitchell Toll Road. Way back when, someone had the idea to charge folks to drive to the top of Mt. Mitchell, the highest mountain in the east. So don't complain about the climb and the rough road; at least you don't have to pay. But partway up, you may be wishing for an alternate means of transport.

Once at the top you'll be near the Blue Ridge Parkway and could continue on up to the top of Mt. Mitchell, but that'd be a different ride. On this route, you'll swing over to Heartbreak Ridge for the descent. It's a beautiful downhill (in more ways than one) and one of the best single track descents in the eastern United States.

Begin the ride from either the Old Fort or Ridgecrest trailhead. Starting from Ridgecrest means you'll have less climbing to start the day, but will finish with a climb when your legs are toast. Start from Old Fort, and the continuous climb at the beginning is longer—you choose. Either way, ride to the entrance of Ridgecrest Conference Center and let them know at the gate that you'd like to ride up their trails to the Old Mitchell Toll Road. Once through the gate, follow the signs up West Ridge Drive toward the tennis courts. You can then take either Rattlesnake Trail or Adventure Trail up to the "toll road." Be ready to climb and don't be ashamed if you have to get off and push at times. What is that pounding noise? It's probably your heart, which is now located between your ears.

Once at Old Mitchell Toll Road, turn right. The grade relaxes substantially and you'll find that the "road" alternates between single track and double track until you reach the Montreat property. Here it becomes more roadlike after passing through a gate.

Climb. Climb. Climb. Soon you'll pass through a bear hunters' camp and be able to take breaks at a number of vantage points. The closest ridgeline to your east is Heartbreak Ridge. Imagine yourself riding down it. Soon enough you will be.

After passing through Pot Cove (there is a pot hanging from a tree here—go figure), the road becomes very rocky. At times it may feel like you are riding up a creekbed. No worries, just keep climbing. You've still got a long way to go.

Finally, after what seems like forever, you'll reach an area where several old abandoned-looking camper trailers are parked. Look for an unmarked trail here splitting off to the right; this is a turn you do not want to miss. (Old Mitchell Toll Road continues to the Blue Ridge Parkway. You'd come in this way if you were going to shuttle the downhill on Heartbreak Ridge.) On this ride, turn right at the trailers on that unmarked trail and head down the hill. Be forewarned and forearmed—the next stretch is very steep, washed out in places, and full of loose rock. Fortunately it doesn't last too long.

After bottoming out of the crazy downhill, the trail climbs back up the ridge a bit before leveling off. Just ahead is the beginning of the Heartbreak Ridge Trail (yellow blazes). Turn right onto it and head down the mountain. The descent starts off pretty steep and loose, but before long it settles into a wonderful ride. The views are out of this world. Behind you is Mt. Mitchell, to your right is the mountain you rode up earlier, and to your left is ridge after ridge along the edge of the Blue Ridge Escarpment. At times the trail goes back up to take you over a knob, but for the most part, you'll steadily descend toward the valley far below.

Eventually you will reach a junction with Star Gap Trail. Turn right here and continue down through a set of challenging switchbacks. They're a hoot—and bring you down to a wet creek crossing where you bear left and continue down to some railroad tracks. Climb up and over these and onto the old road on the other side. A short while later you'll come out onto a paved road. This is Graphite Road; turn left.

At the junction of Mill Creek Road, you have a choice. If you started at Ridgecrest, turn right. You've got about 4 miles still to go and much of it is gradual uphill on alternating paved and gravel road. If you started at Old Fort Picnic Area trailhead, turn left. It's about 3 miles more to your finish and it's all downhill.

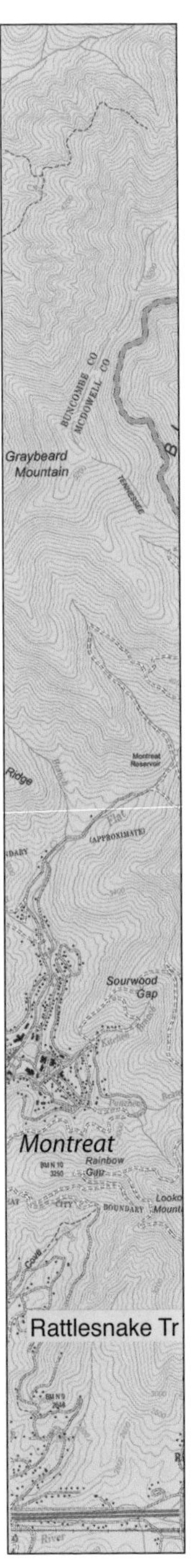

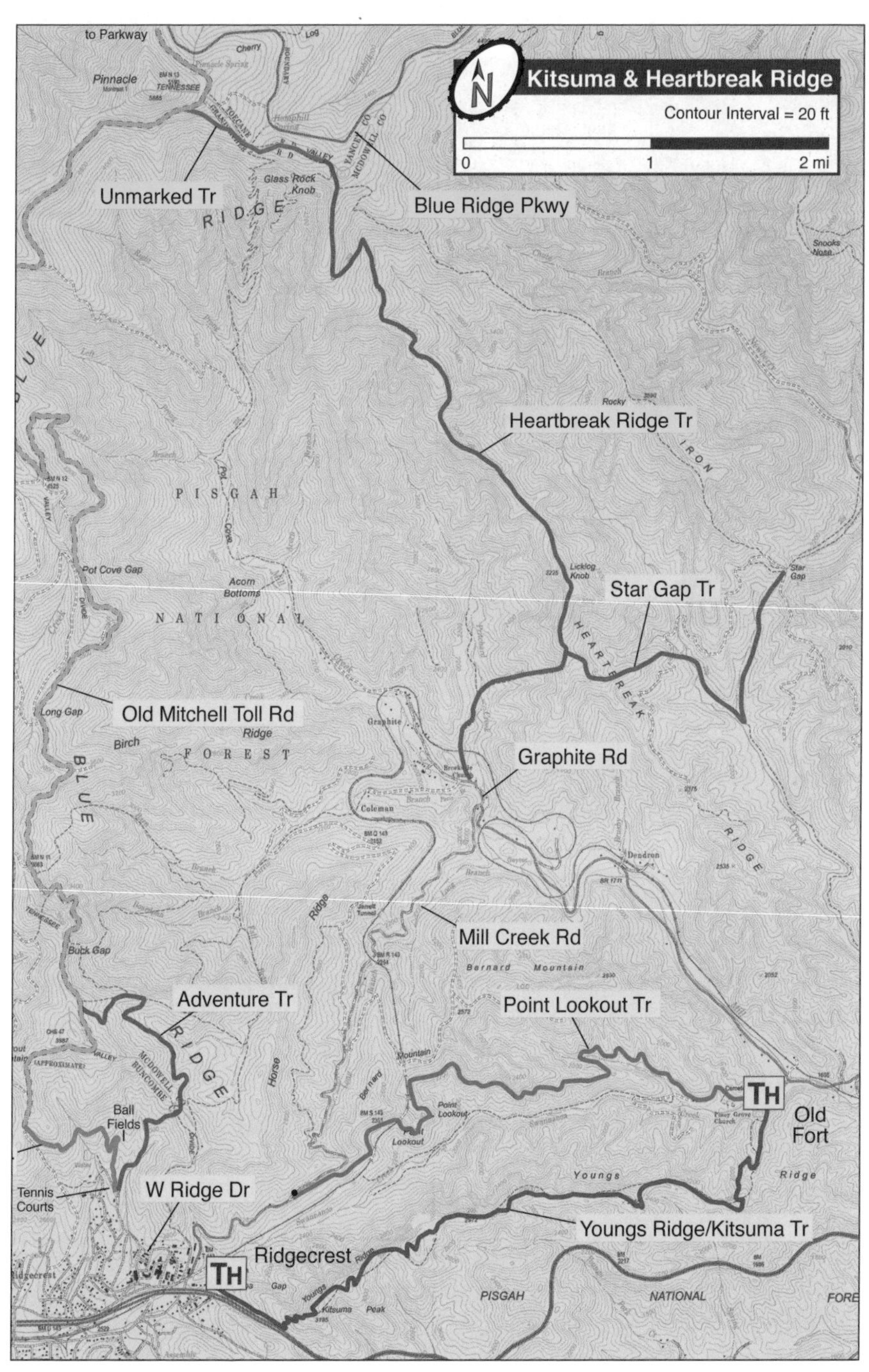
Kitsuma & Heartbreak Ridge
Contour Interval = 20 ft
0
1
2 mi
to Parkway
Unmarked Tr
Blue Ridge Pkwy
Heartbreak Ridge Tr
Star Gap Tr
Old Mitchell Toll Rd
Graphite Rd
Mill Creek Rd
Adventure Tr
Point Lookout Tr
Ball Fields
Tennis Courts
W Ridge Dr
TH
Old Fort
Youngs Ridge/Kitsuma Tr
Ridgecrest
TH

Coleman Boundary

Walker Falls makes a good place to start any of the loop rides at Coleman Boundary.

Type	Backcountry
Parking	Plenty/Limited
Toilets	No
Land Manager	USFS
Fee	None
Access	Gravel road
Special Rules	No

Think of the Coleman Boundary as a big piece of pie. You *can* eat the whole thing at once, but that might be a bit greedy. Or, you can eat it one slice at a time. Yes, that might be a better way.

Many of the riders coming to this area are coming for one thing—the bodacious downhills. The hills are steep, they're rocky, they're tire-flatteners and bike breakers. Those folks with the big-tired, full-suspension, low-seated bikes, sporting elbow and knee pads and full-face helmets love it here. They can shuttle up from the lower trailhead in the backs of their pickup trucks and bomb down the trails all day long. Yee-haw!

Look twice, though; Coleman Boundary has more to offer than that. There are a few routes here that will be of interest to the backcountry cyclists as well. To get started, you'll need to begin most rides on FS 74. This lightly traveled gravel road climbs first up and over Andy Ridge and then up and over Walker Ridge before coming to an end on Bullhead Ridge. It is a beautiful road which passes below a sheer cliff wall and several waterfalls, and the occasional views to the west are stunning. If you start at the Corner Rock trailhead, down at the bottom, know you've got a long climb ahead and the two trail choices for your descent are pretty crazy. If you want, you can skip out on both the big climb and the crazy downhill by driving on up the road a bit farther. There are no more designated trailheads on FS 74, but there is more than one convenient pulloff that makes for a good place to leave your car. Probably the most scenic is the one right at the base of Walker Falls. From here you can hop on your bike and continue out FS 74 to begin your ride.

If you are looking to spend more than a day at Coleman Boundary or want to camp out before or after your ride, there are a number of dispersed-use camping areas located along FS 74. You'll pass a few on the initial climb up Andy Ridge and then several more along the road both before and after Walker Creek Falls. All are available on a first come, first served basis.

Getting to the Trailhead

The drive out through Big Ivy to the Coleman Boundary is beautiful. From I-26, north of Asheville, take exit 15 and head east on NC 197. In the hamlet of Barnardsville, turn right on Dillingham Road and follow it for 5.0 miles until the pavement ends and the road name changes to FS 74. In just a short distance look for a dirt road turning to the right; follow it and turn left into the parking area for the Corner Rock trailhead. To get to Walker Falls, continue up FS 74 for another 4.2 miles. There is a small pulloff just past the waterfall on the left.

GPS Coordinates

Corner Rock TH 35.758, -82.380
Walker Falls TH 35.755, -82.354

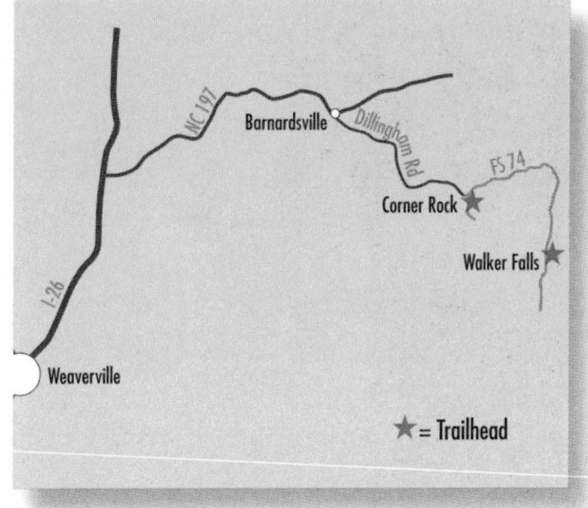

Coleman Boundary Routes

Laurel Gap

Distance 12.5 miles
Difficulty Moderate
Surface Single/double track, forest roads
Trailhead Walker Falls

This is a great loop that's mostly fairly easy riding. The only difficult stretch is the northern end of the loop where you drop down Little Andy Trail. This short section is very steep and rocky; even walking down it with your bike is a bit of a trick. All the rest is either gravel forest road or gated double track.

Start at Walker Falls and continue out FS 74. You'll ride up and over the spine of Walker Ridge, but no worries, it's pretty easy going. At 3.5 miles you'll turn left on Laurel Gap Trail. This is actually a gated road that has been seeded and is now grassy double track with a gravel base. The trail climbs gently for a good while, then descends just as gently as you undulate along Walker Ridge and Andy Ridge. Occasionally you'll get views off to the right of Little Butt and Big Butt Knobs. You'll also pass the turnoffs for Bear Pen Trail and Perkins Trail, either of which can take you (very steeply) back down to FS 74 if you prefer a shorter ride.

After 7.0 miles along Laurel Gap Trail, the double track comes to an abrupt end. Just before this, look for Little Andy Trail cutting off to the left. It's your best bet for returning to FS 74—a steep but ridable half-mile down. Should you decide to continue off the end of Laurel Gap double track, know that the single track that follows is steeper and longer, and will drop you onto a lower portion of FS 74 than Little Andy does. Once on FS 74, it's a pleasant ride back to your car at the falls.

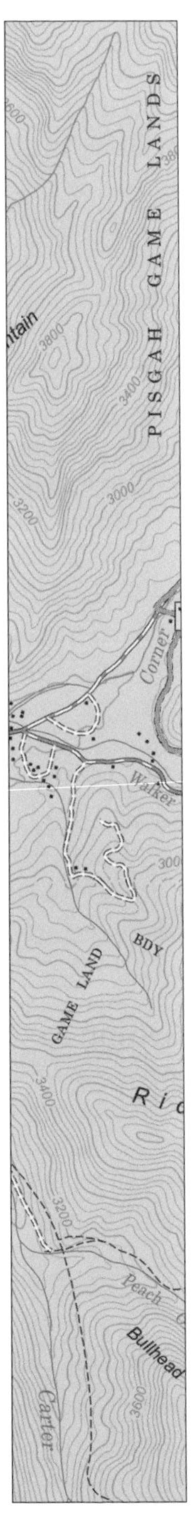

Downhill Routes

Distance 2 to 10 miles
Difficulty Difficult
Surface Single track, forest road
Trailheads Corner Rock

If you're into steep, rocky downhills, you've got a number of trails and routes to choose from here. For the least amount of climbing and/or road riding, you'll want to shuttle or take turns with someone driving you up FS 74 to where either Walker Creek Trail or Staire Creek Trail exits downhill on the right. Just hop on your bike and tear down the mountain for a mile or so until you bottom out at a small parking area, then ride the road down to Corner Rock.

To get the longer downhill runs, you'll have to do a bit more work. Shuttle or get dropped at the junction of FS 74 and Laurel Gap Trail. It's 2.0 miles on Laurel Gap Trail to the turn for Bear Pen Trail and another 2.5 miles farther to Perkins Trail. You can bomb down either of these to FS 74, cross it, and then continue on down to Corner Rock. Have fun, but be careful of your body and your bike, and always be on the lookout for someone coming up.

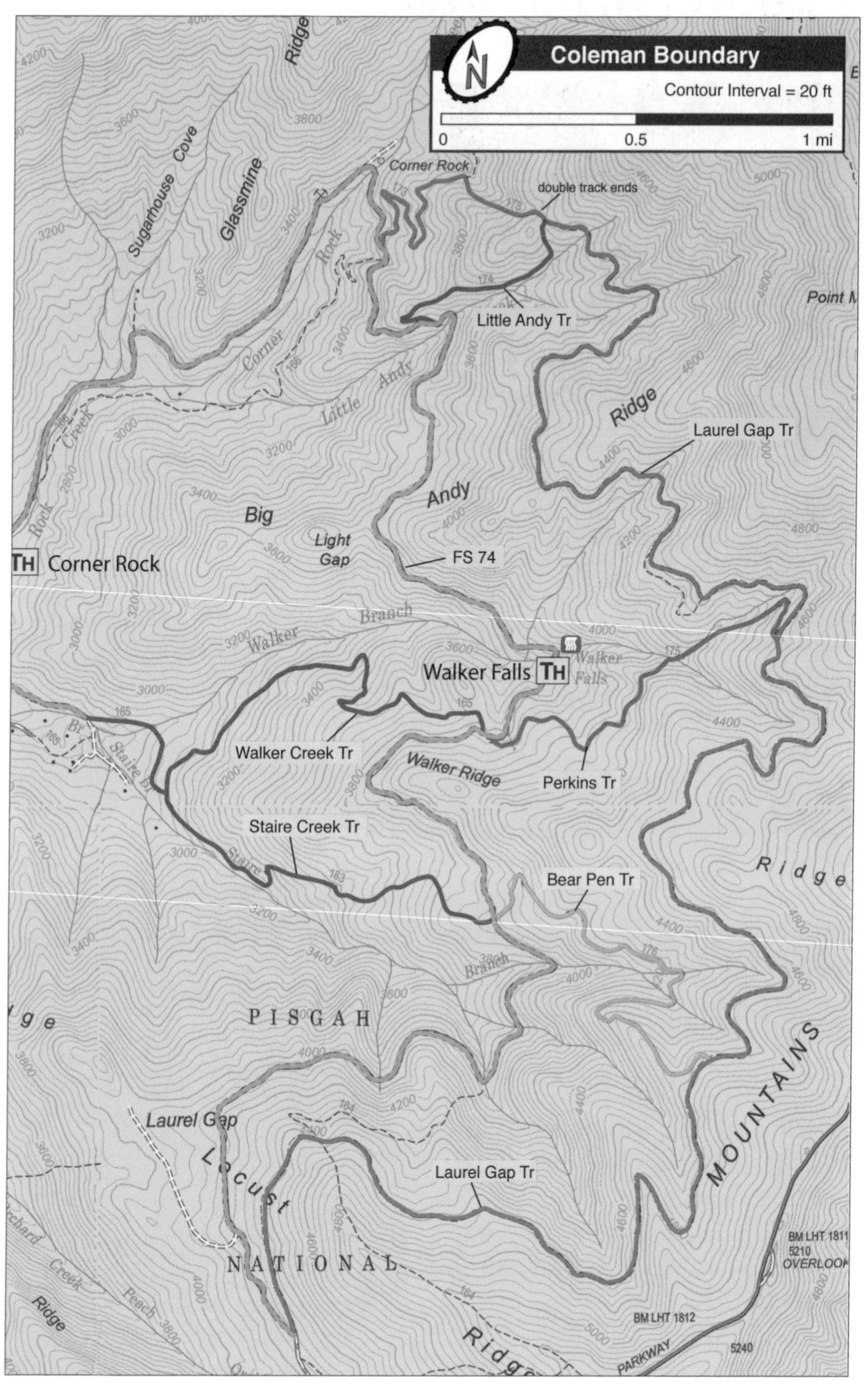

Coleman Boundary
Contour Interval = 20 ft
0
0.5
1 mi
Corner Rock
double track ends
Little Andy Tr
Laurel Gap Tr
Ridge
Andy
Big
Light Gap
FS 74
Corner Rock
Walker Falls
Walker Creek Tr
Walker Ridge
Perkins Tr
Staire Creek Tr
Bear Pen Tr
Sugarhouse Cove
Glassmine
Point M
PISGAH
Laurel Gap
Locust
NATIONAL
Laurel Gap Tr
MOUNTAINS
BM LHT 1811
5210
OVERLOOK
BM LHT 1812
PARKWAY
5240

Laurel River Trail

The quiet trail meanders alongside the turbulent Laurel River.

Type	Backcountry
Parking	Moderate
Toilets	None
Land Manager	USFS
Fee	None
Access	Paved road
Special Rules	None
Distance	7.8 miles
Difficulty	Moderate
Surface	Single track

Laurel River Trail has a reputation for being rocky and rooty. Parts of it certainly are, but much more of it is smooth as can be—and along the entire route the views of the rapids and pools of Big Laurel Creek are awesome. After 3.5 miles in the gorge, you bounce out at the wide French Broad River. What a contrast! Pick a hot day for this ride and plan to swim. You'll find plenty of swimming holes; one is huge, right below a big rapid, and has several rope swings to choose from.

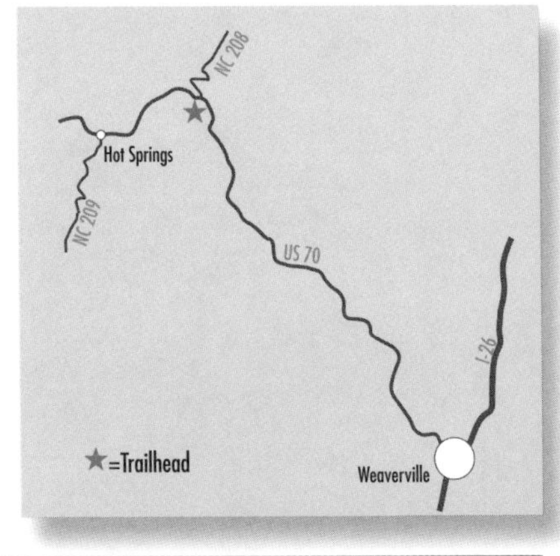

Getting to the Trailhead

From I-26 in Weaverville take US 70 west toward Hot Springs. Drive about 20 miles and the trailhead is on the left, just before the junction with NC 208 where the road crosses the Laurel River.

GPS Coordinates

35.913, -82.757

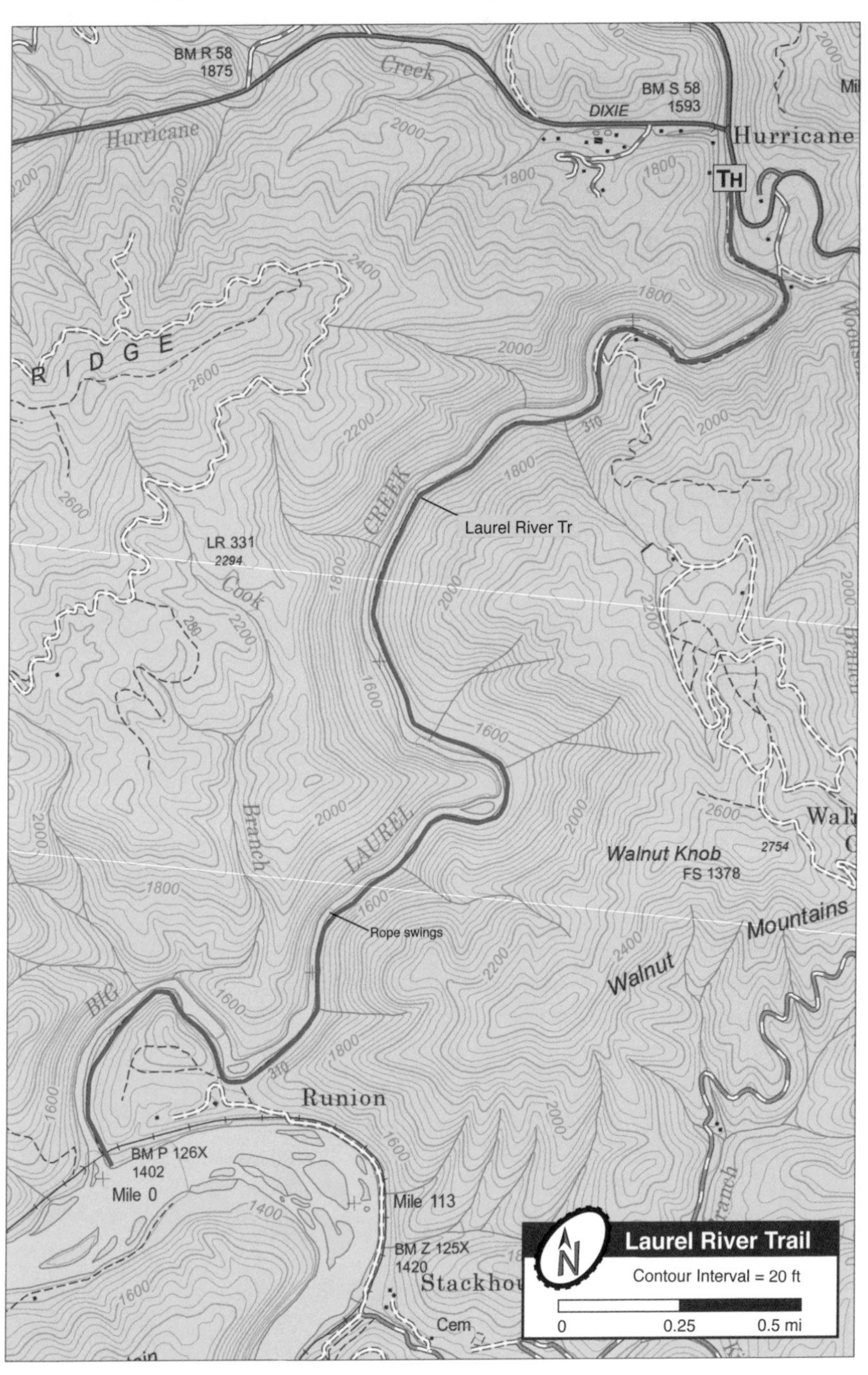

BM R 58
1875
Creek
BM S 58
1593
DIXIE
Hurricane
Hurricane
TH
RIDGE
CREEK
Laurel River Tr
LR 331
2294
Cook
Branch
LAUREL
Walnut Knob
FS 1378
2754
Walnut
Mountains
Rope swings
BIG
Runion
BM P 126X
1402
Mile 0
Mile 113
BM Z 125X
1420
Stackhou
Cem
Laurel River Trail
Contour Interval = 20 ft
0
0.25
0.5 mi

Bent Creek

Deer Lake Lodge Trail connects Ledford Branch to Rice Pinnacle.

Type	Backcountry
Parking	Plentiful
Toilets	Yes
Land Manager	USFS
Fee	None
Access	Paved road
Special Rules	None

Welcome to Bent Creek, Asheville's outdoor sports playground. It's a rare day that you won't find at least one car in one of its numerous parking lots. On nice days at any time of the year you'll see the overflow spilling out onto the adjoining roadways.

Most of the trail users at Bent Creek are split between hikers and bicyclists, but expect to see trail runners, horseback riders, birders, and (in season) hunters, too. On the east side is the North Carolina Arboretum, where native plants and wildflowers are propagated in their natural environment. You can ride your bike right along Bent Creek inside the Arboretum. To the south is the Blue Ridge Parkway, which separates Bent Creek from the rest of the Pisgah District of Pisgah National Forest. Right smack dab in the middle of Bent Creek is Lake Powhatan Recreation Area. There's a large Forest Service campground here and the lake itself, which has a good swimming beach.

Mountain biking at Bent Creek is fabulous. With 25-plus miles of trails and almost as many miles of gated forest roads, there is plenty of room for exploration. The trails are well maintained and well marked with blazes and signs, and there are plenty of choices for all ability levels. Taking your kids out for their first trail ride? Head for Hardtimes Trailhead and roll out onto the trail beside Bent Creek and into the Arboretum. Want a challenging hill-climb followed by a heart-stopping descent with big-air berms? Make your way up to Green's Lick Trail.

Getting to the Trailhead

From NC 191 in southwest Asheville, take Bent Creek Ranch Road, just north of the entrance to the North Carolina Arboretum and the Blue Ridge Parkway. Follow the signs for Lake Powhatan. The road becomes FS 479 and turns to gravel just past the Lake Powhatan Recreation Area entrance. All trailheads are located just off this road. Their GPS coordinates are listed in the order you come to them.

GPS Coordinates

Rice Pinnacle 35.496, -82.615
Hardtimes 35.487, -82.624
Ledford 35.490, -82.628

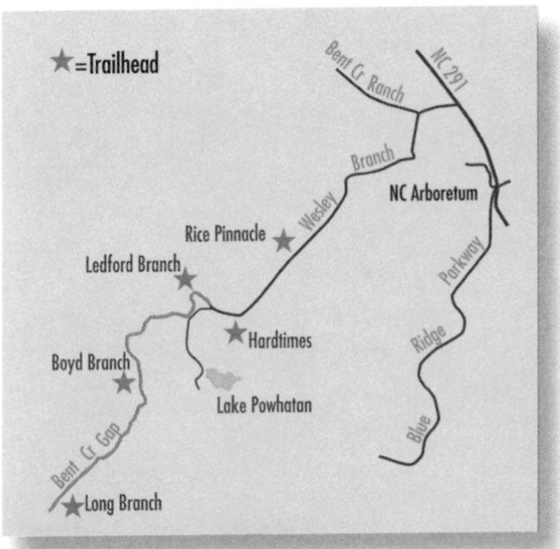

Bent Creek Routes

Hardtimes–Arboretum

Distance 6 miles
Difficulty Easy
Surface Forest roads
Trailhead Hardtimes

For most cyclists, the name of this route does not denote its nature; it's none too hard. You'll start out riding along meandering Bent Creek as it flows into the arboretum. Spring rides when flowers are in bloom are particularly enjoyable. The route then climbs up Hardtimes Road along the same spine as the Blue Ridge Parkway. You'll pass a spring (look for the pipe sticking out of the side of the hill) and get a great view of the Asheville skyline. Enjoy the downhill finish.

Rice Pinnacle–Ledford

Distance 4.8 miles
Difficulty Easy
Surface Single track, forest road
Trailhead Rice Pinnacle or Ledford

The bulk of this ride is on forest roads, which makes it easier, especially the initial climb. Here the descent is on forest road as well, so if you don't care for those dodgy, bumpy downhills, this route is for you. You'll finish up on a section of single track that roughly parallels the road.

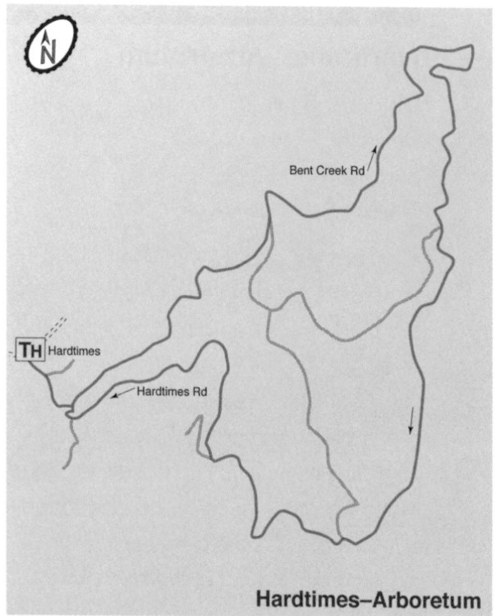

forest. If you're observant, you'll spot plantings of different tree species in different parts of the woods. Some are to attract wildlife while others are selected based on their timber potential. If it's a hot day, you might want to allow time for a swim in the lake at the conclusion of your ride.

Deerfield–Explorer–Pine Tree

Distance 6.8 miles
Difficulty Moderate
Surface Single/double track
Trailhead Hardtimes or Ledford

On these trails you'll stick to the lower elevations of Bent Creek. As they are the closest to the campground, you're likely to see more users during the camping seasons. Nevertheless they make for good riding on this fun loop, with some great single track sections. Early on you'll enjoy the views across Lake Powhatan. Once out on the Deerfield, Pine Tree, and Explorer Loops you can look for interpretive signs describing various aspects of the forest. Note that Bent Creek is an experimental

South Ridge

Distance 11 miles
Difficulty Moderate
Surface Single track, forest road
Trailhead Hardtimes or Ledford

A long, steady forest road climb sets the mood for the first 7 miles of this ride. Your route parallels the Blue Ridge Parkway as it climbs up and away from the French

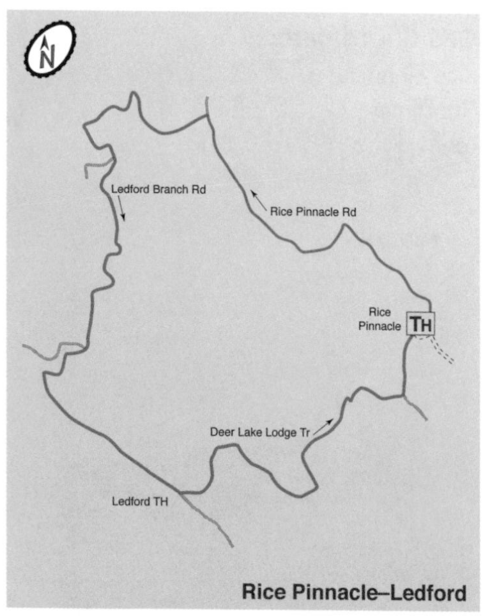

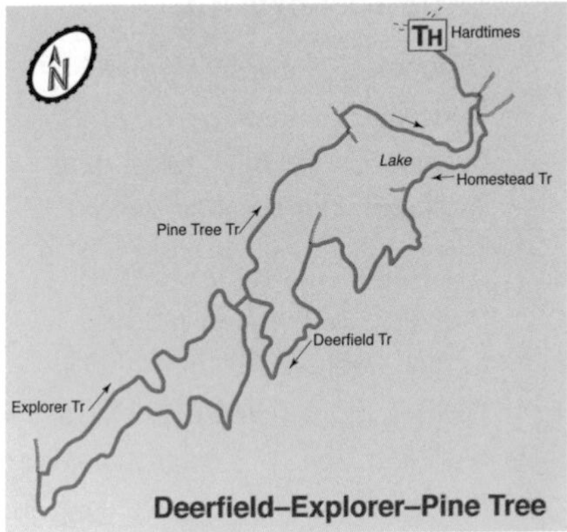

Broad river. When the leaves are off the trees, expect continuous but broken views across the Bent Creek watershed and back to the northeast towards Asheville. You'll also enjoy the big sweeping turns as the road snakes in and out of various coves where small streams rush down the mountain. Listen for the hiccuping pulses of water as it belches out of the pipes passing under the road.

Once at the head of the valley the character of the ride changes considerably. Here, you'll hop over to Lower Sidehill Trail. Maneuvering over logs, rocks, and roots and twisting through the trees on single track has quite a different feel from spinning along on a wide forest road. It's great fun, and for the most part you'll be heading downhill as you work your way through the lower reaches of the Bent Creek valley.

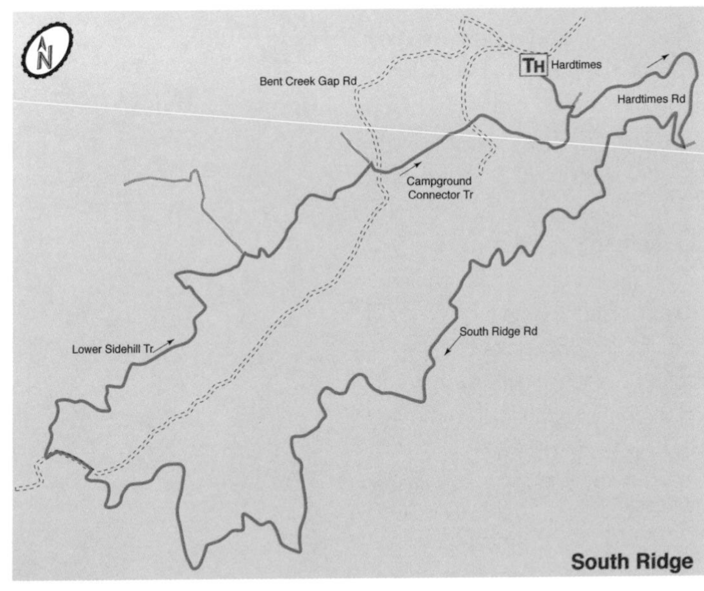

North Boundary

Distance 9 miles
Difficulty Moderate
Surface Single track/forest road
Trailhead Ledford or Hardtimes

No matter how you slice it, to get to the northern boundary of Bent Creek you've got to ride uphill. This route helps spread out that uphill pain to make it more bearable. Some folks enjoy riding up mountain trails, but here you'll ride uphill on a forest road and down on a single track trail. You'll top out on North

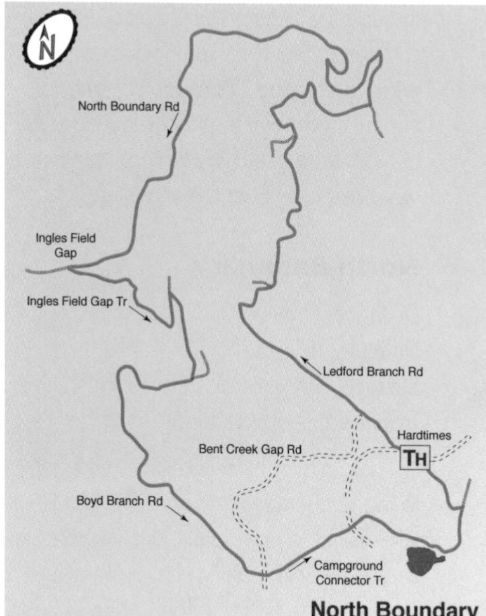

Little Hickory Top

Distance 7.7 miles
Difficulty Moderate
Surface Single track, forest road
Trailhead Hardtimes or Ledford

Want to test your downhill prowess, but not quite ready to tackle Green's Lick? Think of Little Hickory Top as Green's Lick's younger sibling. The uphill's the same, but the descent is tamer.

You'll start out by climbing up Ledford Branch Road (FS 479E) to Ledford Gap. Then work your way up to Ingles Field Gap by taking first FS 479F, then Ingles Field Gap Connector Trail and finally Ingles Field Gap Trail proper. From the gap, head downhill on Little Hickory Trail. This is an awesome trail, relatively

Boundary Road at Ingles Field Gap where five trails/roads converge; make sure to take the correct trail.

Swing hard back to the left on Ingles Field Gap Trail to begin your descent. Keep an eye out for the first right turn onto Ingles Field Gap Connector. It's pretty sweet downhill all the way to Boyd Branch Road (FS 479F) where you'll hang a right. Don't get so carried away that you forget to look out for folks on their way up! From the gate on FS 479F, cross FS 479 and take Campground Connector Trail to Lake Powhatan, skirt the lake, and head back up to Hardtimes trailhead.

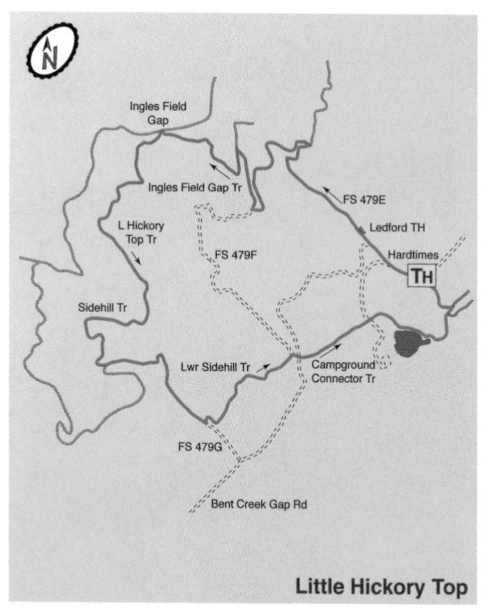

free of rocks and roots. Jump off onto Lower Sidehill Trail and then onto Laurel Branch Road (FS 479G) to continue the descent. Be careful while speeding along the road not to miss the left turn onto Lower Sidehill. Follow Campground Connector Trail to Lake Powhatan. Before you know it, you'll find yourself back near Hardtimes trailhead—that is, if you didn't skip over to Explorer and Pine Tree Trails to extend the ride.

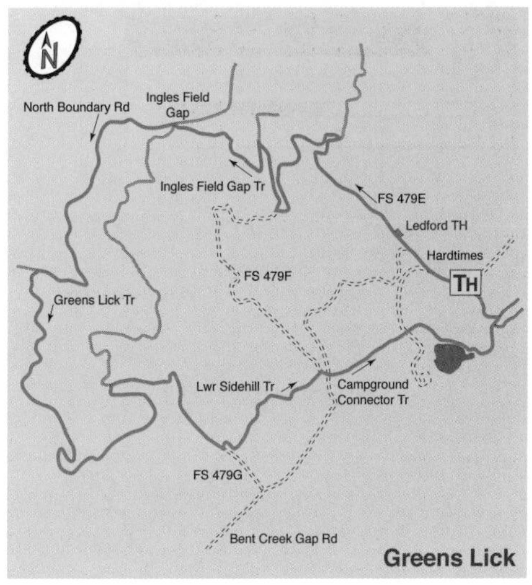

Green's Lick

Distance 8.8 miles
Difficulty Difficult
Surface Single track, forest road
Trailhead Hardtimes or Ledford

"Have you ridden Green's Lick?" If you have not heard that question, you've not talked to enough people who ride at Bent Creek. This is by far the area's most famous trail. Be wary of who you talk to, though. If they've got that sort of crazed look in their eye you'll hear tales of big air and epic crashes. They'll have you believing cyclists frequently find themselves hanging high in the trees after an exceptionally large berm. It's great stuff—or terrifying, depending on your point of view. Well, some of it is true and some of it is exaggerated, *and* you can't make up tales of your own until you've ridden it yourself.

From the trailhead, head up Ledford Branch Road (FS 479E) to Ledford Gap, take a slight jog to the left on FS 479F, then go right onto Ingles Field Connector to Ingles Field Gap Trail. Once at Ingles Field Gap, go straight over onto North Boundary Road (which is more single track than road here) to continue up. A little more than a mile of continued climbing brings you to Green's Lick Trail where the real fun begins. Tighten that helmet strap, lower your seat, check your brakes, and turn it down the mountain.

Eventually you'll end up at the head of Laurel Branch Road. Continue down on Laurel Branch to make a left on Lower Sidehill. Connect it to Campground Connector Trail, skirt the edge of Lake Powhatan, and finally loop back up to Hardtimes trailhead. And make sure you formulate your Green's Lick story well before you get there.

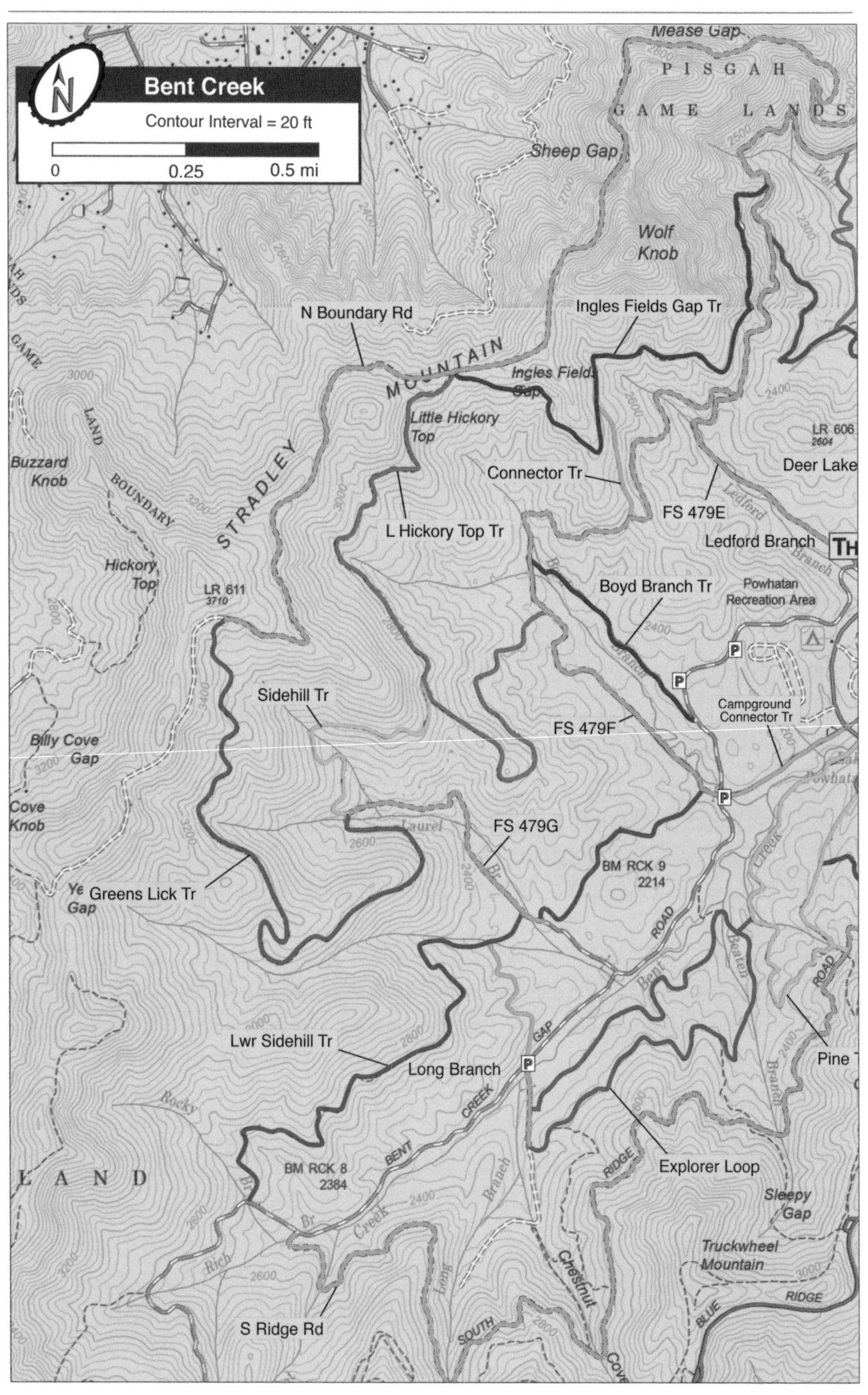
Bent Creek
Contour Interval = 20 ft
0
0.25
0.5 mi
Mease Gap
PISGAH
GAME LANDS
Sheep Gap
Wolf Knob
N Boundary Rd
Ingles Fields Gap Tr
STRADLEY MOUNTAIN
Ingles Fields Gap
Little Hickory Top
LR 606
2604
Deer Lake
Buzzard Knob
LAND BOUNDARY
Connector Tr
FS 479E
L Hickory Top Tr
Ledford Branch
TH
Hickory Top
LR 611
3710
Boyd Branch Tr
Powhatan Recreation Area
Sidehill Tr
Campground Connector Tr
FS 479F
Billy Cove Gap
Cove Knob
FS 479G
BM RCK 9
2214
Greens Lick Tr
Lwr Sidehill Tr
Long Branch
Pine
LAND
BM RCK 8
2384
BENT CREEK GAP ROAD
Explorer Loop
Sleepy Gap
Truckwheel Mountain
BLUE RIDGE
S Ridge Rd
SOUTH
Chestnut
Cove

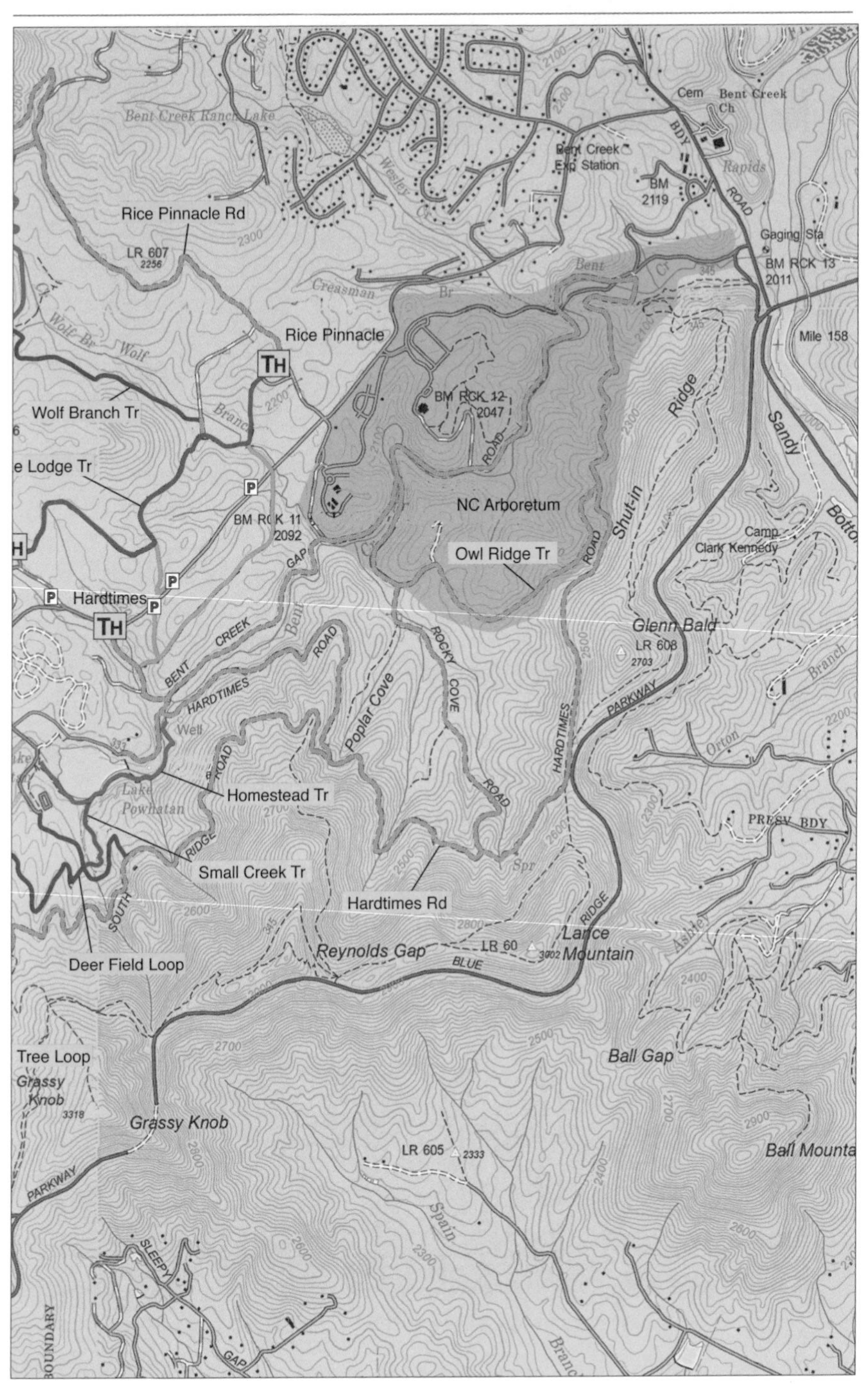

Rice Pinnacle Rd
LR 607
Rice Pinnacle
Wolf Branch Tr
e Lodge Tr
BM RCK 11
2092
Hardtimes
Cem
Bent Creek Ch
Bent Creek Exp Station
BM 2119
Gaging Sta
BM RCK 13
2011
Mile 158
BM RCK 12
2047
NC Arboretum
Owl Ridge Tr
Shut-in Ridge
Camp Clark Kennedy
Glenn Bald
LR 608
2703
Homestead Tr
Small Creek Tr
Hardtimes Rd
Poplar Cove
Lake Powhatan
Reynolds Gap
LR 60
3002
Lance Mountain
Deer Field Loop
Tree Loop
Grassy Knob
3318
Grassy Knob
Ball Gap
Ball Mounta
LR 605
2333

Pisgah District

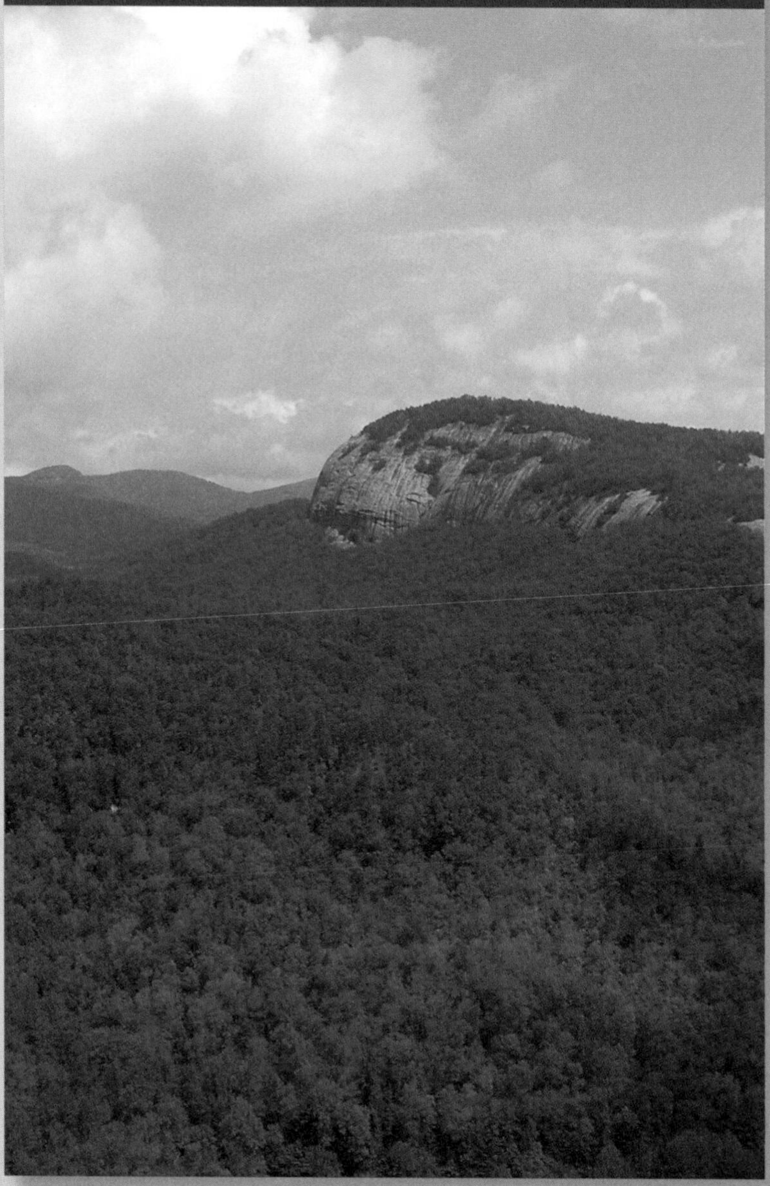

Looking Glass Rock stands like a sentinel in the heart of the Pisgah District.

Nowhere else in the Southeast will you find such a large number of mountain bike trails in such close geographic proximity. The Pisgah District of Pisgah National Forest has over 350 miles of single track trails open to bike use. Add those to the miles and miles of gated forest roads and you've got a lot of territory to explore. You'll find plenty of excitement out there. The locals call the area "the land of waterfalls," and many of the rides listed here take you past more than one.

Once you get out of your car and on your bike, it won't take you long to figure out that these trails are pretty tough. The trails of the Pisgah District are generally more difficult than most other riding destinations in the Southeast. This is mainly due to the rugged terrain and the differences in elevation. Trails around the Ranger Station begin at around 2,000 feet. Those up close to the Blue Ridge Parkway are close to 6,000 feet. In general, these trails were developed many years before the advent of mountain bikes; an uphill route that would dictate a switchback elsewhere is likely to point straight up around here. It's a national forest, so there are plenty of rocks and roots to dodge as well. Keep all that in mind when looking at the difficulty ratings.

If you are looking for lodging, places to stay are plenty. Campers will find two USFS-developed campgrounds: Davidson River Campground near the entrance in Pisgah Forest and North Mills Campground located on the east side, north of Mills River. Free camping options are also plentiful. Along FS 475B, 477, and 1206 there are numerous dispersed-use sites to choose from. Just be aware they get snapped up quickly on weekends and holidays. For the closest lodging, look first in Brevard, the closest real town. There are good eats in Brevard and also in Pisgah Forest.

Bike shops are excellent and close by; there are two just outside the national forest entrance in the town of Pisgah Forest and both offer rentals as well as repairs and merchandise. See Appendix D for bike shop details. Farther afield is Hendersonville and of course, Asheville.

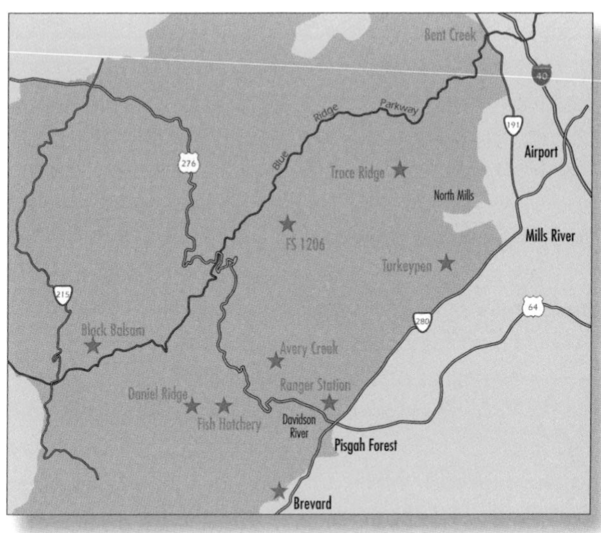

Ranger Station

Sycamore Cove Trail travels through fern-filled glades.

Type	Backcountry
Parking	Plentiful
Toilets	Yes
Land Manager	USFS
Fee	None
Access	Paved road
Special Rules	*Yes

* Seasonal trails can be ridden between October 15 and April 15 only.

If this is your first time riding in the Pisgah District of the Pisgah National Forest, your first stop should be the district ranger station and visitors center. This place holds a wealth of information. Workers staff the desk during the day, ready to answer questions and offer advice. They can tip you off about any closed trails and recommend a good place to camp. They even have a small store where you can pick up guidebooks (like this one), maps, t-shirts, and more. You'll find large restrooms with flush toilets, and spigots outside where you can top off your water containers. And be sure to check the kiosk featuring a large trails map of Pisgah and current forest alerts.

The ranger station has all the above amenities, and several rides leave from there or near there, but when you park, it's best to leave your car at the Black Mountain trailhead (see *Getting to the Trailhead*, below). This trailhead is the southern terminus of Black Mountain Trail, which begins near the Pink Beds and is one of Pisgah's longer trails. It's also the best access point for the Thrift Cove and Sycamore Cove loop rides. In addition, it provides access to North Slope Trail (a seasonal trail), which is across the highway and above Davidson River Campground. You can base much longer rides from Black Mountain trailhead as well;

FS 477 is just up the road and allows you to access Black Mountain Trail much farther up for a big loop.

You'll quickly learn that all these trails are favorite haunts of local bikers living in nearby Brevard and Pisgah Forest. There are bike and outfitter shops just down the road and they also typically send visitors to these nearby trails.

Getting to the Trailhead

You'll find the Black Mountain trailhead parking lot located on the east side of US 276, just south of the Pisgah Ranger Station and Visitors Center.

GPS Coordinates

35.283, -82.721

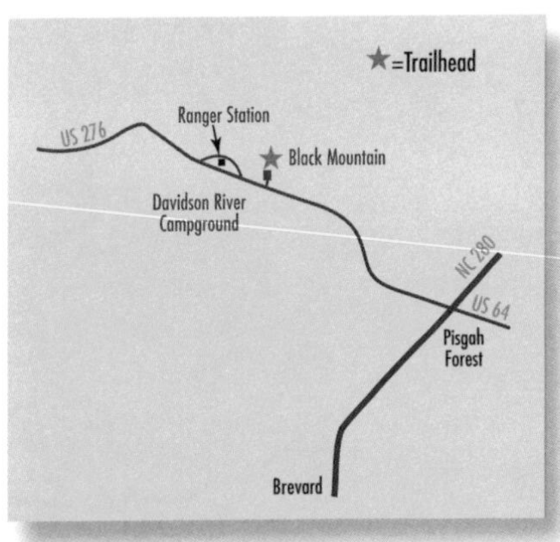

Ranger Station Routes

Thrift Cove

Distance 4 miles
Difficulty Moderate
Surface Single track
Trailhead Black Mountain

The Thrift Cove loop is an excellent introduction to riding in Pisgah, featuring many of the elements that make the area such a magnet for cyclists. The great thing is that it's fairly short, allowing you to try your Pisgah wings, so to speak, before committing to one of those all-day death marches.

The route starts out with a classic abandoned-forest-road-turned-single-track climb. Don't worry, it is very gradual. You can even push some of those bigger gears at times. At the head of the cove, you'll turn back down along Thrift Branch on the tail end of Black Mountain Trail. Then things get interesting. It's a fast descent, but don't get carried away. Smooth single track can quickly lead into a rocky jumble or a series of jumps that you might not be expecting. Some turns are banked and there are a few fun wall rides—one leading right onto a bridge. Soon enough, you'll be back at the trail-head with time to spare for another ride.

Sycamore Cove Loop

Distance 5 miles
Difficulty Moderate
Surface Single track, pavement
Trailhead Black Mountain

This is the first trail you come to as you enter Pisgah National Forest from the town of Pisgah Forest; its southern end represents one of the lowest elevations in the forest. The best way to do this loop and keep the time spent on US 276 to a minimum is this. Begin as if you are riding the Thrift Cove Loop. After just a few tenths of a mile, take the second right at the top of the hill to turn onto Grass Road Trail. Follow Grass Road all the way around until it dumps you out on Sycamore Cove Trail. Take a left. Now you'll highside Sycamore Cove all the way down to US 276. Take a right here, follow the highway briefly, then jump back down on the other end of Sycamore Cove Trail.

Back on Sycamore Cove, you'll ride briefly through the bottom land. In summer this area is filled with fluorescent green ferns. After crossing the creek, be sure not to miss the hard left that leads uphill to the Thrift Cove Trail; you've been here before. The trailhead is just down the hill to the left or, if you've got the time, take a right and circle Thrift Cove for an all-out ride.

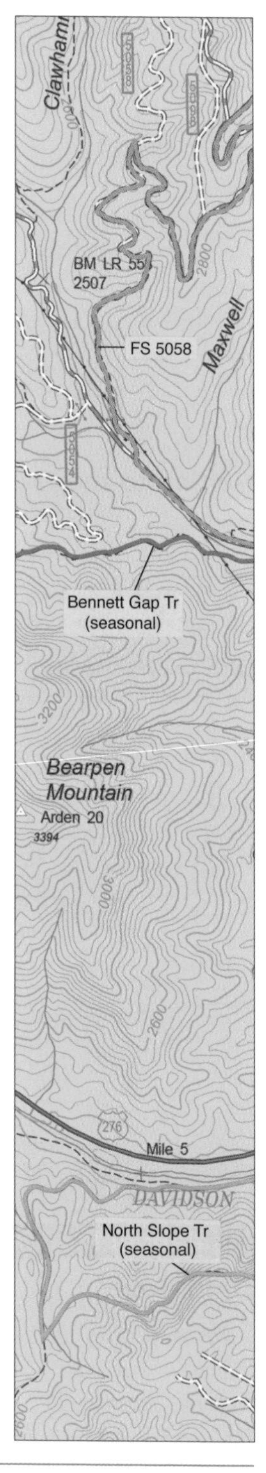

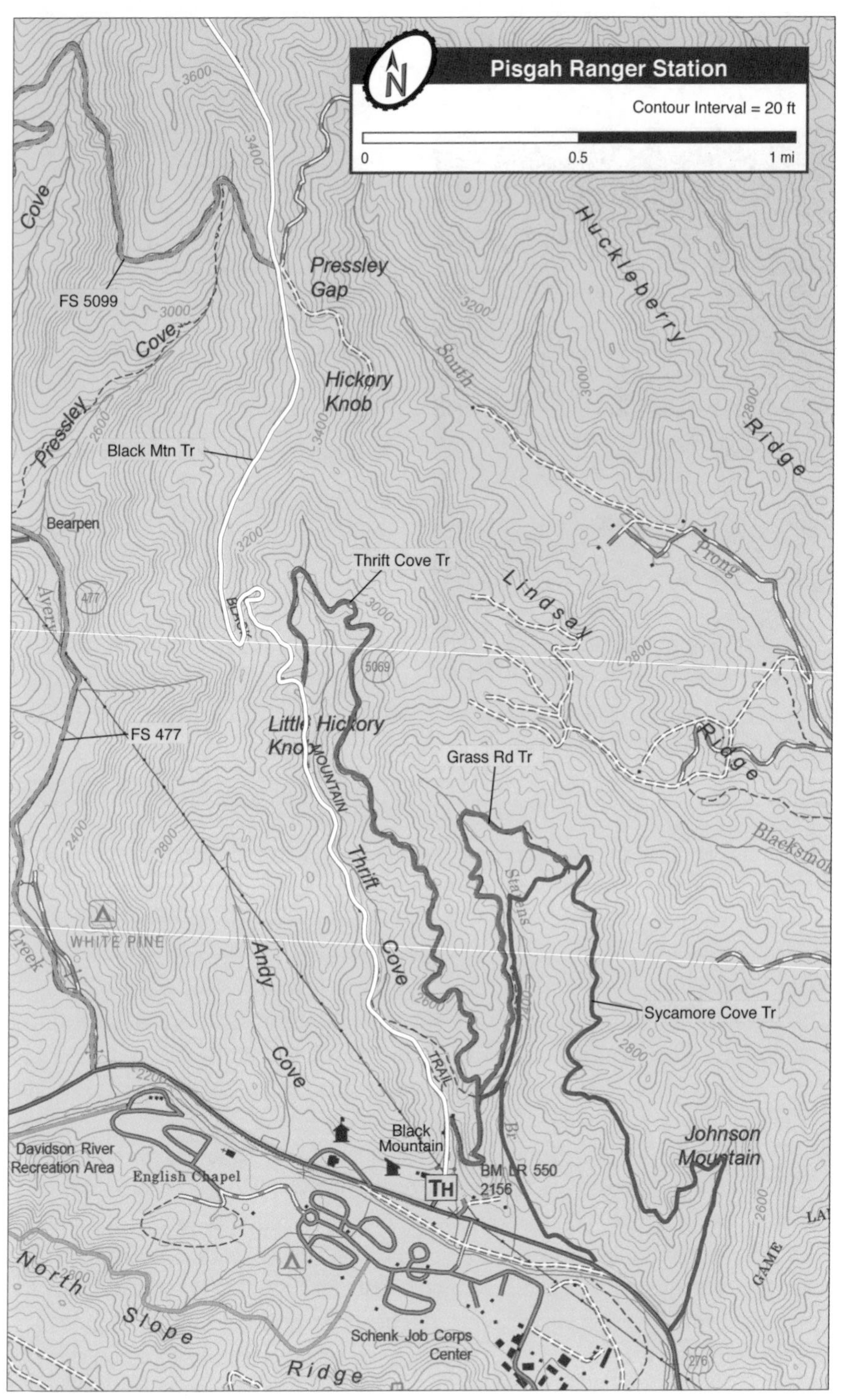
Pisgah Ranger Station
Contour Interval = 20 ft
0
0.5
1 mi
Cove
FS 5099
Cove
Pressley
Pressley Gap
Hickory Knob
Huckleberry
South
Ridge
Black Mtn Tr
Bearpen
Avery
Thrift Cove Tr
Lindsay
Prong
Little Hickory Knob
FS 477
Grass Rd Tr
Ridge
Blacksmo
Thrift
Cove
Andy
Cove
WHITE PINE
Creek
Sycamore Cove Tr
Johnson Mountain
Black Mountain
Davidson River Recreation Area
English Chapel
TH
BM LR 550
2156
North
Slope
Ridge
Schenk Job Corps Center
GAME

Fish Hatchery

Grogan Creek Falls, right beside Butter Gap Trail, makes a nice break spot.

Type	Backcountry
Parking	Plentiful
Toilets	Yes
Land Manager	USFS
Fee	None
Access	Paved road
Special Rules	*Yes

* Seasonal trails are open to bikes between October 15 and April 15 only.

The Fish Hatchery trailhead is one of the largest in Pisgah, and once you get here you'll quickly see why. Not only does this parking lot serve the visitors coming to see the hatchery, it is the location for the Pisgah Center for Wildlife Education, a major asset of the North Carolina Wildlife Resources. There are outdoor classrooms, a small museum, and a gift shop. You'll also find large restrooms with running water, *and* a pay telephone. A telephone may seem silly to some in this day and age, but good luck finding cell coverage anywhere nearby. On a busy warm day you'll see lots of folks picnicking, pulling on waders to fish in the Davidson River, donning packs for a hike, and generally milling around. You can even buy little bags of fish food here to feed the trout in the hatchery. Go ahead, it's fun.

The rides that begin here are pretty good, but if you find the lot to be too crowded for your taste, you can access some of the same rides (and many more) by starting out just a few miles farther down FS 475 at the tiny Cove Creek lot or the larger Daniel Ridge trailhead. Also note that Cat Gap Trail, the major artery to the nearest trails to the south, is designated as a seasonal trail. The lower portion of Butter Gap Trail is also seasonal. So, to really get the best of the fish hatchery trails, you'll want to use this trailhead between October 15 and April 15.

Getting to the Trailhead

From US 276 turn west onto FS 475, following signs for Pisgah Fish Hatchery and Wildlife Center. Continue on FS 475 until you see the humongous parking lot across the bridge to your left. You can't miss it.

GPS Coordinates

35.284515, -82.791834

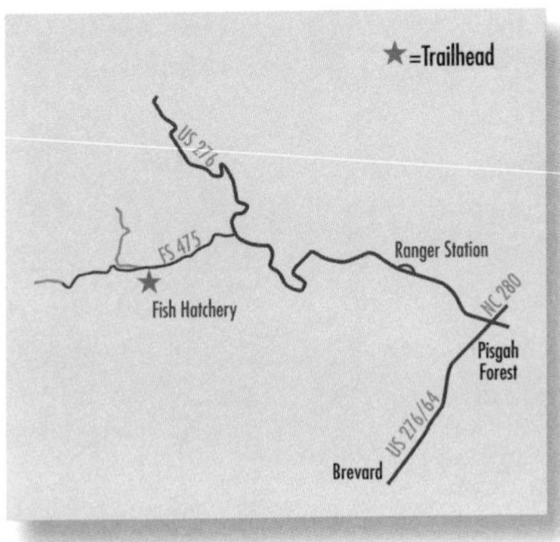

Fish Hatchery Routes

Headwaters Loop

Distance 9.8 miles
Difficulty Moderate
Surface Single track, forest road
Trailhead Fish Hatchery

This route covers a lot of territory, and views of Looking Glass Rock, John Rock, and several high waterfalls make it an appealing scenic ride. It's also one you can do any time of the year.

The first part of the loop follows FS 475B as it twists, winds, and climbs around the side of Looking Glass. This is not a gated road; you can expect to be passed by a car or two, but they generally are infrequent. Once you've worked your way up to Gumstand Gap you'll turn onto FS 225 briefly before skirting onto a side trail leading down the mountain. At the bottom, turn onto Cove Creek Trail to begin a 3-mile stretch of great single track. Most of it is downhill; along the way you'll cross over log bridges, ride over some jaw-rattling rooty stretches, and pass near the top of a high waterfall.

Cove Creek Trail ends on the entrance road to Cove Creek Group Campground. Follow this out to FS 475 and cross over onto Davidson River Trail, which enters the road just 30 feet or so up the paved road from the parking lot. But if it's a super-hot day, don't leave this little parking lot too soon. Follow the trail out the back of it a short distance to the river and a great swimming hole. It's known as Whaleback, and it's an awesome spot to cool off.

You might not notice it, but Davidson River Trail is actually an abandoned roadbed. This stretch used to be FS 475, but part of it kept falling in the river so it was replaced by a higher section of road. It's short and goes by quickly; before you know it you'll be back at the Fish Hatchery trailhead.

Long Branch

Distance 8.4 miles
Difficulty Moderate
Surface Single track, forest road
Trailhead Fish Hatchery

You'll want to ride this loop in the off-season, since it uses portions of Cat Gap and Butter Gap Trail that are open only between October 15 and April 15. That is the best time in any case, since there are fewer cars on FS 475 at that time of year.

Begin by heading west on FS 475. Turn off onto the Davidson River Trail, which bypasses over a mile of road and a significant hill. You'll come back out onto FS 475 just as it turns to gravel. Follow it out past the Daniel Ridge trailhead and then up the long hill which climbs to Gloucester Gap. About halfway up, be on the lookout for the far end of Long Branch Trail. It is just past the gated road marked as Cemetery Loop Trail. You'll be on Long Branch Trail for close to 3 miles as it gradually climbs and descends along the contour lines. It's a fun trail with log bridges, but beware of a few mucky areas.

Long Branch Trail deadends into Butter Gap Trail where you'll take a left (downhill). Just before this trail meets Cat Gap Trail, you'll ride through Picklesimer Fields. There are a few fields here as well as an area of beaver ponds and marshes. The trail meanders through this low-lying area, then picks up steam again once you drop down onto Cat Gap Trail. Listen closely and you can hear a waterfall down on the creek. After crossing a road above the fish hatchery, the trail follows the fenceline around the wildlife center back to the trailhead.

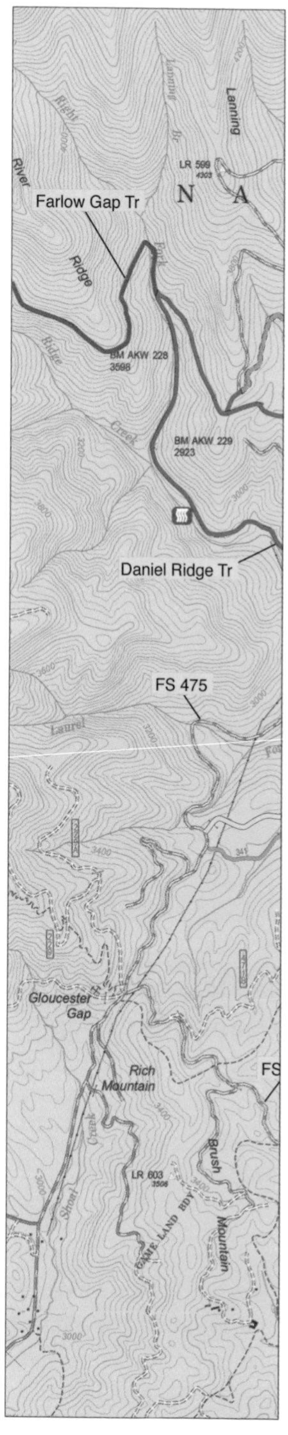

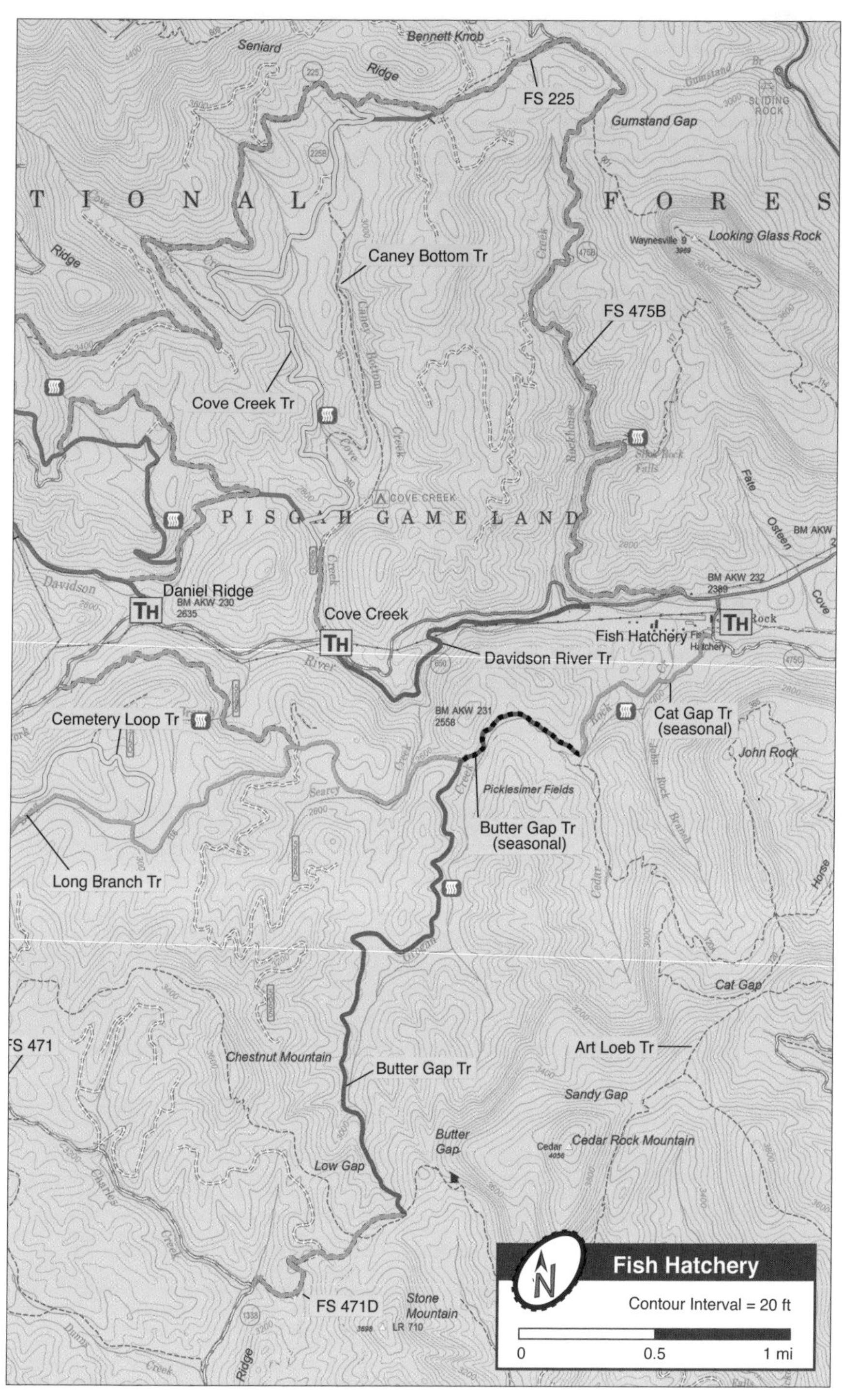

Fish Hatchery
Contour Interval = 20 ft
0
0.5
1 mi
Bennett Knob
Seniard
Ridge
FS 225
Gumstand Gap
SLIDING ROCK
T I O N A L
F O R E S
Looking Glass Rock
Caney Bottom Tr
FS 475B
Cove Creek Tr
PISGAH GAME LAND
COVE CREEK
Daniel Ridge
BM AKW 230
2635
Cove Creek
BM AKW 232
2389
Fish Hatchery
Davidson River Tr
Cemetery Loop Tr
BM AKW 231
2558
Cat Gap Tr
(seasonal)
John Rock
Pickelsimer Fields
Butter Gap Tr
(seasonal)
Long Branch Tr
Cat Gap
FS 471
Art Loeb Tr
Chestnut Mountain
Butter Gap Tr
Sandy Gap
Butter
Gap
Cedar Rock Mountain
Low Gap
FS 471D
Stone
Mountain

Daniel Ridge

You can ride above and below Toms Spring Falls on Daniel Ridge Trail.

Type	Backcountry
Parking	Moderate
Toilets	None
Land Manager	USFS
Fee	None
Access	Gravel road
Special Rules	None

You could spend days riding from the Daniel Ridge trailhead and still discover places you have not been. The variety of routes is astounding. If you're looking for a quick heart-pounder, you can find more than one here. Want to just ride out and take in a waterfall or two? No problem, there's more than one route where you can do that. Looking to spend an entire day on just one ride? There are several options for that as well. Looking to set up a base camp and ride for the week? This is good place to do that. There are some walk-in, dispersed-use campsites on the river—right out from the trailhead.

Daniel Ridge represents what most cyclists coming to Pisgah are looking for. The parking lot is just off a dusty gravel road and looks more like a very large pullout, with cars facing every which way. It's fairly easy to get to, but don't expect flush toilets and a water fountain (you'll find those back down the road at the fish hatchery). Ride five minutes down the trail in any direction and you are in the backcountry. There are no flat rides. Everything goes up and then comes back down.

Getting to the Trailhead

From US 276, follow FS 475 (paved at this point) toward the fish hatchery and wildlife center. Continue past that trailhead as the road twists up and over a ridge. At the entrance to Cove Creek Group Campground the road turns to gravel. Continue another 0.8 mile to the trailhead on the right.

GPS Coordinates

35.284673, -82.829191

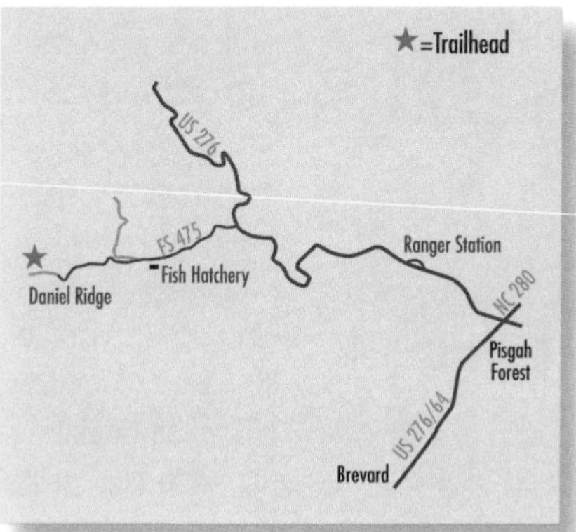

Daniel Ridge Routes

Short Daniel

Distance 3 miles
Difficulty Moderate
Surface Single track, forest road
Trailhead Daniel Ridge

If you're looking for a quick warm-up or want to check that everything is working properly before starting out on a longer circuit, this is a great choice. It also makes a nice addition to any other ride in the area.

Start by riding out across the bridge on Daniel Ridge Trail, which is a road at this point. After the bridge, instead of turning left on the trail, bear right to continue on the gated road; it quickly becomes double track. Keep an eye out on your left for a view of Toms Spring Falls. The road twists and turns as it climbs up and around the spine of the ridge. Those brambles that occasionally grab your legs are heavy with blackberries in July.

Just when your legs are saying, "Enough already!" Daniel Ridge Trail crosses the roadway. Turn left here, down the mountain, and hang on. What seemed to take you eons to climb will take moments to descend. Be ready for rooty drop-offs, a jaw-rattler or two, and some funky bridges on your way down.

Daniel Ridge

Distance 4.1 miles
Difficulty Moderate
Surface Single track, forest road
Trailhead Daniel Ridge

This is just over a mile longer than Short Daniel, but it seems a lot longer than it really is—why is that? Mainly it's due to the hard fact that it includes some gnarly single track climbing.

Things start out tame enough. Follow Daniel Ridge Trail out of the parking lot by going around the gate and out across the bridge. Just before you run into the mountain ahead of you, turn left to begin the single track portion. The trail parallels the river for about a mile before coming to a sheer drop-off, the location of an old bridge. Turn right here, shift into granny

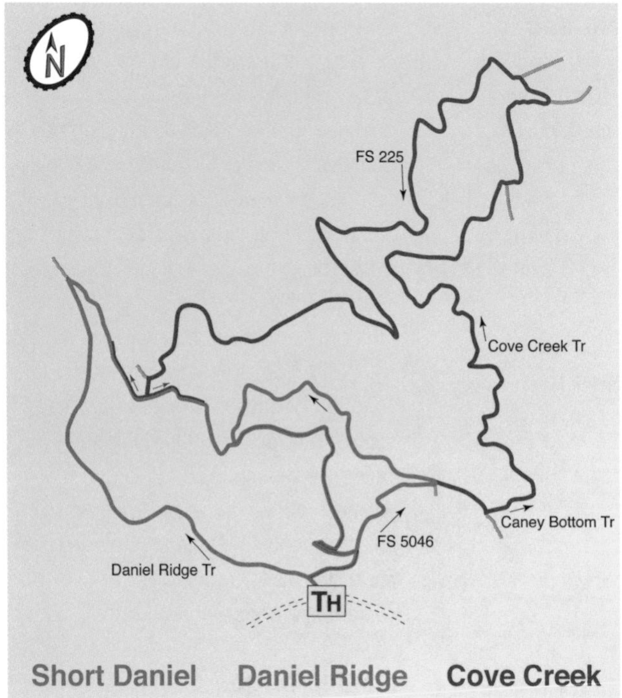

gear, and head up (*really* up) the mountain. It's steep and ridable—but don't be surprised if either your lungs, your legs, or both give out and you're forced to push. A series of log steps lead to the junction with Farlow Gap Trail. Bear right here and you can ride again—at least for a while. Eventually you'll top out where an unmarked trail comes in from the left (see the Cove Creek route).

From here it's a hang-onto-your-socks (or better yet, your brakes) blitz to the bottom at the base of Toms Spring Falls where you'll swing right to zoom on back to the trailhead.

Cove Creek

Distance 8 miles
Difficulty Moderate
Surface Single track, forest road
Trailhead Daniel Ridge

On this ride you'll hop over the ridge to Cove Creek, gain a fair amount of altitude on the single track trail there, then skip onto a gated forest road to gain even more elevation, and finally jump down to the high point of Daniel Ridge Trail for an all-out run back to the bottom. So really it's just a hop, skip, and jump sort of ride.

Begin by riding out and over the bridge on Daniel Ridge Trail. On the far side, bear right to stay on the double track and continue up past Toms Spring Falls. You'll climb a bit farther past the falls, but when the road makes its first switchback to the left, continue straight into the woods and down the single track trail. As the trail opens up and you can see the open fields of the group camp ahead, look for a sharp left turn that crosses a small creek. This is Caney Bottom Trail and you don't want to miss it. Turn left and follow to where it intersects with Cove Creek Trail which you'll follow for close to 3 miles as it gradually climbs into the hills.

Cove Creek Trail terminates at gate onto FS 225. Turn left on this road. At the next series of gates, be sure to stay on FS 225 as it ascends the mountain farther still. You will climb for a long time. Eventually, when it looks like the road ahead is completely grown over and you're sure you went the wrong way, you'll see an unmarked single track trail snaking into the woods on the left. This takes you down to connect with the Daniel Ridge Trail. At this point you can go left or right to follow the Daniel Ridge Trail back to the trailhead—the choice is yours. Either way you can't go wrong.

Butter Gap

Distance 10.5 miles
Difficulty Moderate
Surface Single track, forest road
Trailhead Daniel Ridge

This route accesses the trails on the south side of Davidson River watershed. But first you're going to head over the mountain to get at them from the other side. You'll spend a little time on some forest roads that are also accessible to cars in the early part of the ride, so take care and keep an ear out for those pickups with Bubba at the wheel.

Head out from the trailhead on FS 475. You might as well go ahead and shift into a low gear, it's a bit of a climb up to Gloucester Gap. Once at the gap, swing left onto FS 471 and climb a little more. You're almost to the top.

Once you've topped out, the road angles down and you'll pick up speed quickly. It's a rush, but keep it under control; gravel does not make for a soft landing. You'll also need to be paying attention so as not to miss your turn. You are looking for FS 471D. It may or may not be marked, but it is the second gated road on your left after starting down the hill and 2.2 miles from Gloucester Gap.

This road quickly becomes trail-like as it gains back all that elevation you just lost. Partway up you'll bear right at

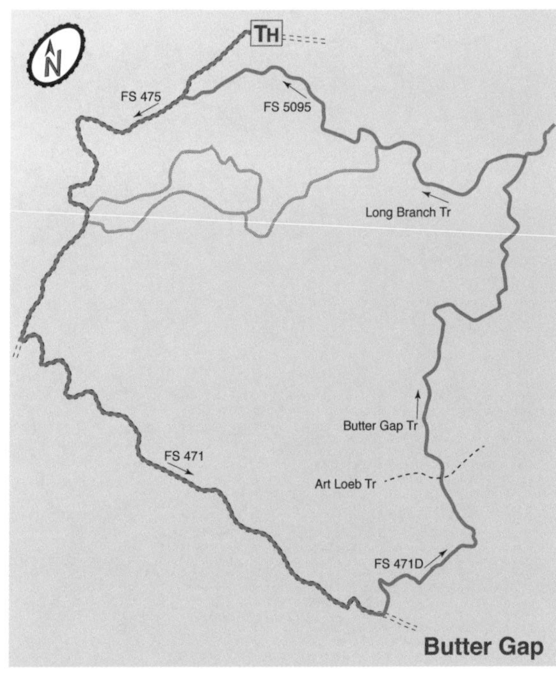

an unmarked junction and soon you'll find yourself at a junction with Art Loeb Trail. Cross straight over it and when you reach Butter Gap, bear left down the mountain on Butter Gap Trail.

Butter Gap starts out with some tricky sections, including some pretty big drop-offs. Soon enough it settles down. You'll pass a waterfall down off the trail to the right and some distance beyond that the route makes a left turn onto Long Branch Trail. This is another turn you don't want to miss, but it should be well marked.

Follow Long Branch until it intersects with the far end of FS 5095. Turn right and cruise down the easy grade until it ends at a gate on FS 475. The trailhead is just down the road to the right.

Farlow Gap

Distance 10.4 miles
Difficulty Difficult
Surface Single track, forest road
Trailhead Daniel Ridge

Farlow Gap Trail has by far the steepest, most technical descent in all of Pisgah. Some trails might have sections

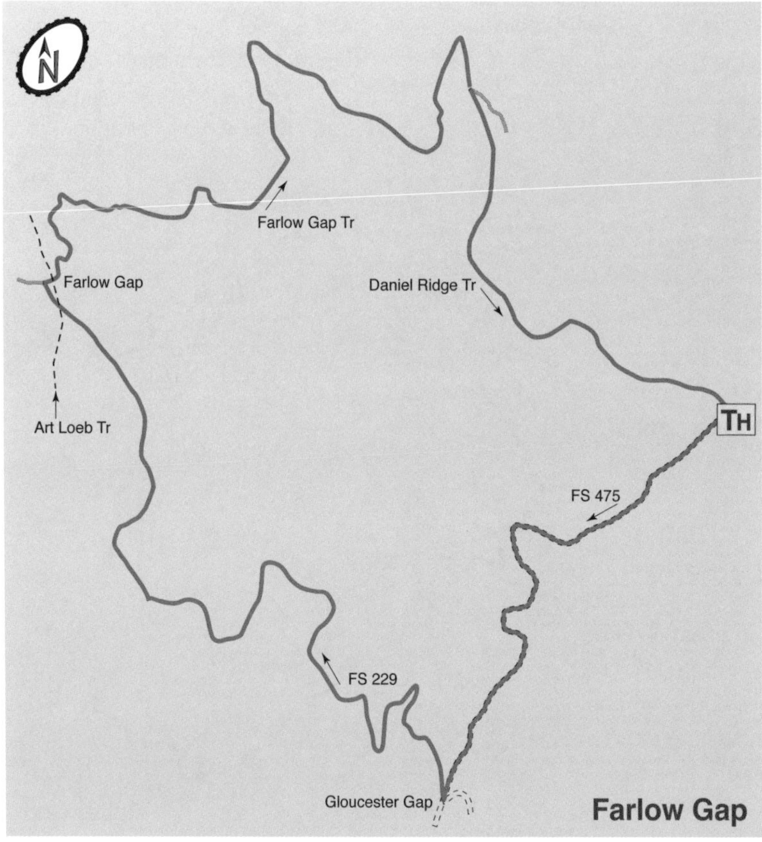

that are steeper, and some might have sections that are more technical, but none have both for such a long stretch.

If that statement scares you off this route, that is its intent. You will not enjoy this ride if you don't have the skills to ride safely down a steep trail with loose rocks, drop-offs, and serious consequences. If you do, you'll love it—that is, if you don't mind climbing for hours first.

Begin by riding up FS 475 to Gloucester Gap. Remember that cars also use this road. At the gap, turn right on FS 229 and continue to climb up the side of Pilot Mountain. Normally this is a gated road, but during some seasons the gate is open. You'll climb on this road for 2.5 miles to a turnout. Continue around the berm on the upper left side of the turnout and follow the old woods road along the ridge. This double track road does not climb so much now, as you are well over 4,000 feet. After a mile or so, the Art Loeb Trail crosses. Stay on the road a little farther as it swings around the west side of the ridge and comes to Farlow Gap. Here, Art Loeb Trail will be on your right following the ridgeline and Farlow Gap Trail heads off downhill to the east (right). You'll get on Farlow Gap Trail here. And whatever you do, don't continue to follow the old woods road downhill to the west side (left) of the ridge.

Farlow Gap Trail rolls off the ridge gently at first, and then drops like a roller coaster, straight down the mountain. Don't be too proud to take a break every now and to rest your brake hands. Eventually things will settle down and you can breathe a little easier. What follows is several more miles of sometimes technical, sometimes not, but all fantastic trail. Along the way you'll cross the top of a waterfall, hop down log steps, and probably do some whooping for joy.

Eventually you'll end up on Daniel Ridge Trail where you'll turn right down the log steps and on down through Daniel Ridge's technical section before finally returning to the trailhead.

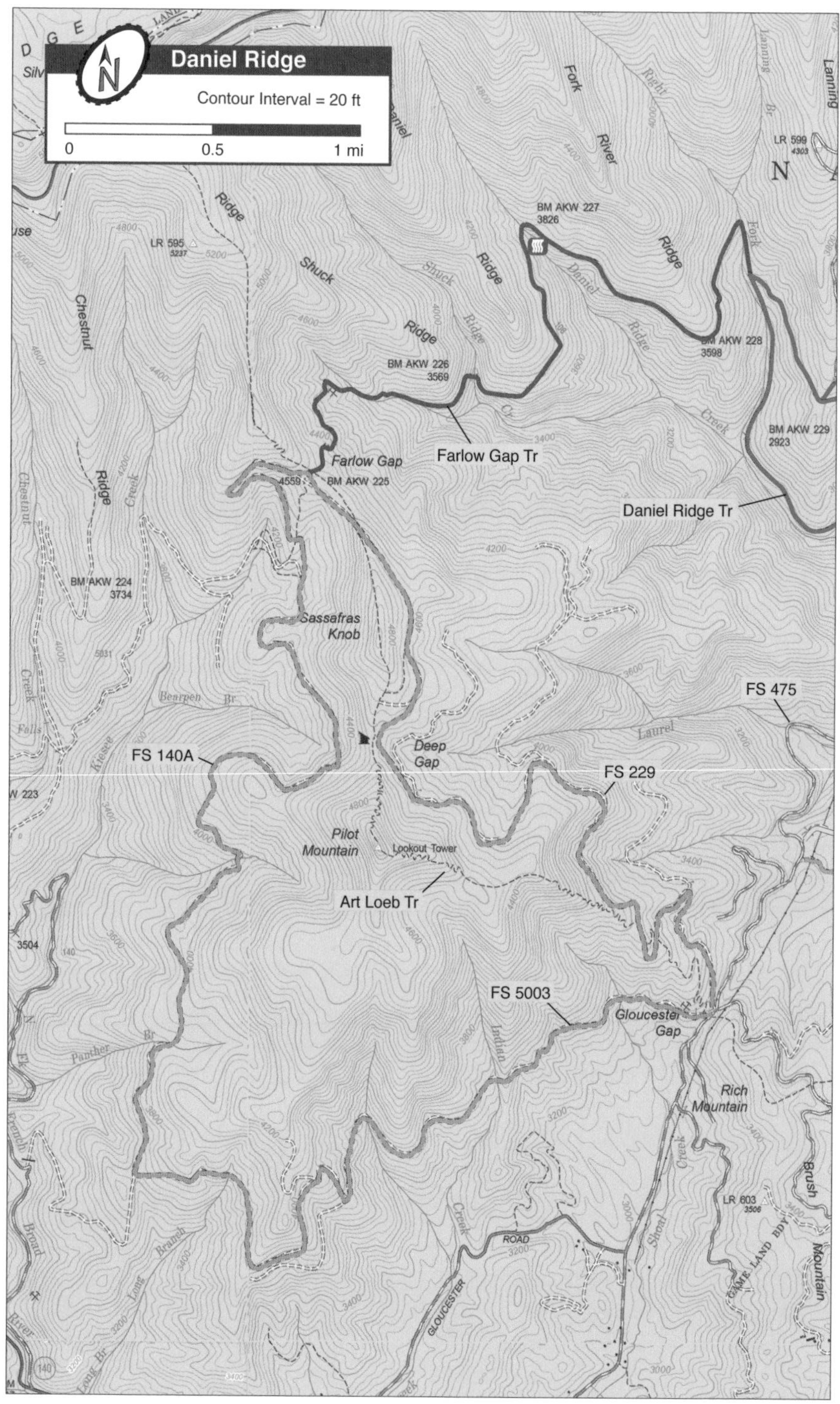

Daniel Ridge
Contour Interval = 20 ft
0
0.5
1 mi
Farlow Gap Tr
Daniel Ridge Tr
Farlow Gap
BM AKW 225
4559
BM AKW 226
3569
BM AKW 227
3826
BM AKW 228
3598
BM AKW 229
2923
BM AKW 224
3734
LR 595
LR 599
LR 603
Sassafras
Knob
Deep
Gap
Pilot
Mountain
Lookout Tower
Art Loeb Tr
FS 475
FS 229
FS 140A
FS 5003
Gloucester
Gap
Rich
Mountain
Chestnut
Ridge
Shuck
Ridge
Fork
River
GLOUCESTER
ROAD
GAME LAND BDY
Brush
Mountain

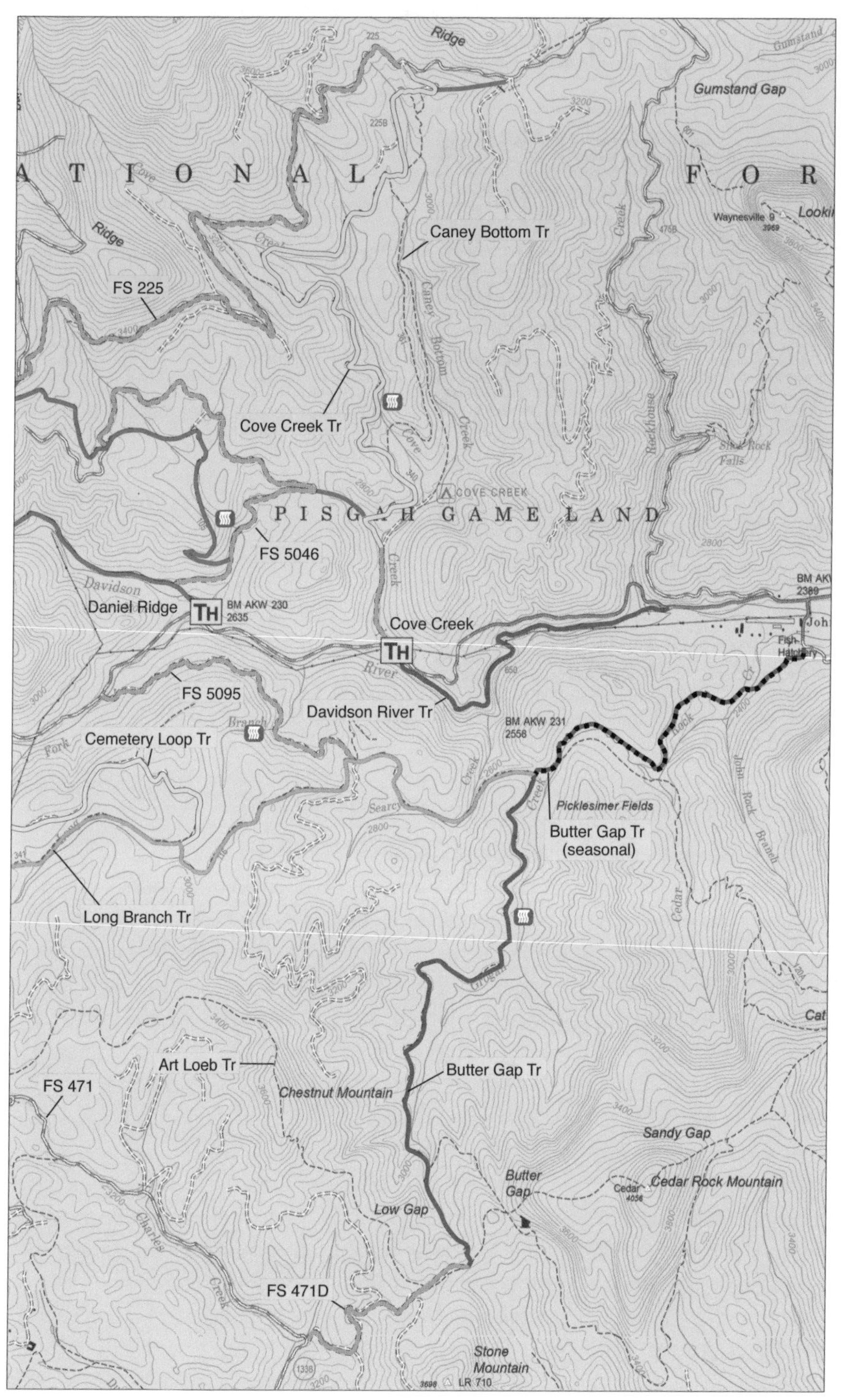
Gumstand Gap
Caney Bottom Tr
FS 225
Cove Creek Tr
Waynesville 9
PISGAH GAME LAND
FS 5046
Daniel Ridge
BM AKW 230
2635
Cove Creek
FS 5095
Davidson River Tr
BM AKW 231
2558
Cemetery Loop Tr
Picklesimer Fields
Butter Gap Tr
(seasonal)
Long Branch Tr
Art Loeb Tr
FS 471
Chestnut Mountain
Butter Gap Tr
Sandy Gap
Butter Gap
Cedar Rock Mountain
Low Gap
FS 471D
Stone Mountain
LR 710

Avery Creek

Trails in the Avery Creek area are well signed and blazed.

Type	Backcountry
Parking	Limited
Restrooms	None
Land Manager	USFS
Fee	None
Access	Gravel road
Special Rules	*Yes

* Seasonal trails are open to bikes between October 15 and April 15 only.

Avery Creek is right in the heart of Pisgah, with three small trailheads all within a long stone's throw of each other. One is adjacent to a horseback riding concessionaire that operates in the warmer months, with the other two just up the road. You might find it best to leave the lower lot to the horse folks when they are operating. Whichever you choose, they all serve as staging points for the many trails in the Avery Creek watershed. None of these rides could be rated easy; all involve a fair amount of climbing, some on gated forest roads and some on steep single track trails. Basically you'll choose a route that heads up to a ridge. You'll ride along that ridge, maybe link over to another ridge, and then loop back down. They are all great.

Several trails here are designated as seasonal—the south side of the Coontree Loop, Bennett Gap Trail, and to the north, the upper portion of the Pink Beds Loop. There is still plenty of riding for the warmer months, but in the off-season you can add those trails to make additional loops. And if you don't want to drive all the way in to the trailhead on the gravel road in the off-season you can park at Coontree Picnic Area on US 276 and access the Avery Creek trails from there.

Looking for a half-day ride? You have many choices around Avery Creek; a few suggestions follow. You can hardly go wrong however you do it; just don't try riding up Avery Creek Trail—unless you're a glutton for punishment. If you're looking for a really long tour, head up to Buckhorn Gap via FS 5058 and drop over into the South Mills watershed. From there you can jump onto the northern side of the Pink Beds Loop in the off-season or swing into the maze of trails on the east side of South Mills River any time of the year. Or make your way up to the Black Mountain Trail and take it all the way to the ranger station.

If you are looking for a campsite to set up a base camp for several days' riding in the area, there are quite a few dispersed-use sites next to FS 477. All are right along Avery Creek.

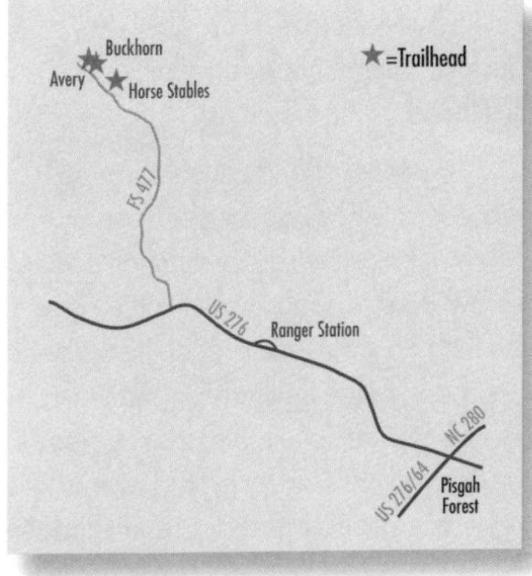

Getting to the Trailhead

From US 276 just north of the ranger station, take FS 477 for 1.5 miles. This will get you to the trailhead adjacent to the horse riding concession. Continue on up the hill on FS 477 to a small lot at the end of the Avery Creek Trail and then another small lot up the road just beyond, at the end of the Buckhorn Gap Trail.

GPS Coordinates

35.308613, -82.745367

Avery Creek Routes

Buckhorn Gap

Distance 10 miles
Difficulty Moderate
Surface Single track, forest road
Trailhead Buckhorn

This route is 10 miles total and at least 4 of those are straight-out climbing, but if you can take that in stride, you'll love what follows. Spotty views, an old trail shelter with a cold spring out back, places where the ridge drop-off on either side of you is so close it's scary, a downhill that rocks, a waterfall—it's all here.

Begin the ride from any of the three trailheads. If you choose Avery or Buckhorn, head downhill first on FS 477, turn left on FS 5058 and start the climb. You may share the road with some horses, but if you do you'll likely not be around them too long. It is always a bit of a trick to pass horses safely on the way up a hill. Trail etiquette says cyclists yield right of way, but what do you do when they're climbing a hill so much more slowly than you? Get the lead rider's attention and ask him or her the best way to proceed. Most likely they'll gather everyone together so you can pass. You should then dismount and walk on by while making polite conversation with both the riders and the horses.

After the forever uphill, you'll arrive at Buckhorn Gap. Take the stairs to the left and guess what—you've still got a mile of climbing to go, now on the single track Black Mountain Trail. It's not so awful as you might expect. Once you hit the high point your climbing is over. Drop steeply down to Club Gap, turn left on Avery Creek Trail, and drop steeply some more.

Eventually you'll bottom out down near a crossing of Avery Creek. Turn right here onto Buckhorn Gap Trail and follow it back to your car.

Clawhammer

Distance 10.7 miles
Difficulty Difficult
Surface Single track, forest road
Trailhead Horse Stables

If necessary you can start this ride from one of the other two trailheads, but it works best to start at the stables. It saves a short uphill at the end, when, trust me, you won't want to ride uphill any more.

Like most of the rides around here, it starts with a big climb. This is the biggest. Of a total 6 miles of climbing, the first 4.5 miles you can actually ride. Much of the last 1.5 miles is more hike-a-bike than ride-a-bike. Is it worth it? You bet!

After spinning up to Buckhorn Gap on FS 5058, you'll turn right on Black Mountain Trail to go up and over Clawhammer Mountain. At the top is an amazing clifftop view that looks west to Looking Glass Rock and all the mountains beyond. The downhill that follows is superb. Make sure to keep your bike under control, your body on your bike, and your bike on the trail and you'll be good.

Once down at Pressley Gap you'll turn right on FS 5099, a grassy double track that leads most of the way back to the trailhead. Watch your speed and keep an eye out for horses. Finish on the short stretch of FS 5058 you rode up before.

Bennett Gap

Distance 6.5 miles
Difficulty Moderate
Surface Single track, forest road
Trailhead Horse Stables

This seasonal ride should not be missed. From any trailhead, head up FS 477 to Bennett Gap. Turn left and follow Bennett Gap Trail all the way back to FS 477 where a left turn takes you back to the trailhead.

These are simple directions for an awesome ride. Expect great views, some tight, boulder-y single track, and a downhill that goes on forever.

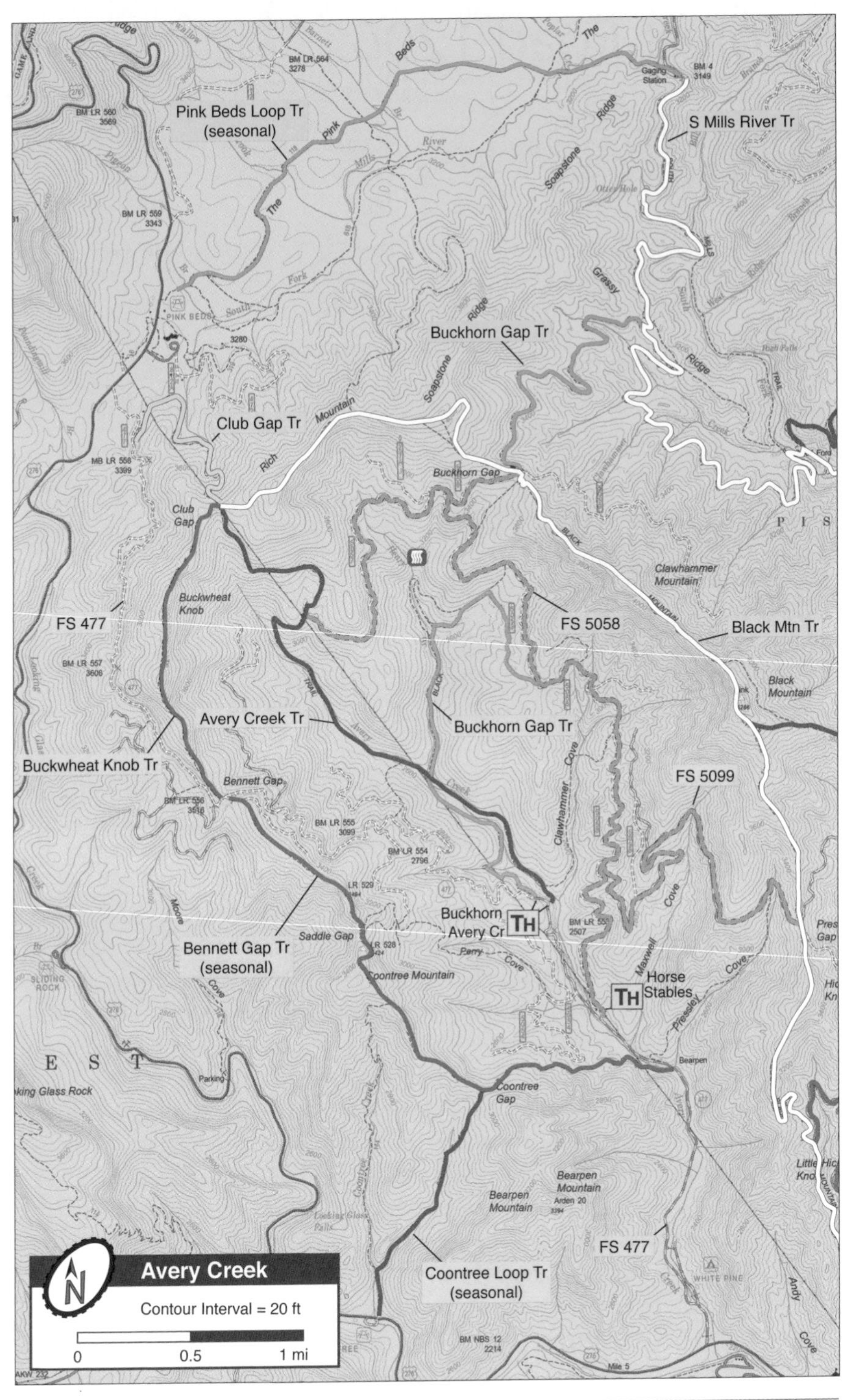
Avery Creek
Contour Interval = 20 ft
0
0.5
1 mi
Pink Beds Loop Tr
(seasonal)
S Mills River Tr
Buckhorn Gap Tr
Club Gap Tr
FS 477
FS 5058
Black Mtn Tr
Avery Creek Tr
Buckhorn Gap Tr
Buckwheat Knob Tr
FS 5099
Buckhorn
Avery Cr
TH
Bennett Gap Tr
(seasonal)
TH
Horse
Stables
FS 477
Coontree Loop Tr
(seasonal)
Club
Gap
Buckwheat
Knob
Buckhorn Gap
Clawhammer
Mountain
Black
Mountain
Bennett Gap
Saddle Gap
Coontree Mountain
Coontree
Gap
Bearpen
Mountain
Bearpen
Mountain
Looking Glass Rock
Parking

Forest Road 1206

The view from the top of Slate Rock is definitely worth the climb to get there.

Type	Backcountry
Parking	Limited
Toilets	None
Land Manager	USFS
Fee	None
Access	Gravel road
Special Rules	None

From Forest Service Route 1206, you have access to some of Pisgah's most remote trails. You can climb thousands of feet, all the way to the Blue Ridge Parkway. You can dip down into the lowest of the river bottoms. And you can ride everywhere in between. There are waterfalls where you can hang out and soak in the scenery. There are cliff faces and rock outcrops you can ride across or sit on and watch the birds soar by. You can wade across rivers up to your waist or get lost on trails so far out in the backcountry you might not be found for days. Okay—you don't want to do that last thing.

For the most part, this entire area drains into the South Mills River. The river and its tributaries define the geography. It seems as if most anywhere you ride, there is water. Even high up on Laurel Mountain you'll find springs bubbling across the trail. Carry a filter and you'll never go thirsty. At different times of year, some of the coves you ride through are like green oases, from the ferns on the forest floor to the bright green leaves of the trees.

Here is a place where it is doubly important to pay attention to the weather. Pisgah is famous for its summer thunderstorms. It's not nicknamed Pisgah National "rain forest" for nothing! Don't be caught unprepared. A hot day at 5,000 feet can get frigid fast when rain, hail, or both starts pounding down. And, needless to say, you shouldn't linger on Slate Rock to watch lightning dancing across the sky.

Looking for a campsite? There are dispersed-use sites located along Bradley Creek on FS 1206, and more down FS 476 on the way to the South Mills trailhead.

Getting to the Trailhead

Four small trailheads are located along FS 1206 and there's another just off 1206 on the back side of the Pink Beds at the end of FS 476. FS 1206 is a long gravel road that traverses Pisgah from US 276, just north of the Pink Beds, all the way to the North Mills Recreation Area. The recreation area is accessed from NC 191 via North Mills River Road in Mills River. You can come in from either direction. Just know you'll be driving a long way on a gravel road.

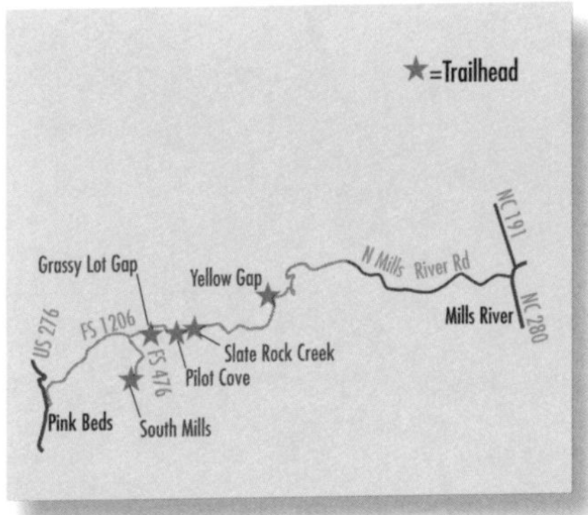

GPS Coordinates

Grassy Lot Gap 35.382, -82.735
South Mills 35.367, -82.740
Pilot Cove 35.383, -82.714
Slate Rock Creek 35.385, -82.691
Yellow Gap 35.394, -82.675

Forest Road 1206 Routes

Pilot Cove–Slate Rock Creek

Distance 7.1 miles
Difficulty Moderate
Surface Single track, forest road
Trailhead Slate Rock Creek

At least two things stand out about this ride: you'll get a great view from top of the cliff that is Slate Rock, and riding down the mountain along Slate Rock Creek is a hoot. Though this route is rated moderate, there is still a short hike-a-bike to get to the top of Slate Rock and some tight single track through the trees just after that. It's easy to blow past the waterfall near the end, so keep an ear out for it.

You'll begin by riding up to the Pilot Cove Loop trailhead on FS 1206. Once on the loop trail, be sure to take the first right you come to. It'll take you straight up the mountain to bare rock riding and an amazing clifftop view. Once you've trudged up to Slate Rock and taken in the scenery, continue along the ridgetop until you reach the 3-way junction with Slate Rock Creek Trail. Turn right and follow Slate Rock Creek all the way back down to your car.

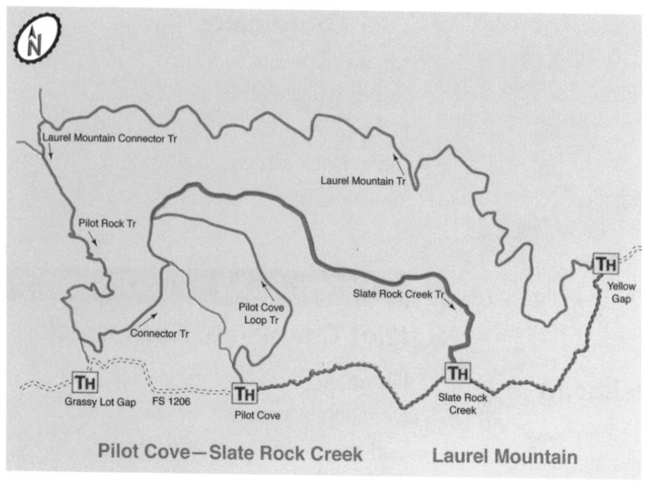

Laurel Mountain

Distance 13.5 miles
Difficulty Difficult
Surface Single track, forest roads
Trailhead Slate Rock Creek

This route is a famous ride in Pisgah—it's one of those rite of passage things. If you are in Pisgah for a week's vacation, it is the one you want to end your trip with. Yes, it's that awesome. What makes it so great? It just seems to capture the essence of Pisgah. There's a short bit of uphill forest road riding to start out with and then a long, *long* climb up a single track trail. The climb is gradual enough that you can ride almost the entire thing. Way up high, there are several pitches where you can slip it into granny and then spin like crazy to see just how far up you can go before stalling out and having to hoof it.

After it seems like you will do nothing but ride uphill and the temperature is a good 15 degrees cooler than down below, you top out and the ride changes character considerably. The ride down Pilot Rock Trail is at times a twisty, log-strewn, switchback-y rock garden. It's one of those descents when your triceps start to burn and your hands get tired from working the brakes. If you can peel your eyes off the trail in front of you, the views are pretty awesome; stop every now and then and take a look. A short ways before reaching FS 1206, turn left on an unmarked connector over to Pilot Cove. From there take the Pilot Cove/Slate Rock Creek Trail for a fun

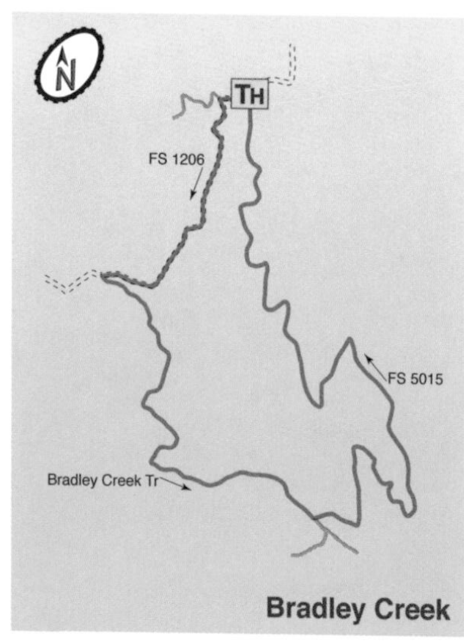

downhill back to the trailhead.

Directions for this ride are simple. Take FS 1206 down and then up to Yellow Gap. Turn left on Laurel Mountain Trail and ride uphill long enough to drink all the water you brought. At Turkey Spring Gap turn left on Laurel Mountain Connector Trail. At the top of the climb, turn left on Pilot Rock Trail. Follow it down to unmarked Connector Trail, turn left, and then climb some more. Turn left on Pilot Cove/Slate Rock Creek Trail, climb a little farther, and then bomb down the trail to your car.

Bradley Creek

Distance 7 miles
Difficulty Moderate
Surface Single track, double track
Trailhead Yellow Gap

If you don't mind getting your feet wet you'll love this ride. The route crosses and recrosses Bradley Creek 12 times in a mile and a half. Why would anyone want to do that? The rivers and streams of Pisgah are pretty special. The water is clear and cold, the rocks are mossy green, and there is just something about splashing around in the water that gets your blood pumping and makes you feel good. Don't worry—you end the ride with a spinning climb on a gated forest road, and plenty of time for your shoes to go from dripping to damp.

Begin by riding down FS 1206 to the first pullout on the left. Turn left on Bradley Creek Trail here. It's a very short, but very steep downhill to the creek. Now just follow the creek downstream. Finally, after many back and forth crossings, you pass a small reservoir and cross over to the east side of the creek. Look for an open area and a forest road entering from the left. This is your road, FS 5015. Turn left on it to follow it back up to Yellow Gap.

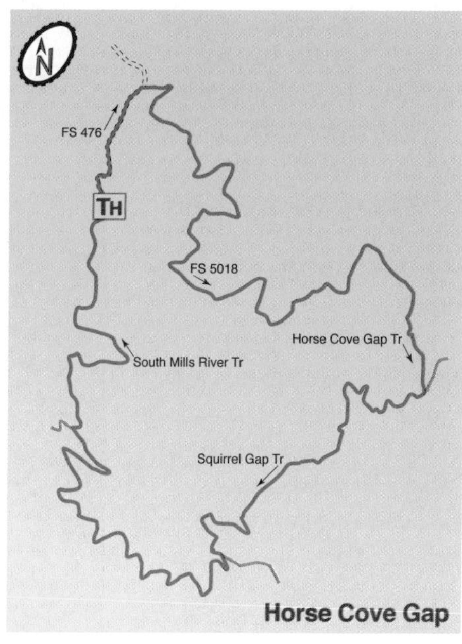

Horse Cove Gap

Distance 12.2 miles
Difficulty Moderate
Surface Single track, forest road
Trailhead South Mills or Grassy Lot Gap

This ride begins with a forest road climb and views that rival any in Pisgah. The only catch is, to see them you'll need to look back over your shoulder as you spin up the road. Hanging on the mountain behind you are the bold cliff faces of Pilot Rock and Slate Rock. High above you can make out the grooved line that is the Blue Ridge Parkway, but once you leave the forest road, the single track that follows will command your attention.

Begin by taking FS 476 to gated FS 5018. You'll ride this road for 4 miles. At the end, Horse Cove Gap Trail heads straight off into the woods and down the mountain to its namesake gap. Turn right on Squirrel Gap Trail for more downhill to a stream ford. The trail eventually leads to the South Mills River and, thank goodness, a narrow suspension bridge. Cross the bridge and continue onto South Mills River Trail as it climbs a low ridge, bumps into the far end of Buckhorn Gap Trail, and then drops back to the river. You'll stay by the river all the way back to the trailhead.

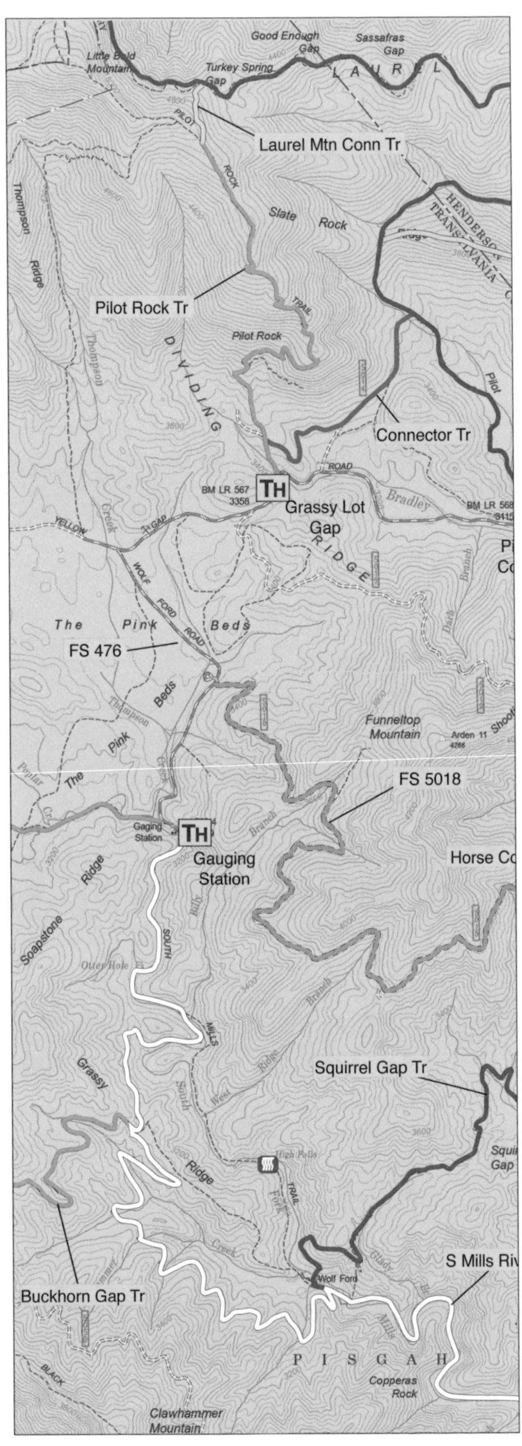

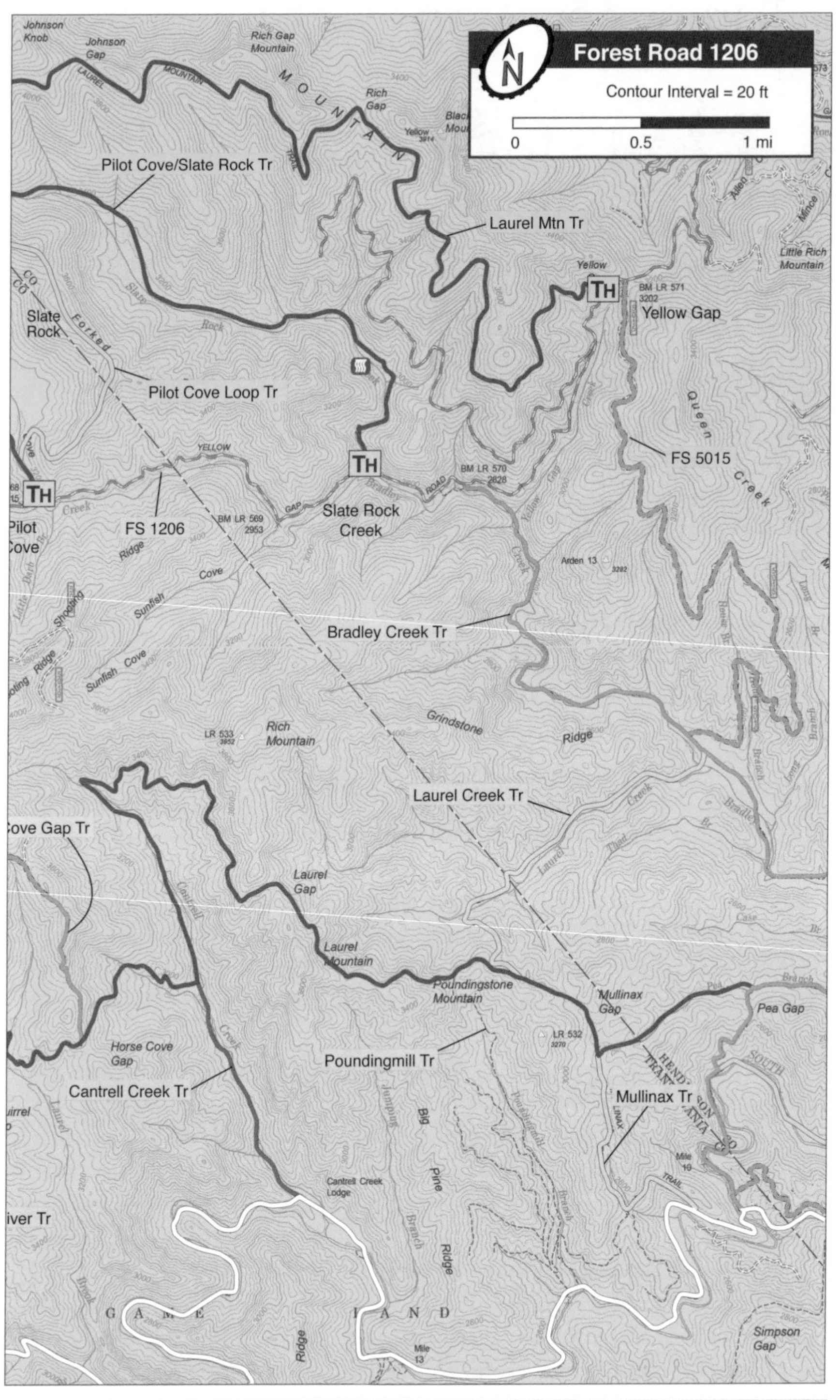
Forest Road 1206
Contour Interval = 20 ft
0
0.5
1 mi
Pilot Cove/Slate Rock Tr
Laurel Mtn Tr
Yellow Gap
Pilot Cove Loop Tr
FS 5015
FS 1206
Slate Rock Creek
Bradley Creek Tr
Laurel Creek Tr
Cove Gap Tr
Poundingmill Tr
Cantrell Creek Tr
Mullinax Tr
Pea Gap
Simpson Gap
Rich Mountain
Laurel Gap
Laurel Mountain
Poundingstone Mountain
Mullinax Gap
Horse Cove Gap
Cantrell Creek Lodge
Slate Rock
Pilot Cove
Johnson Knob
Johnson Gap
Rich Gap Mountain
Rich Gap
Little Rich Mountain

Turkeypen Gap

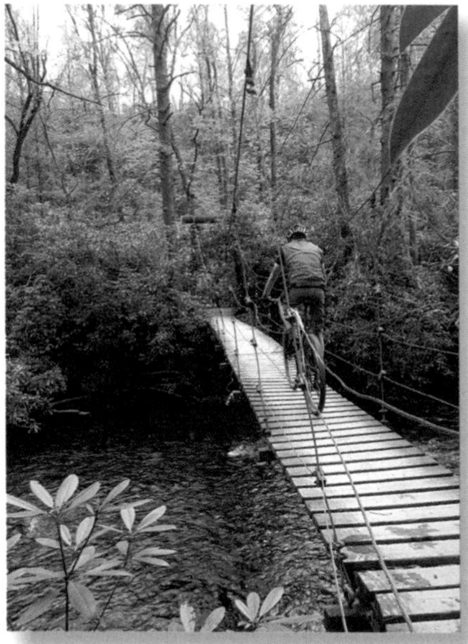

Crossing South Mills River on the bouncy suspension bridges is fun.

Type	Backcountry
Parking	Moderate
Toilets	None
Land Manager	USFS
Fee	None
Access	Gravel road
Special Rules	None

The Turkeypen Gap trailhead and the trails that branch out from it are probably frequented more by the horse crowd than any other users. On a pretty weekend you are likely to see a number of horse trailers in the lot and plenty of equestrian groups on the trail. For the most part these folks are just like you, people who enjoy getting out on the trails. But it's not like you're riding around the grounds of Churchill Downs. Once in the woods, the various user groups tend to spread out, and encounters are few.

The biggest draw to this area is the lower portion of the South Mills River and the associated South Mills River Trail. From it, you can branch off on a number of different rides. The great thing is that there are several suspension bridges across the river, alleviating what would be some pretty wet crossings. In places the river is 20 or more feet across and can get pretty deep. It's a beautiful stream with numerous small rapids.

If you look at the map, it appears there are any number of long routes you could put together leaving from Turkeypen Gap, but here's the reality. Many of the trails are open to bikes, but not all of them make for decent riding. Those along the ridge where the trailhead is located have so many steep sections, you end up walking more than riding. Try to make a loop out of the length of the South Mills River Trail and you're going to have a long, wet day with lots of scratches on your legs.

Still, between all the tough spots and potential horse groups there are a number of trails you don't want to miss. If you're up for it, you can connect some of the routes listed here with those farther to the north or even to the west to make for a real epic adventure. Before planning the big one though, spend some time exploring the trails closer in. Once you've got a feel for them, the sky is the limit.

Getting to the Trailhead

Drive 5 miles east on NC 280 from the highway junction in the town of Pisgah Forest and look for FS 297 on the north side of the road. You'll find the trailhead at the end of this gravel road.

GPS Coordinates

35.342157, -82.658860

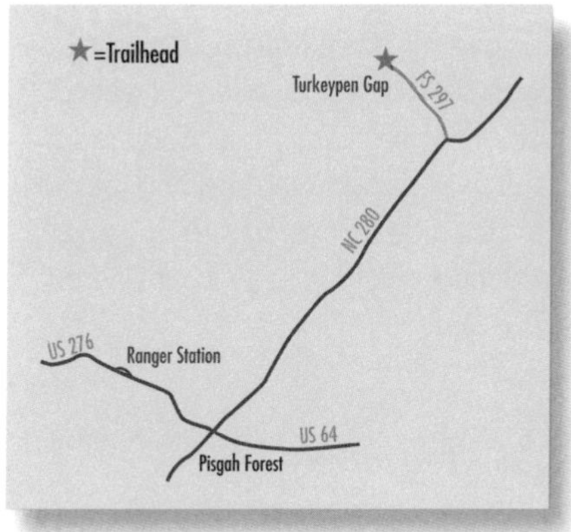

Turkeypen Gap Routes

Old Cantrell Creek Lodge

Distance 7.2 miles
Difficulty Easy
Surface Single track
Trailhead Turkeypen Gap

This should be said right up front: There is no longer a lodge located on Cantrell Creek. It was moved years ago to the Cradle of Forestry, up near the Pink Beds. What remains is an old chimney and a grown-over lawn with some bushes and flowers. Still, it makes for an interesting destination and the ride to get there is really not that difficult—especially for Pisgah.

One of the neatest characteristics of this route is the suspension bridges across the river. They're fun to ride across, make for great photos, and keep your feet dry. South Mills River is also a highlight. Find a sunny spot on a rock and hang out by the water for a while.

Begin by riding around the gate and down the old roadway to the river. At the trails junction go left to follow the trail up to the first bridge. Cross it and continue to follow the river upstream on South Mills River Trail. Two bridges later you'll come to the lodge site; there should be a historical sign near the chimney. Can you imagine years ago, folks riding out here in wagons? They would have taken the same route you did. It's not a bad place for a little rest and relaxation. From here, just retrace your route to return to the trailhead. Or you can use this as your

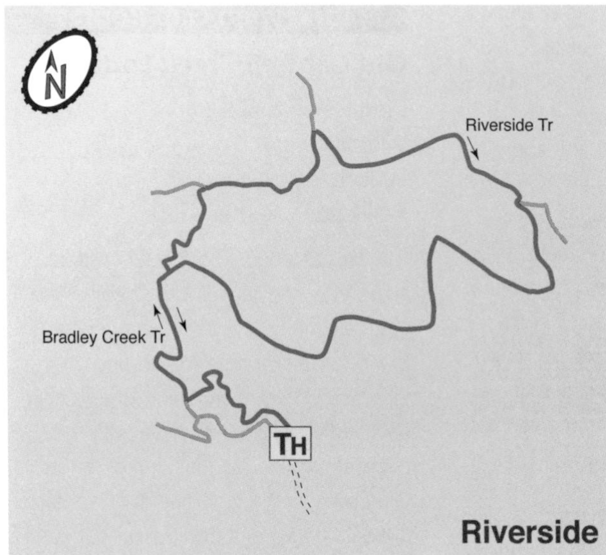

the junction on Bradley Creek Trail. Ride downstream, cross the river, go a bit farther and then turn left up the hill as Riverside Trail enters from the right. You'll climb up to Pea Gap. It's not a difficult climb, nor is it long.

After dropping down from Pea Gap and after splashing through a small stream, turn right on Riverside Trail to cross Bradley Creek. In the warmer seasons there are some amazing fields of ferns along this trail. They make for good photos, too. Just as you reach South Mills River again, turn right to stay on Riverside Trail. You'll cross the river several more times on this trail and have to negotiate some rooty and deep sand sections. It's these and the river crossings that give this route its moderate rating. Eventually you'll slosh back to the junction of Bradley Creek Trail. You should recognize that you've been here before. Turn left, ride to that last river crossing, and retrace your route to the trailhead.

starting point for a much longer tour into the backcountry.

Riverside

Distance 7.8 miles
Difficulty Moderate
Surface Single track
Trailhead Turkeypen Gap

This is the ride to do if you want some photos of yourself crossing a hip-deep river with your bike on your shoulder. You probably should not do it in winter, though the pictures might be more impressive. All told, there are 10 river and stream crossings along the route and some are more difficult than others. Use good judgment and whatever you do, don't attempt to cross any stream that's in flood stage.

To start, ride down to the river on the old road behind the gate. Turn right at

Poundingstone Mountain

Distance 14 miles
Difficulty Moderate
Surface Single track
Trailhead Turkeypen Gap

You'll want to pack a lunch for this one. The route takes you out and over the flank of Poundingstone Mountain. Though difficult enough, it makes for a really nice full day of riding. Be aware that on Squirrel Gap and Laurel Creek Trails you are way out in the backcountry (*read*: a long way from help if you need it, so be careful). Once out there, you'll notice that these trails don't see near the amount of use of those closer in. That means there's a greater chance of trees or debris across the trail— things that could do damage to you or your bike. In other words, be prepared and know that you have some wet river crossings late in the trip.

You'll start out by riding out to the Cantrell Creek Lodge site as described a few pages back. From the lodge you leave the river behind, head up Cantrell Creek Trail, and gradually climb up to meet Squirrel Gap Trail. Hang a right, ride up the flank of Rich Mountain, through Laurel Gap, and then up and around the flank of Poundingstone Mountain. There is a bailout option here if you need it, via Mullinax Trail.

If you hang in there for this route, though, the next step is to drop off the mountain down Laurel Creek Trail to the banks of Bradley Creek, a sizable stream. Cross the creek, turn right, and follow Bradley Creek Trail, crossing the creek several times more before heading up through Pea Gap and back across South Mills River to complete the loop.

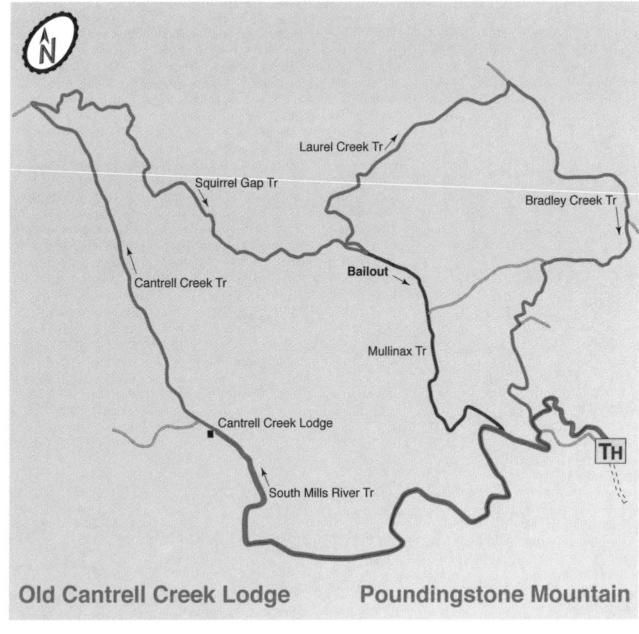

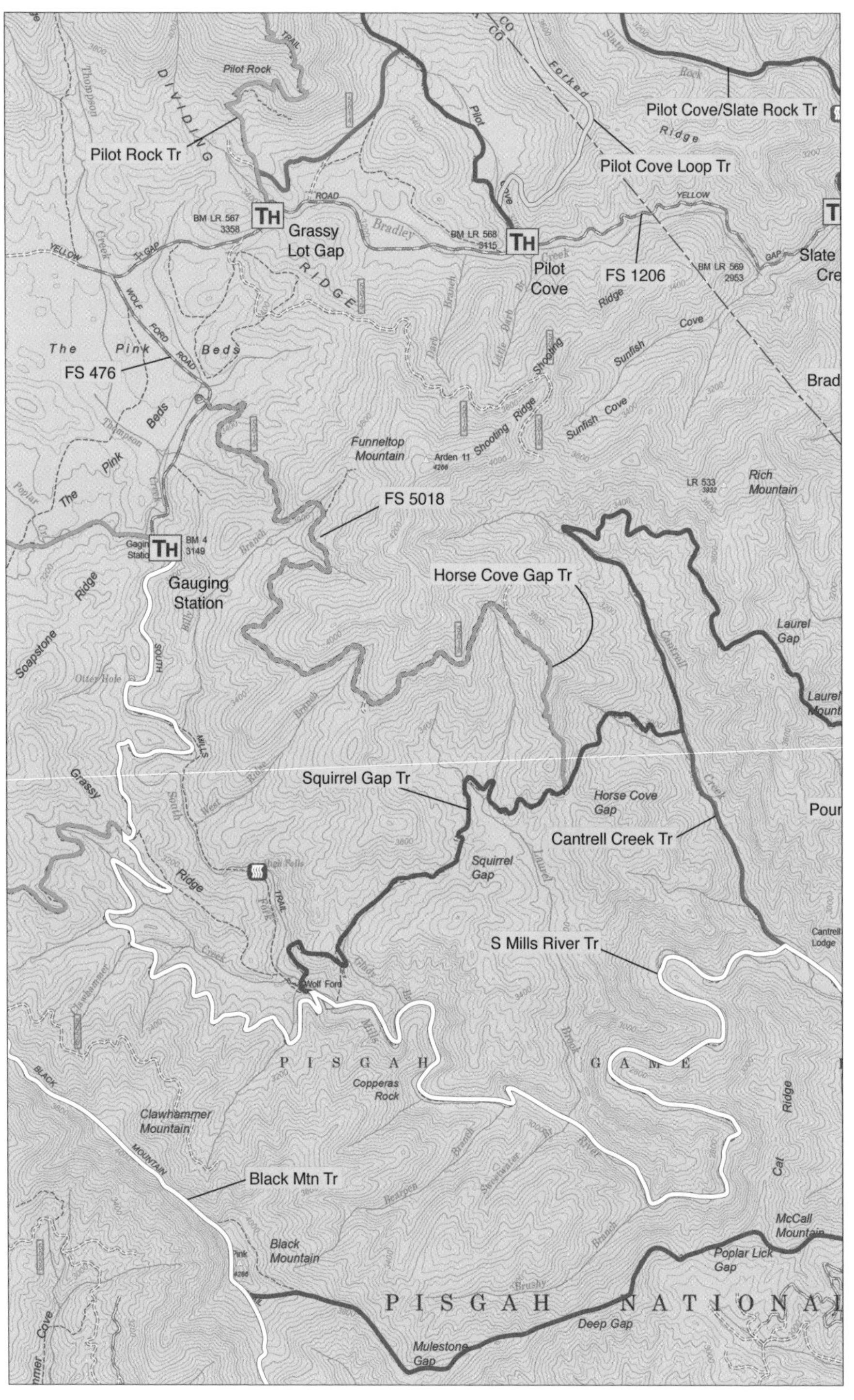
Pilot Rock Tr
Pilot Cove/Slate Rock Tr
Pilot Cove Loop Tr
Grassy
Lot Gap
Pilot
Cove
FS 1206
Slate
FS 476
FS 5018
Horse Cove Gap Tr
Gauging
Station
Squirrel Gap Tr
Cantrell Creek Tr
S Mills River Tr
Black Mtn Tr
Funneltop
Mountain
Rich
Mountain
Laurel
Gap
Horse Cove
Gap
Squirrel
Gap
Copperas
Rock
Clawhammer
Mountain
Black
Mountain
McCall
Mountain
Poplar Lick
Gap
Deep Gap
Mulestone
Gap
P I S G A H   N A T I O N A L
P I S G A H   G A M E

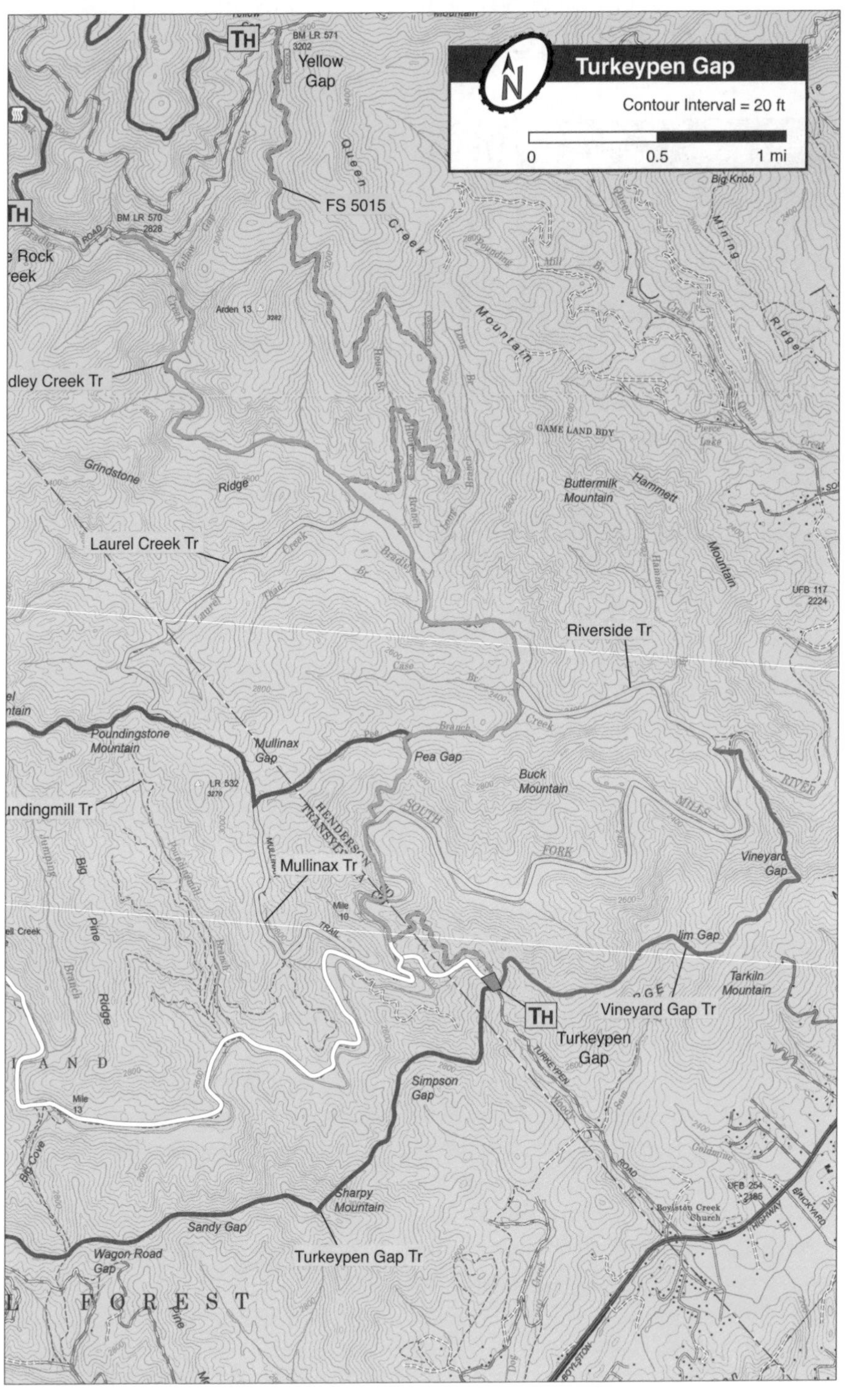
Turkeypen Gap
Contour Interval = 20 ft
0
0.5
1 mi
Yellow Gap
FS 5015
Bradley Creek Tr
Laurel Creek Tr
Riverside Tr
Poundingmill Tr
Mullinax Tr
Pea Gap
Buck Mountain
Vineyard Gap
Jim Gap
Vineyard Gap Tr
Tarkiln Mountain
TH
Turkeypen Gap
Simpson Gap
Sharpy Mountain
Sandy Gap
Turkeypen Gap Tr
Wagon Road Gap
Buttermilk Mountain
Big Knob

Trace Ridge

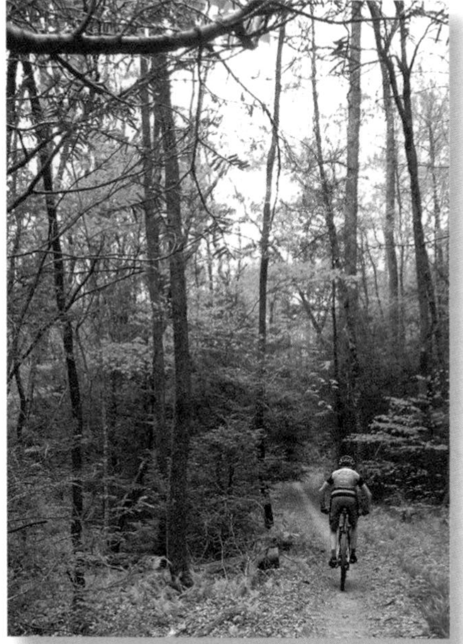

Fletcher Creek Trail is smooth and fast as it gently descends to the creek itself.

Type	Backcountry
Parking	Moderate
Toilets	None
Land Manager	USFS
Fee	None
Access	Gravel road
Special Rules	None

Trace Ridge is the trailhead to use to access the rides of the North Mills River watershed. This broad area is situated between Laurel Mountain to the south and the Blue Ridge Parkway to the north. You'll find a lot of trails here *and* a lot of diversity, including easier routes where you just meander out the impossibly long Forest Service Route 5097. It did not get the nickname Never-Ending Road for nothing; it just goes on and on. Branching off this road are a number of trails that bring you right back to the trailhead, each following a different creek. None of these is super difficult.

There are some more difficult rides to be found here as well. Take a turn up onto Trace Ridge Trail and you'll find all the hill climbing you'll ever want, right from the trailhead. Getting off the mountain is just like getting on: steep.

You'll drive to the trailhead on FS 5000. Just before the trailhead turnoff you'll find a horse camp; behind the horse camp are a few easier trails. Folks tend to skip these in favor of the Never-Ending Road routes, but if you're looking for something short and sweet, follow Lower Trace Ridge and Wash Creek to connect over to Bear Branch.

Want to head out on an all-day epic adventure? You can do that from Trace Ridge. Try circling up the Blue Ridge Parkway (don't forget those headlamps for the tunnels!) and returning on Big Creek Trail. Be aware that you are not allowed to actually *ride* your bike on the portion of trail that crosses National Park Service land and connects directly to the Blue Ridge Parkway; it's a very short stretch right at Little Pisgah Mountain tunnel. The Forest Service recommends you carry your bike here. The descent down Big Creek starts out pretty rocky and crazy, but tames down the farther you go.

Want even more? You can snake over to Yellow Gap via the Yellow Gap Trail and a gated forest road. Once over there, you've got nearly endless options.

If you need a campsite, you're in luck. There are dispersed-use sites just back of FS 142 from the trailhead and more can be found on FS 5000. It's not too far down the road to the North Mills River Campground. If you want picnic tables, toilets, running water and lots of company, this is the place.

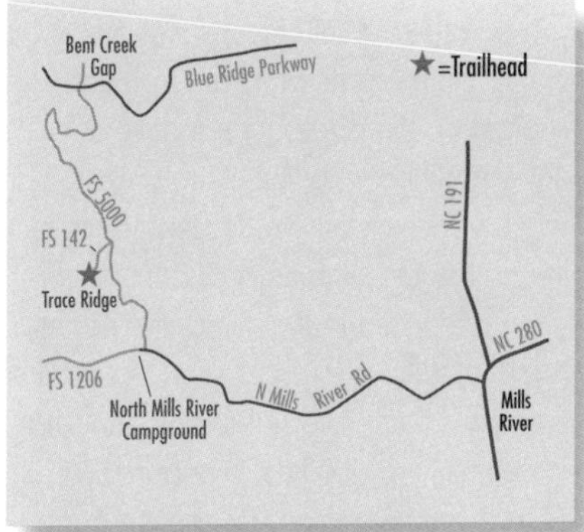

Getting to the Trailhead

Drive 2 miles north on FS 5000 from North Mills River Campground or 3 miles south from Bent Creek Gap and the Blue Ridge Parkway. Yes, you can drive here straight from Bent Creek. Whichever way you come in, turn west on FS 142 and drive a half-mile to the trailhead.

GPS Coordinates

35.420612, -82.656909

Trace Ridge Routes

Fletcher Creek

Distance 9 miles
Difficulty Easy
Surface Single track, forest road
Trailhead Trace Ridge

If you're looking for a route in Pisgah that's not too hard but also not too short, give this ride out Never-Ending Road to Fletcher Creek at try. The forest road portion follows the contours, so there are no big hill climbs to contend with, and the return along Fletcher Creek is a pretty gentle downhill as well.

Directions are easy. Ride around the gate and onto FS 5097, a.k.a. Never-Ending Road. Follow it for about 5.5 miles as is twists and turns and bobs up and down. Start looking for a carsonite wand sign marking the entrance onto Fletcher Creek Trail.

Fletcher Creek Trail runs through beautiful woods with ferns and wildflowers; you might have to hop a log or two. Eventually you'll make a wet crossing of Fletcher Creek to meet up with Spencer Gap Trail. Turn right (downstream) to follow Fletcher Creek Trail up and over a hill that has a short technical section. You should be ready for that by now.

When the trail dumps you out on FS 142, turn left and ride up the hill to the trailhead.

Variation Instead of turning onto Fletcher Creek Trail, stay on Never-Ending Road another 2 miles or so and turn down Middle Fork Trail, which is very similar to Fletcher Creek Trail. To finish the same way, just make the jog over to Fletcher Creek Trail when you reach Fletcher Creek; this makes a 12-mile route.

Spencer Gap

Distance 8 miles
Difficulty Moderate
Surface Single track, forest road
Trailhead Trace Ridge

Spencer Gap starts out exactly like the Fletcher Creek route, but once on Spencer Gap Trail you'll find the ride to be completely different. It is more difficult due to the creek crossings (all in the ankle-to-shin-depth category) and there are a number of places where you negotiate narrow hillside trails.

Begin by riding out Never-Ending Road. You'll be looking for a trail crossing the road around the 4.5-mile mark. Since the trail crosses here, there will be a trail sign on each side of the road. It is also the first major stream you will cross on the route. Turn left onto Spencer Gap Trail. For the next mile you'll follow and sometimes cross the branch until you reach the junction with Fletcher Creek Trail. Cross the trail and then the creek several more times before finally ending at Hendersonville Reservoir, a small dammed-up body of water that collects drinking water for the masses.

Just below the dam, continue onto FS 142 and follow it back up the hill to the trailhead.

Trace Ridge

Distance 6 to 10 miles
Difficulty Difficult
Surface Single track, forest road
Trailhead Trace Ridge

Notice the variable mileage above. You can tag Trace Ridge onto any of the other routes along Never-Ending Road. Follow Spencer Gap back for 6, Fletcher Creek for 7.3, and Middle Fork for 10. However you decide, it's the ride up to, and then the traverse and descent of, the ridge that makes it so difficult.

Begin by riding over the dirt mound to the right of the gate for Never-Ending Road. This leads onto Trace Ridge Trail. Go ahead and shift into granny gear; you're going to need it. The trail goes straight up the ridge. It's not quite a never-ending climb, but it feels like it. Just when you think you've made it to the top, the trail starts climbing again.

Compared to the climb, the ridge ride that follows is pretty short. About the time your heart rate stops registering up in helmet-land, it's time to head down. Take a break, tighten your helmet strap, lower your seat, and turn left on Spencer Gap Trail. Your heart beat will be back where it's supposed to be, but your stomach is suddenly going to jump up to your throat. The short descent that follows is rocky and steep, so take care.

It's not too far down to Never-Ending Road. Continue straight across to follow Spencer Gap Trail, turn right for Fletcher Creek Trail or Middle Fork Trail. Or if you've had enough single track for the day, turn left for the trailhead.

Bear Branch

Distance 3 miles
Difficulty Easy
Surface Single track, forest road
Trailhead Trace Ridge

Check out the Horse Camp at the entrance to FS 142 on your drive into the trailhead. If it's full to overflowing with equestrians, know that you'll be heading into horse territory if you do this ride. You're not likely to encounter any more horses on the trail itself than anywhere else, but you'll be riding beside their campsite and you don't want to spook a lot of horses.

The ride is great—just enough single track, just enough hill climbing, just enough descent. Nothing too difficult. Scenery equals a solid B. Distance is short and sweet.

Begin by riding out the far end of the parking lot onto lower Trace Ridge Trail. It's a downhill start but watch your speed, as soon you'll be taking a 300-degree left turn onto Wash Creek Trail to continue down the hill. Here's a dirty little secret: One of the biggest mud-holes in Pisgah is located after a blind turn, so watch out.

In no time, you're back at FS 142 and just down the hill from the trailhead. Cross Wash Creek on the bridge and cross over to the horse camp. Go 20 feet or so up the entrance road and turn immediately left to hop up on to Bear Branch Trail. Follow it through the woods along the edge of the campground (It's a big field).

After half a mile turn left at the fork and climb up to the woods road above. Take a left here and then a right at the next road junction. Follow FS 5001 up to the head of Bear Creek. Turn right onto the other end of Bear Branch Trail and follow it all the way back to the horse camp. From there you can just ride FS 142 to the trailhead or retrace your route from the beginning to finish up on single track.

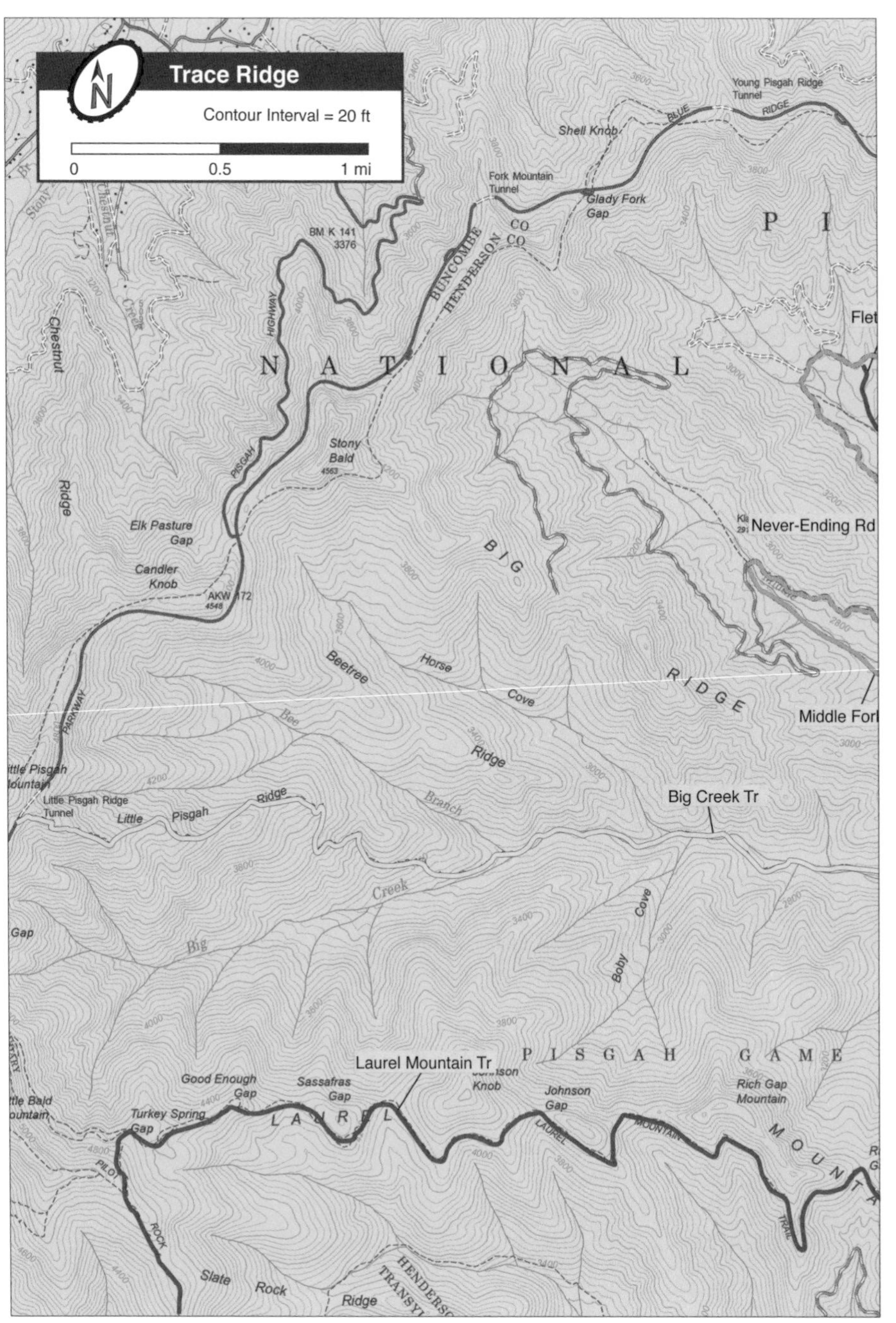
Trace Ridge
Contour Interval = 20 ft
0
0.5
1 mi
Never-Ending Rd
Middle Fork
Big Creek Tr
Laurel Mountain Tr

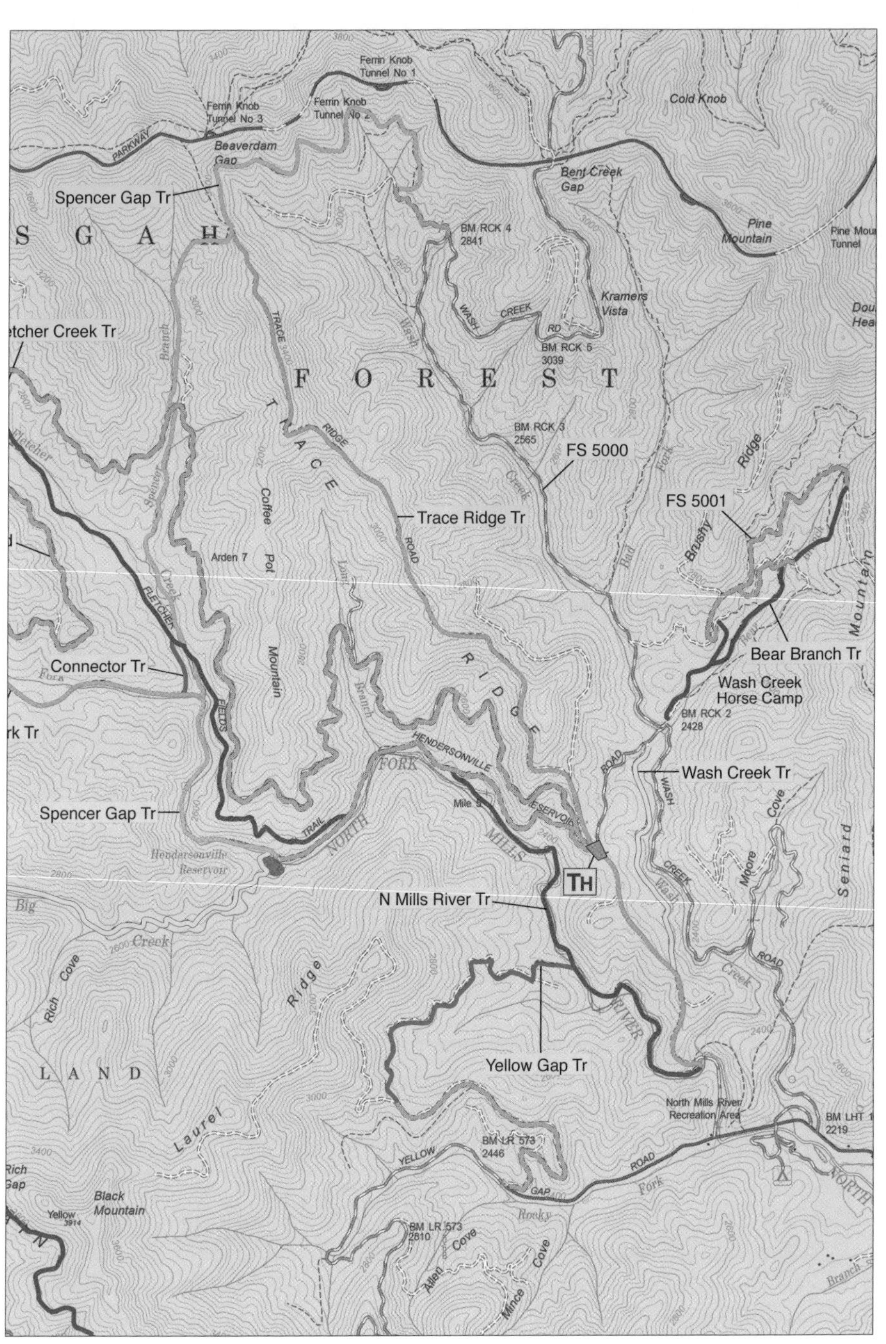

Ferrin Knob Tunnel No 1
Ferrin Knob Tunnel No 3
Ferrin Knob Tunnel No 2
Cold Knob
PARKWAY
Beaverdam Gap
Bent Creek Gap
Spencer Gap Tr
BM RCK 4 2841
Pine Mountain
Kramers Vista
WASH CREEK RD
BM RCK 5 3039
F O R E S T
TRACE RIDGE
BM RCK 3 2565
FS 5000
FS 5001
Trace Ridge Tr
Coffee Pot Mountain
Arden 7
Brushy Ridge
Bear Branch Tr
Connector Tr
FLETCHER
FIELDS
Wash Creek Horse Camp
BM RCK 2 2428
HENDERSONVILLE
Wash Creek Tr
Spencer Gap Tr
Mile 5
RESERVOIR
Hendersonville Reservoir
TH
N Mills River Tr
Moore Cove
Seniard Mountain
Rich Cove
Ridge
Yellow Gap Tr
L A N D
Laurel
North Mills River Recreation Area
BM LR 573 2446
YELLOW
GAP
ROAD
Black Mountain
Yellow 3914
BM LR 573 2810
Allen Cove
Mince Cove
Rocky Fork

Black Balsam

Much of the Black Balsam area is devoid of tall trees, with expansive views.

Type	Backcountry
Parking	Moderate
Toilets	Yes
Land Manager	USFS
Fee	None
Access	Paved road
Special Rules	None

Black Balsam Trailhead is a major destination for day hikers and overnight backpackers. For that reason, you may get some hairy eyeball looks when you pull up and start getting your bike ready to ride. Never fear, the rocky old rail-grade that heads north from this trailhead toward the Wilderness boundary and continues in the other direction, south, all the way down to NC 215, is open to bikes year-round. It's really the best mode of travel on these grades, much more interesting than walking.

Ever wanted to ride a mountain bike in the Scottish highlands? Want an alternative to sweating like a cold water bag in humid, near 100-degree weather? Like riding in the great wide open with views in every direction? That's what you get and more up at Black Balsam. Okay, you don't really get to ride in the Scottish Highlands, but it can sure feel like it—especially when a cloud rolls in and you are enveloped by the mists. At a little over 5,000 feet, this trailhead is one of the highest around. As soon as you get out of your car you can feel it; things are just different. The temperature is much lower, the air is clearer without all the humidity, even the vegetation has changed. The big stand of spruce fir behind the trailhead makes it smell like Christmas.

The views. The views are amazing, stunning, exquisite, extensive. They're great. But you'll need to come to a complete stop to take a long look because the trails are pretty darn rocky. Rocks come in all different shapes and sizes and these are the good kind—large and generally smooth. It's fun to weave in and out of them with no worries about mowing down some hiker; it's hard to go fast. There are not a lot of options up here for routes—basically just two.

Camping opportunities up here are not so good. If you're lucky you can snag a spot back in the spruce grove. If you don't mind hoofing it a ways, you could camp down on Flat Laurel Creek. Other than that, you're a long way from a car camping spot.

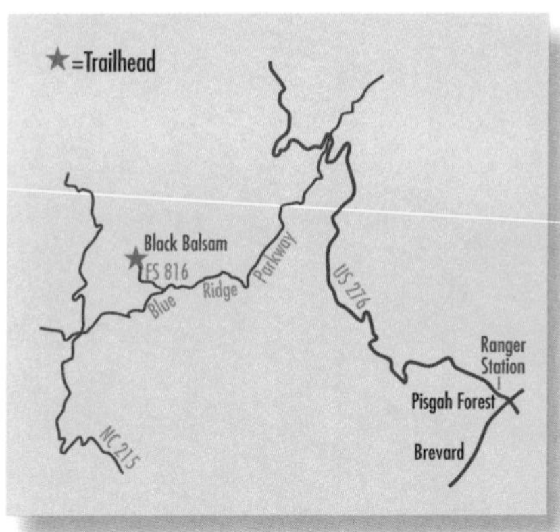

Getting to the Trailhead

Head up to the Blue Ridge Parkway—go south from US 276 or north from NC 215. You're looking for milepost 420. Two tenths of a mile north of this marker turn north on FS 816. The trailhead is at the end of the road.

GPS Coordinates

35.325474, -82.881960

Black Balsam Routes

Ivestor Gap

Distance 4 miles
Difficulty Easy
Surface Single track (kinda)
Trailhead Black Balsam

This out-and-back ride is along the Ivestor Gap Trail. What you'll see when you get there is that it's more road than trail, but so rocky there's no definite track. Just pick your route through the rocks and around the wet spots. You'll probably ride out differently than you'll ride back.

You start out at just over 5,000 feet in elevation and that is pretty much where you stay; the trail is practically level. There will be no coasting and no climbing. It's best just to spin along at a reasonable pace to keep from getting bounced around.

You'll know you've reached Ivestor Gap when you arrive at the big sign for Shining Rock Wilderness. Turn around here.

Flat Laurel Creek

Distance 5 or 7 miles
Difficulty Moderate
Surface Single track, pavement
Trailhead Black Balsam

On this route you'll encounter a whole lot more gradient than on the Ivestor Gap ride. Flat Laurel Creek Trail drops all the way down to NC 215 to a tiny trailhead, one you could possibly use in winter when the Parkway is closed. It's not in any way steep, just a gradual descent.

Flat Laurel Creek Trail starts on the far end of the parking lot, away from the toilet and up next to the road. Just get on it and ride. Along the route, you'll cross over a couple of streams and down near the bottom you'll ride past over waterfall while crossing a bridge. Once you hit NC 215, either return the way you came or loop up to the Parkway and come back past Devil's Courthouse to FS 816, turn left, and return to the trailhead.

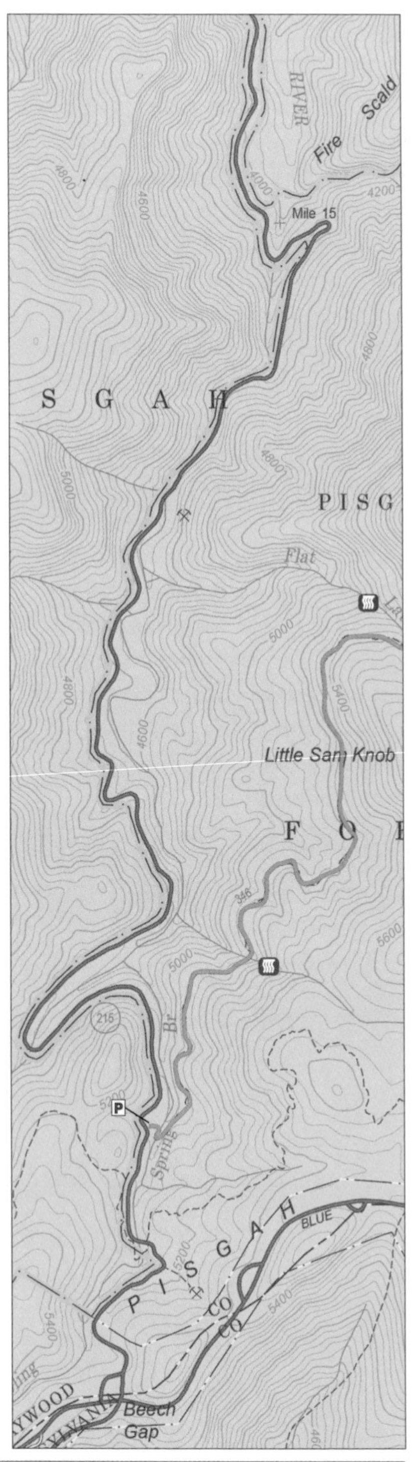

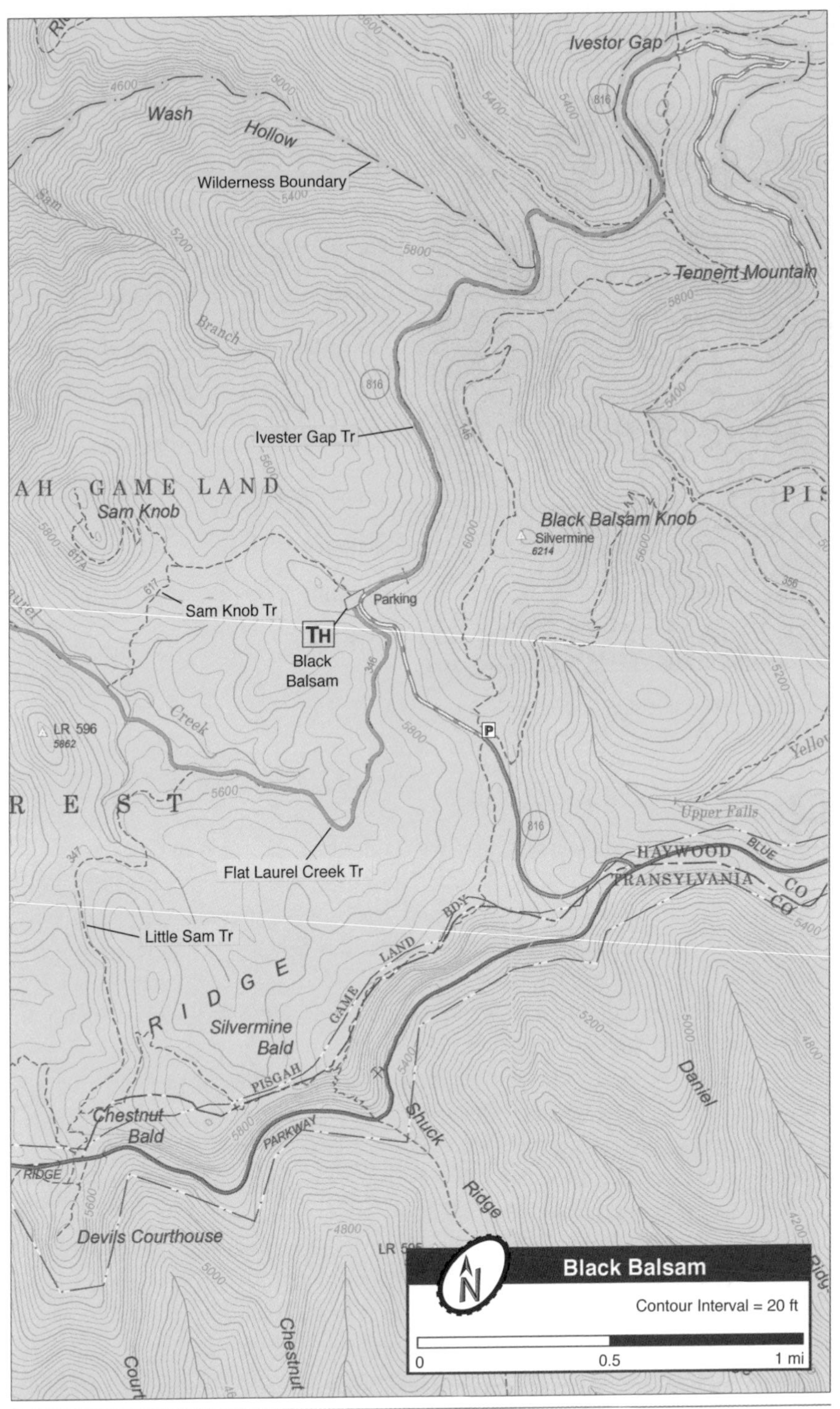

Ivestor Gap
Wash
Hollow
Wilderness Boundary
Sam
Branch
Tennent Mountain
Ivester Gap Tr
AH GAME LAND
Sam Knob
Black Balsam Knob
Silvermine
6214
Parking
Sam Knob Tr
TH
Black
Balsam
Creek
LR 596
5862
R E S T
Upper Falls
HAYWOOD
TRANSYLVANIA
BLUE
CO
CO
Flat Laurel Creek Tr
Little Sam Tr
R I D G E
Silvermine
Bald
GAME
LAND
BDY
PISGAH
Chestnut
Bald
PARKWAY
Shuck
Ridge
Daniel
RIDGE
Devils Courthouse
Chestnut
Court
Black Balsam
Contour Interval = 20 ft
0
0.5
1 mi

Bracken Mountain

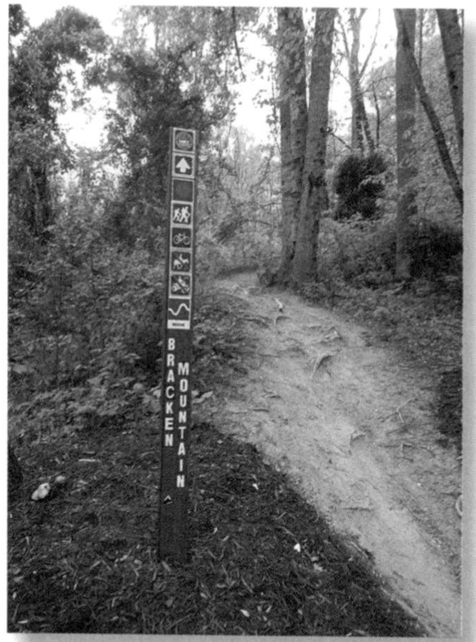

Once you leave this sign, it's all uphill for a good long climb.

Type	Backcountry
Parking	Moderate
Toilets	None
Land Manager	City of Brevard
Fee	None
Access	Paved road
Special Rules	None
Distance	5+ miles
Difficulty	Difficult
Surface	Single track

Be sure to bring your climbing legs with you when you come to Bracken Preserve. From the parking lot, it's all uphill for half a mile without any letup, and then more climbing and then more climbing. You'll be sucking air in a serious way before you've gone a couple of hundred yards. The old rule, "what goes up must come down" definitely applies here—and the down is pretty awesome. From the top of Bracken Mountain back down to the trailhead is one of the best downhills in the area with high, banked turns and plenty of dips and whoops.

Technically Bracken Preserve is not part of Pisgah National Forest. It's a park managed by the City of Brevard. However, it does adjoin the national forest and if you are up for a really big ride, you can ride all the way to the Pisgah Fish Hatchery and back by connecting to FS 475C. Most folks will just want to do the 5-mile-plus loop that is all within the preserve.

From the trailhead, ride uphill on Bracken Mountain Trail. At a little over a half-mile you'll reach the junction with Brushy Creek Trail. At this point you can ride the loop in either direction, but for the smoothest downhill, go right here on Brushy Creek. The trail goes down a little, and then climbs a good bit more before connecting with Mackey Ridge Trail. Go right on Mackey Ridge and then left back onto Bracken Mountain. Hang onto your socks; it's mostly downhill from here for the next 2.5 miles.

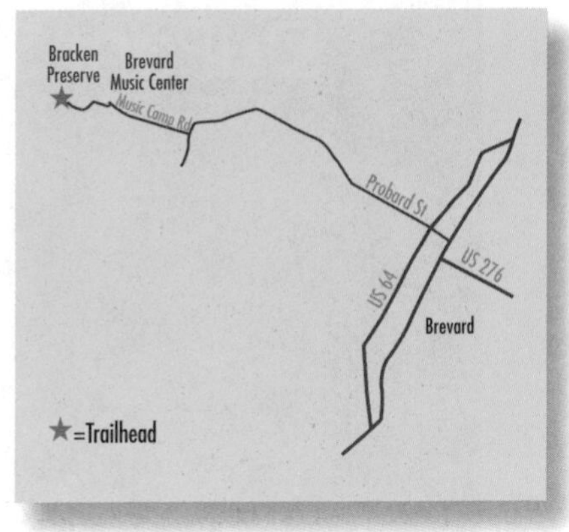

Getting to the Trailhead

From US 64 in Brevard, take Probart Street, following the signs to the Brevard Music Center. After a mile, turn right on Music Camp Road and at the turn into the Music Center bear left up the hill on Pinnacle Road to the trailhead at the top.

GPS Coordinates

35.241, -82.756

Bracken Preserve
Brevard Music Center
Music Camp Rd
Probard St
US 276
US 64
Brevard
★=Trailhead

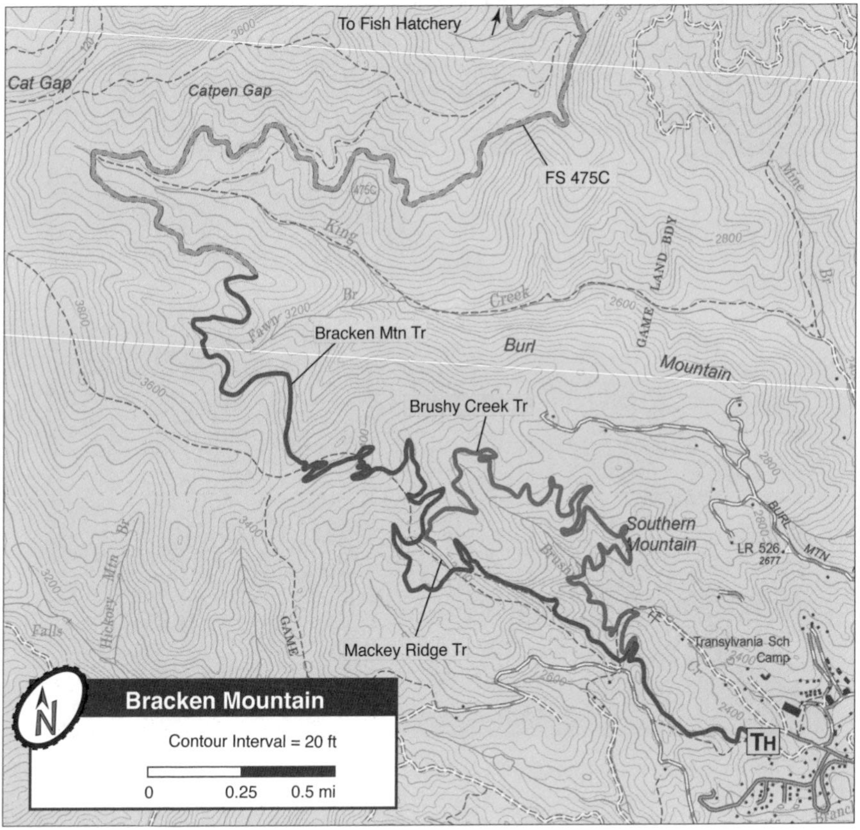

To Fish Hatchery
Cat Gap
Catpen Gap
FS 475C
475C
King
Creek
Fawn
Br
Bracken Mtn Tr
Burl
Mountain
GAME LAND BDY
Brushy Creek Tr
Southern Mountain
LR 526
2677
BURL MTN
Mackey Ridge Tr
Hickory Mtn Br
Falls
Transylvania Sch Camp
Mine Br
TH
Bracken Mountain
Contour Interval = 20 ft
0
0.25
0.5 mi

DuPont State Forest

Triple Falls is a major attraction in DuPont State Forest and makes for a great destination on a bike ride.

You'll be hard pressed to find a better collection of mountain bike trails anywhere in the Carolinas; DuPont truly has the cream of the crop. Forest managers here know they have a world-class destination for cyclists and they spare no expense in keeping the trails here in top-notch condition. Turns are banked, grades are bermed and dipped, and swooping turns replace tight switchbacks. Grades are maintained to make all uphills ridable. It's just an awesome place to ride a mountain bike.

Of course the stunning scenery is also a huge draw. There are six major waterfalls, four mountain lakes, and a number of mountainsides with exposed rock riding surfaces and amazing views up top. You can rip it up on the single track or you can slowly cruise the dirt roads. There is something for everyone. While you're at it, take a break and swim below a waterfall or jump off the dock at a quiet lake.

First-timers to DuPont may find all the trails and roads a bit confusing—there are 84 named trails adding up to 84 miles. That's a lot of really short trails and roads. Don't worry, the signage is excellent. Just be sure to bring your map, or in a pinch you can ask one of the many other users you're bound to run into.

Same as Pisgah, the closest town is Brevard. Hendersonville is nearby as well. If you need a bike shop for repairs, rentals, or supplies, head first to Pisgah Forest where you'll find a couple to choose from (see Appendix D for shops listed by town). Or you could zip over to Hendersonville or even up to Asheville, neither of which are very far away. DuPont is also just up the mountain from Travelers Rest and Greenville, SC. So if you're coming up that way, you might stop in and shop there first.

Lodging and food are plentiful in those towns as well, but if you're looking for somewhere nearby to camp for free, you're out of luck. Your best bet for that is to base out of Pisgah.

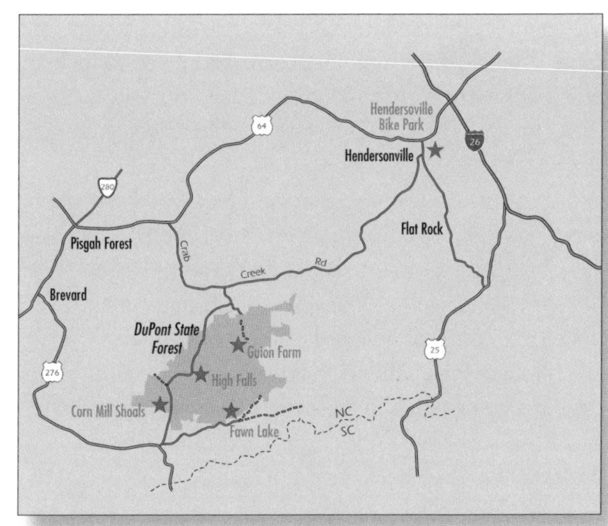

Guion Farm

Small and secluded Wintergreen Falls has a nice plungepool for cooling off.

Type	Backcountry
Parking	Plentiful
Toilets	Portable
Land Manager	NC Forest Service
Fee	None
Access	Gravel road
Special Rules	None

The area surrounding the old Guion Farm is traditionally known as the flatwoods. Flat is not what comes to mind when you think about the mountains of western North Carolina. Relatively speaking, though, the woods here are pretty level. That makes this an ideal trailhead if you're looking for an easier ride. Just start out on Buck Forest Road and circle back by way of White Pine, Hickory Mountain, or Thomas Cemetery Road and you'll be riding the easiest there is in the forest.

The flatwoods only go so far. Once you leave them, the terrain gets a bit more rugged. From this same trailhead you can head up a mountain or drop down a ridge, or ride over to other parts of DuPont for an all-day epic adventure. Take a spin down to Wintergreen Falls and go for a swim in the pool below. There are plenty of options for riders of all stripes.

Right at the trailhead, hidden in the woods, is a mountain bike skills course. This is a great place to mess around while you're waiting for your group to get ready or in between rides. You'll find a fun obstacle course of logs, ramps, teeter-totters, and more. It's great fun.

Getting to the Trailhead

From Pisgah Forest, go east on US 64. At the rock quarry turn right onto Crab Creek Road and continue several miles. Turn right onto DuPont Road and then take the first left you come to as you head uphill. This is Sky Valley Road, and it will turn to gravel not long before reaching the trailhead.

GPS Coordinates

35.211677, -82.587929

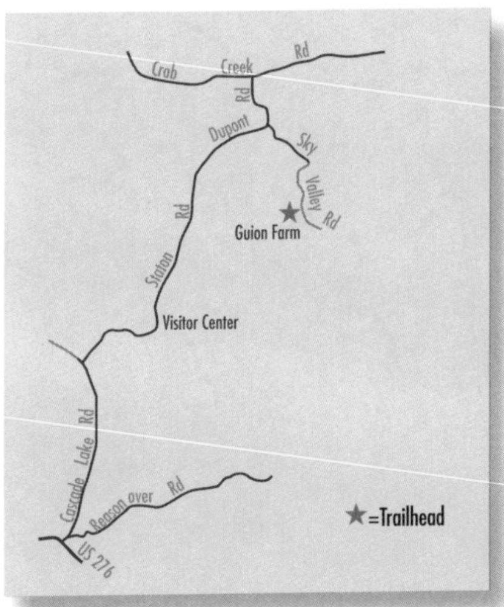

Guion Farm Routes

Wintergreen Falls

Distance 8.5 miles
Difficulty Easy
Surface Single/double track
Trailhead Guion Farm

You can get to Wintergreen Falls any number of ways, the most direct obviously being to ride straight to it. However, if you want to get in a nice ride first and treat yourself to a view or a swim at the end, this is the way to go.

Begin by riding south out Sky Valley Road to the first trail junction on the left. Go left on Shoal Creek Trail and ride down the hill. Follow this trail all the way to where you intersect again with Sky Valley Road.

Back on the road, turn right and after a very short distance, turn left up the hill on Rifle Trail. You'll need your granny gear for the next half-mile, as it's a good climb with some berms thrown in just to add agony to the misery. When Rifle Trail hits Guion Trail, go left and then turn right on Hickory Mountain Road.

The double track road leads out to the rifle range in a big field. Turn left here on Ridgeline, ride down the hill, and then turn left on Hooker Creek Trail which leads down to the creek. It's a fun, swooping downhill. Enjoy it, because the climb that follow is a sweatmonger.

Eventually you'll top out back in the flatwoods. Turn right on White Pine Road and then a bit farther on cross Buck Forest Road onto Thomas Cemetery Road. This next stretch is a hoot as you gradually head downhill. Put it in that big gear and roll. Just when you've had enough big-gearing, look for a left turn onto Tarklin Branch Road. A downhill leads to a fun, fast, splash-water-everywhere shallow creek crossing and—surprise!—a steep but short climb that follows.

Turn right at the top of the hill onto Sandy Trail, which lives up to its name as it travels alongside the creek. Stay on it all the way to the right turn to Wintergreen Falls. Follow this trail to a small open area just beyond a horse tie-up. Leave your bike here and follow the footpath to the falls. This is a great spot and does not see near the crowds of the other waterfalls in the forest.

To return to the trailhead, head back down Wintergreen Falls Trail and turn right to go uphill on a road that's still called Wintergreen Falls Trail. Turn right on Tarklin Branch Road partway up and eventually you'll bear left on the trail leading across the big field surrounding the trailhead.

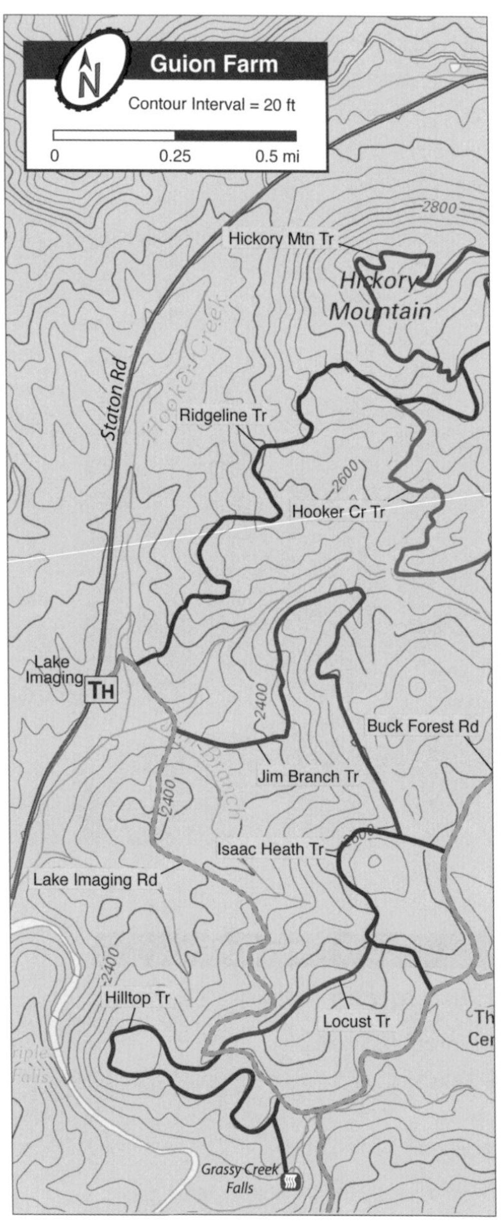

Ridgeline

Distance 6.5 miles
Difficulty Moderate
Surface Single/double track
Trailhead Guion Farm

There are people who do shuttles between the Guion Farm and Lake Imaging trailheads just for the downhill run on Ridgeline Trail. Yes, it's that good. It's not super steep, just a fun trail with sweeping turns, tight singletrack, wall rides, and small berms. The fun seems to go forever.

From the trailhead, ride across the field behind the farmhouse and then onto Hickory Mountain Road. At the rifle range field, turn left onto Ridgeline Trail, put it in a big gear, and start pumping. You'll finally bottom out on Lake Imaging Road. Now you have to regain all that elevation you lost. Turn left and then left again on Jim Branch Trail. Follow it back up the mountain to Buck Forest Road. Turn left on Buck Forest to head back to the trailhead.

Variation At the rifle range, add in the Hickory Mountain Loop Trail.

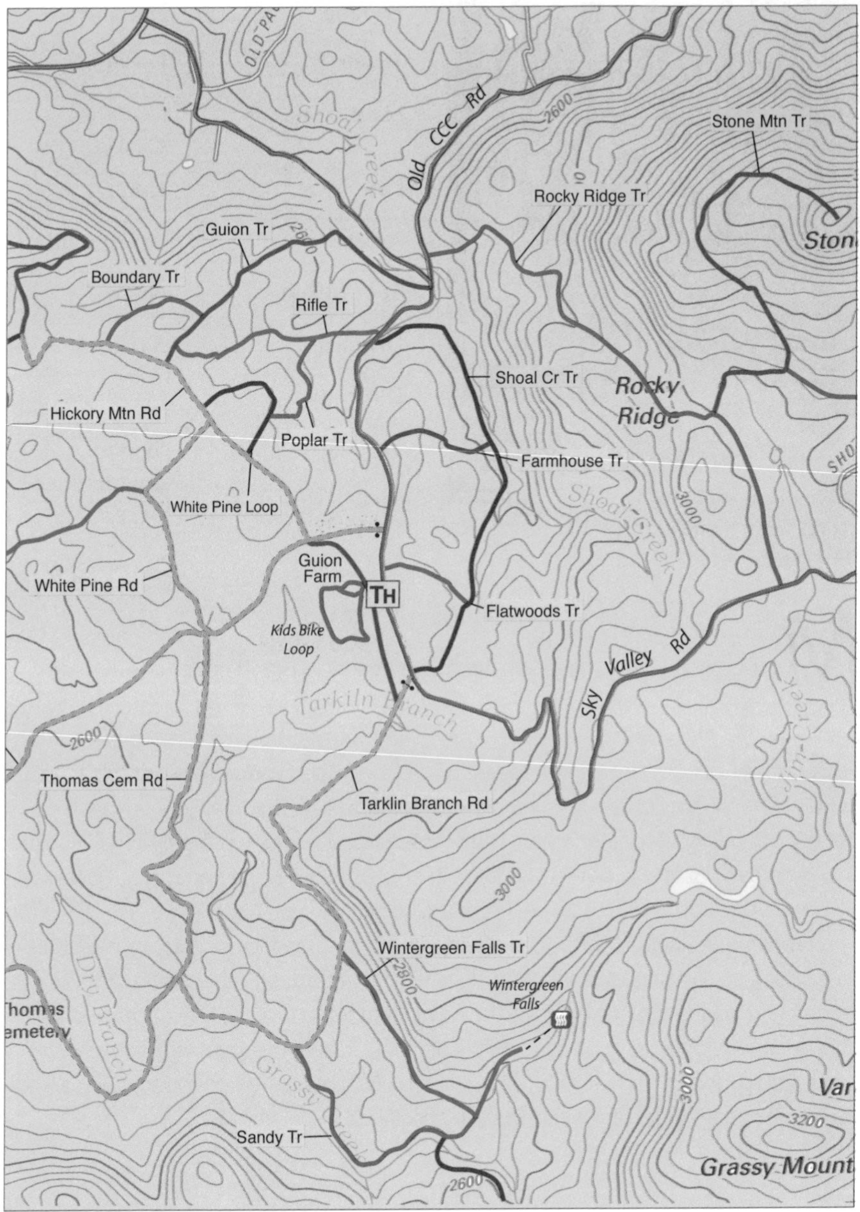

Lake Imaging

Flying down Ridgeline Trail in close quarters is a lot of fun.

Type	Backcountry
Parking	Plentiful
Toilets	Portable
Land Manager	NC Forest Service
Fee	None
Access	Paved road
Special Rules	None
Distance	5 miles
Difficulty	Moderate
Surface	Single/ double track

Most cyclists who use the Lake Imaging trailhead are there for one reason and one reason only—Ridgeline Trail. On busy days this parking lot can get quite hectic. Many of the vehicles belong to mountain bikers, but you'll see quite a few horse trailers as well; this is the easiest and closest trailhead for equestrians to pull their trailers to. Not only is this the closest trailhead to Ridgeline, you have the benefit of ending up at the bottom after making your run down the mountain. Take a lap, or two, or three. Yes, you can do plenty of other loops from here, but most of those are better accessed from other trailheads.

From the trailhead ride out Lake Imaging Road, passing the bottom of Ridgeline Trail. Just past tiny Lake Imaging, turn left on Jim Branch Trail and take it up the hill and all the way to Buck Forest Road. Turn left on Buck Forest, follow it to Hickory Mountain Road, and turn left. Both these roads are fairly flat and you can pump a big gear if you want to. Ride Hickory Mountain Trail all the way to its end and continue left onto Ridgeline Trail. It's mostly downhill from here for a total of about five miles. Enjoy.

Getting to the Trailhead

From Pisgah Forest, go east on US 64. At the rock quarry turn right onto Crab Creek Road and continue several miles. Turn right onto DuPont Road, heading up and over the mountain. DuPont Road becomes Staton Road. Continue to the Lake Imaging trailhead on the left.

GPS Coordinates

35.209376, -82.615741

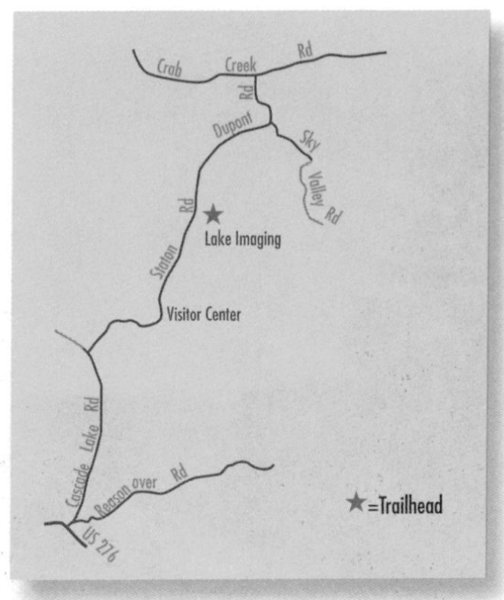

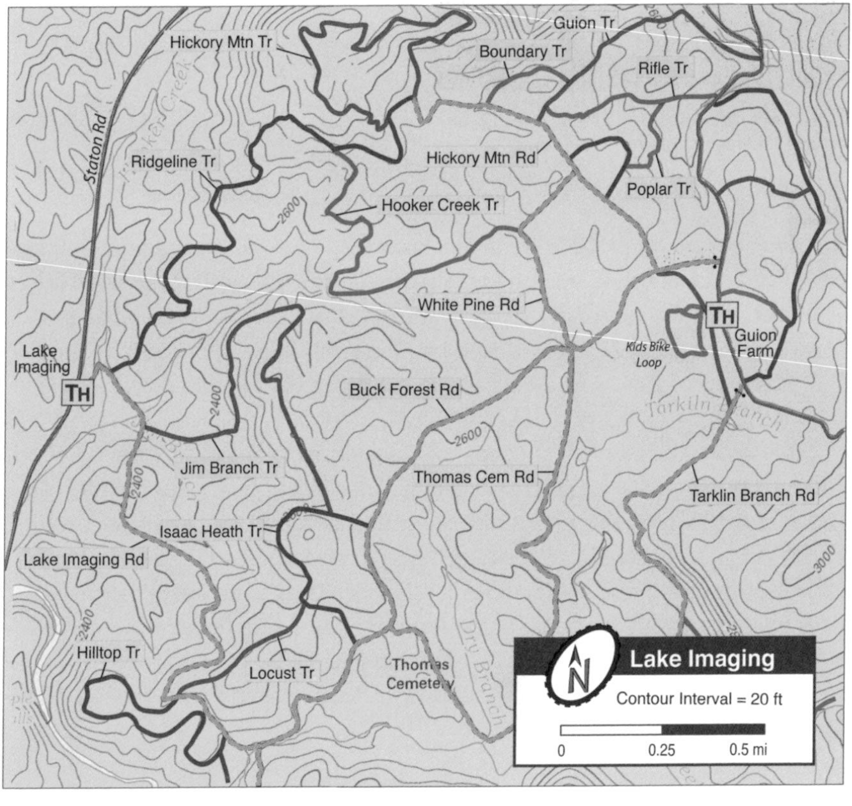

High Falls

You'll ride out to great views of the big waterfalls from High Falls trailhead.

Type	Backcountry
Parking	Moderate
Toilets	Yes
Land Manager	NC Forest Service
Fee	None
Access	Paved road
Special Rules	*Yes

* Bike riding is prohibited on white gravel foot trails.

High Falls is the place to go for the latest details on the goings-on in DuPont State Recreational Forest. You'll find a visitors center here, most days staffed by volunteers who are more than happy to answer your questions. Even when it is closed, look to this kiosk for what is usually the most current information of any in the forest. This is also the best trailhead to use if you want to ride out to see the big waterfalls.

You'll see there are only a couple of route recommendations for this trailhead. There's a good reason for that; it's a very popular place. Spectacular High Falls is only a short walk away and is also the access trailhead for the easiest hike to Bridal Veil Falls. So of course you're going to see a lot of the hiking crowd, often families with young kids and perhaps not so much backcountry experience. Take care riding around them; being passed suddenly by a bike from behind can be startling. But if you want to spin out to the falls this is easy access for bikes; if you want more, this trailhead is also a good place for exploring the southwestern side of the forest.

Getting to the Trailhead

From Pisgah Forest go east on US 64. At the rock quarry turn right onto Crab Creek Road and continue several miles. Turn right onto DuPont Road, heading up and over the mountain as it becomes Staton Road. Continue down and across Little River. You'll find the High Falls trailhead a bit farther on the left.

GPS Coordinates

35.191057, -82.623356

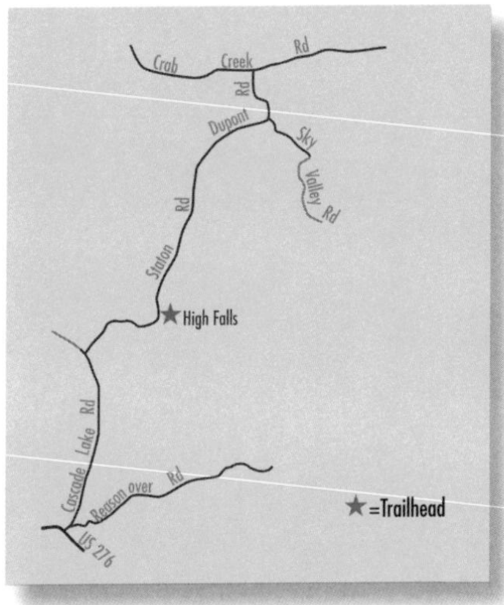

High Falls Routes

DuPont Waterfalls

Distance 1 to 8 miles
Difficulty Easy
Surface Forest road
Trailhead High Falls

Do you want to see some of the major features of DuPont, including the big waterfalls, without working too hard? Here are some ride options for you. Most of them are on wide dirt roads and are a great introduction to both the forest itself and to mountain biking in general.

First up is High Falls, just a half-mile from the trailhead—straight out Buck Forest Road. You can view it from the top by riding over a covered bridge or swing over for a frontal view from High Falls Trail.

Getting a look at Triple Falls requires a slightly more difficult ride: downhill going out on Triple Falls Trail and uphill on the return via High Falls Trail. It's 1.4 miles from the trailhead to the viewing shelter.

Grassy Creek Falls, though not so huge or spectacular as the others, makes a good destination as well. Take Buck Forest Road to Lake Imaging Road and turn left. You'll have to climb a bit to get there and then walk down to view the falls, but it's worth it. This waterfall is another 0.8 mile from the covered bridge.

Bridal Veil Falls is something else. Located in the heart of DuPont, it takes your breath away to watch it racing down a huge slab of rock. From the covered bridge, ride south on Conservation Road. Cross below the dam to Lake Julia, and the first road on the right is Bridal Veil Falls Road. Follow this a little ways until it dead-ends. From here a short trail leads to the base of Bridal Veil Falls. If this falls looks familiar, perhaps it's because you've watched *The Hunger Games* or *The Last of the Mohicans*. You can stand on the rock at the base where Katniss Everdeen stood with her bow and arrow, or run up the angling slab to the left of the falls as Hawkeye did in *The Last of the Mohicans,* to see the "bridal veil" at the top.

You might want to cruise out and have a look at Lake Julia. It's a beautiful mountain lake and makes a great spot for a picnic. To get there, ride as if you're going to Bridal Veil Falls. Instead of turning right on Bridal Veil Falls Road, continue on up the hill a bit, turn left on Lake Julia Road, and follow it down to the lake and a picnic spot where you can kick back, relax, and enjoy the view.

You can check out some single track on any of these forays. Circle around Hilltop Trail on your trip to Grassy Creek Falls. Out near Bridal Veil Falls you can make a short loop by connecting Corn Mill Shoals Trail to Shelter Rock Trail; there is a fun little stretch in there with boulders and other obstacles. On the way back from Lake Julia or Bridal Veil Falls try hopping onto Three Lakes Trail to view Lake Julia, tiny Lake Alford, and Lake Dense. Then take Pitch Pine Trail to end up back at the covered bridge.

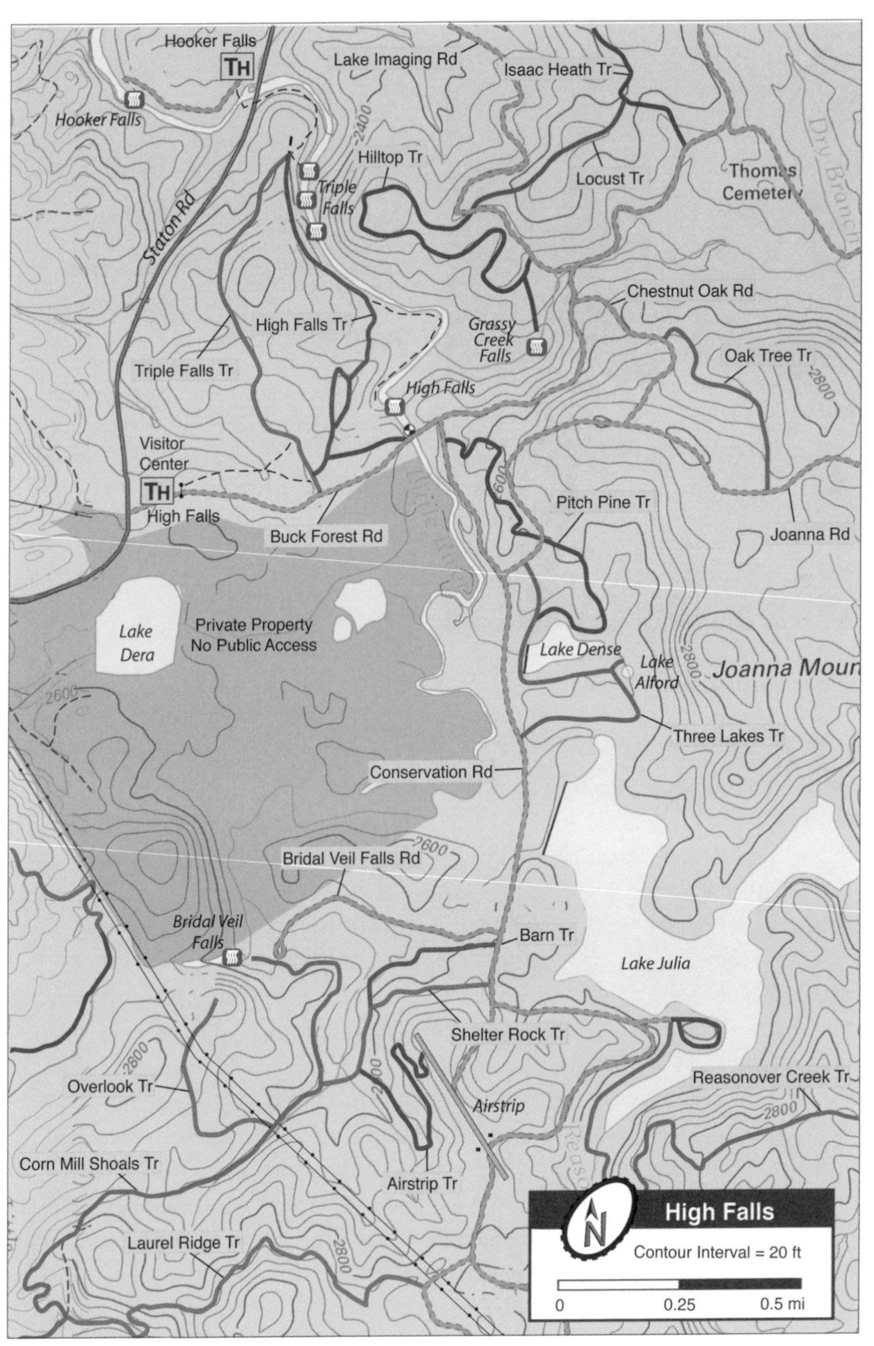
Hooker Falls
TH
Lake Imaging Rd
Isaac Heath Tr
Hooker Falls
2400
Hilltop Tr
Triple
Falls
Locust Tr
Thomas
Cemetery
Dry Branch
Staton Rd
Chestnut Oak Rd
High Falls Tr
Grassy
Creek
Falls
Triple Falls Tr
Oak Tree Tr
2800
High Falls
Visitor
Center
TH
High Falls
Buck Forest Rd
Pitch Pine Tr
Joanna Rd
Lake
Dera
Private Property
No Public Access
Lake Dense
Lake
Alford
2800
Joanna Moun
2600
Three Lakes Tr
Conservation Rd
2600
Bridal Veil Falls Rd
Bridal Veil
Falls
Barn Tr
Lake Julia
Shelter Rock Tr
2800
Overlook Tr
Reasonover Creek Tr
Airstrip
2800
Corn Mill Shoals Tr
Airstrip Tr
Laurel Ridge Tr
2800
N
High Falls
Contour Interval = 20 ft
0
0.25
0.5 mi

Corn Mill Shoals

The trail up Cedar Rock is like a paved sidewalk—after an earthquake.

Type	Backcountry
Parking	Plenty
Toilets	Portable
Land Manager	NC Forest Service
Fee	None
Access	Paved road
Special Rules	None

Wow, oh wow—the rides heading out from Corn Mill Shoals trailhead are like none other in the Southeast. Here you can ride up and over mountains on trails of solid granite. Imagine a concrete sidewalk tilted to a twenty-degree angle, rough it up a bit, gouge out some depressions, break off some slabs and overlap them, and then plant grass in the crevices. Now intersperse these hundreds-of-yards-long sections with baby head-sized rocks, throw in some roots and a few big drops, make some tight twisting turns through the trees, and you're starting to get the idea. But now quit trying to imagine it and just go to Corn Mill Shoals, get on your bike, and experience it for yourself.

This is not the trailhead for the inexperienced mountain biker. Even Corn Mill Shoals Road is, in most places, a single track trail with its own set of difficulties. People sometimes arrive back at the parking lot with scraped elbows, skinned knees, or worse. Go down on those rocks and you'll find they aren't very forgiving.

For the most part, though, it's just a really fun place to go for a bike ride. You get to test the limits of what your multi-thousand-dollar bike was designed for and see some really neat sights as well.

The routes included here are those most immediate to the trailhead. But really, the sky is the limit. If you're looking for an epic adventure, this is as good a place to start as any. Try heading over to the Fawn Lake/Reasonover area via Mine Mountain,looping back past the visitor center, and continuing on to Sheep Mountain and Cascade Trails before finishing up.

Getting to the Trailhead

From Pisgah Forest, go east on US 64. At the rock quarry turn right onto Crab Creek Road and continue several miles. Turn right onto DuPont Road, heading up and over the mountain as it becomes Staton Road. Pass three trailheads and the visitor center before reaching the T-intersection with Cascade Lake Road; turn left. The trailhead is just down the road on the south side. You can also come in on Cascade Lake Road from the tiny town of Cedar Mountain on US 276.

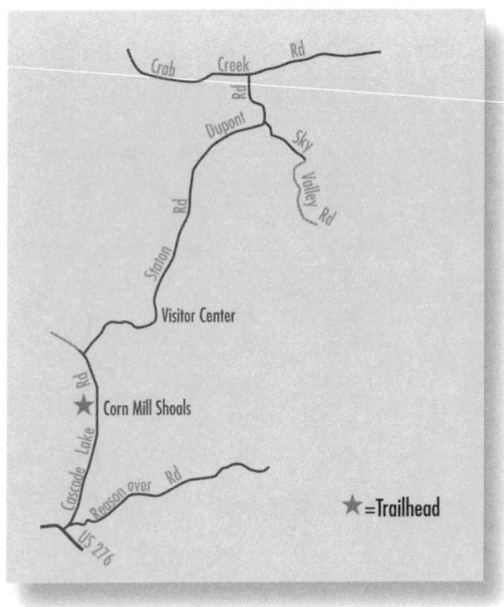

GPS Coordinates

35.172798, -82.638778

Corn Mill Shoals Routes

Burnt Mountain–Cedar Rock

Distance 6.8 miles
Difficulty Difficult
Surface Single/double track
Trailhead Corn Mill Shoals

If you do only one ride in DuPont State Recreational Forest, make it this one. You'll get to experience what everyone raves about and what some call the Moab of the East: the bare-rock riding over Cedar Rock. It's pretty cool.

Begin by riding across the road, around the gate, and onto Corn Mill Shoals Road. Just down the trail a bit you'll see Big Rock Trail heading up to the left. A lot of people get excited and turn to go up the mountain here. Resist that urge and continue down Corn Mill Shoals Road.

About a half-mile farther down the road you'll come to an intersection where Burnt Mountain Trail enters from the right. Just a short ways farther, Little River Trail (which looks like a road) exits to the left. Continue on Corn Mill Shoals Road by bearing right.

At the next intersection, angle slightly right onto the other end of Burnt Mountain Trail and get ready for some fun. Ahead is a series of big berms that big-air lovers dream about. Let it fly or keep your tires firmly on the ground—whichev-

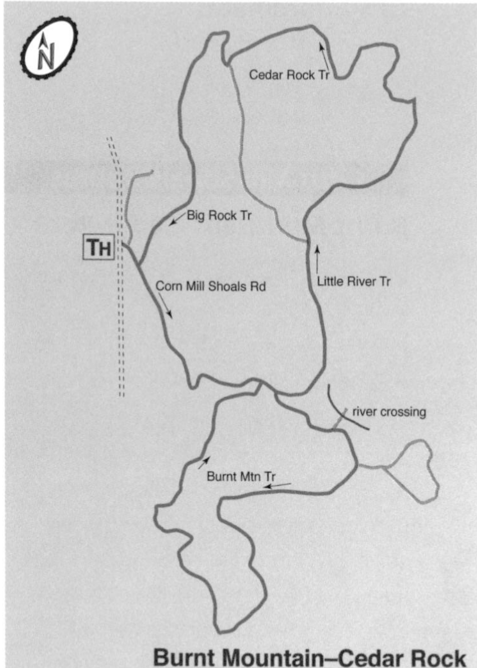

Burnt Mountain–Cedar Rock

er you choose, it's a hoot. Following the berms, the trail climbs up and along the ridge of Burnt Mountain. It's somewhat of a slog, but you can handle it. After a cruise along the side of the ridge up top, the trail drops like a stone back down to Corn Mill Shoals Road. Watch your speed, there's a serious drop-off into a rocky section two-thirds of the way down. Remember the "or worse" mentioned above? This is where it happens.

Back down on Corn Mill Shoals Road (you were at this spot earlier), turn right and then left onto Little River Trail, which is quite roadlike here. Follow it down along the river until it ends in a brush pile. This is where you turn up the mountain on Cedar Rock Trail.

Enjoy your ride to the summit. It's a huffer-puffer, but much of it is on bare rock.

Up top at the big rock cairn and sign, angle right onto Big Rock Trail after soaking in the view. This is your path down and it's a blast. Hang on and watch for folks coming up. Hang a right at the bottom to finish the ride.

Buck Ridge Add-on

Distance 3.5 miles
Difficulty Moderate
Surface Single track, forest road
Trailhead Corn Mill Shoals

You can add this short loop onto just about any ride you choose from Corn Mill Shoals Trailhead. It makes for a great warmup and it's a good way to test that all is in order with your bike before heading farther afield. The stretch leading down to the trailhead at the end has a short section of bare rock similar to Cedar Rock Trail.

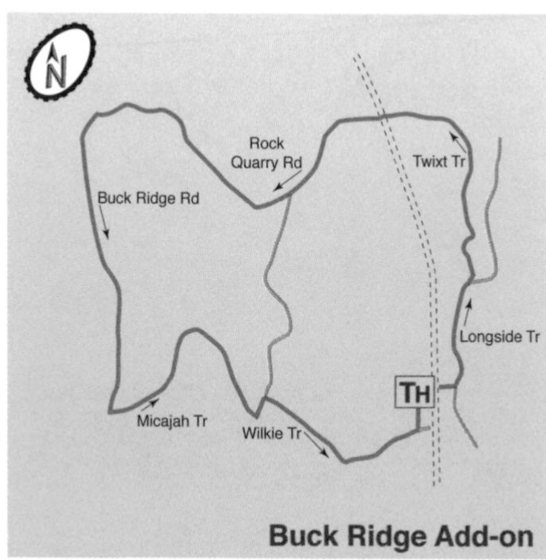

Buck Ridge Add-on

Start out by riding across the road and onto Corn Mill Shoals Road. After the gate take an immediate left on Longside Trail. Just 0.2 mile later, bank left onto Twixt Trail which takes you down to Cascade Lake Road. Cross the road and ride up Rock Quarry Road, passing one end of Micajah Trail, and then farther up turn left on Buck Ridge Road.

After 0.7 mile on Buck Ridge turn left down the other end of Micajah Trail and head down the mountain. When you get to Wilkie Trail, turn right onto it and head for the parking lot.

Bridal Veil Falls

Distance 5 miles
Difficulty Moderate
Surface Single/double track
Trailhead Corn Mill Shoals

This is the fun route to Bridal Veil Falls. It's an out-and-back ride, but it has so much variety that coming back seems quite different than heading out. Be aware that it includes a crossing of Little River where you will get your feet wet.

The directions are pretty simple, since you follow Corn Mill Shoals Trail all the way to the falls, and a good part of it is a road. Begin by crossing Cascade Lake Road onto Corn Mill Shoals Trail. Stay on it.

At one mile, cross Little River at Corn Mill Shoals, a pretty little rapid and a fun spot to hang out. It's a tiny version of Sliding Rock in Pisgah. The route crosses just above the shoals where it is shallow. It is also very slippery. Dismount and walk across in your socking feet (for best traction), pushing your bike and using it for balance. This way just your socks and lower legs will get wet. Insist on riding across? When your bike skitters out from under you, your whole body will get soaked. It's your choice.

After the ford you'll ride up and over a ridge with some interesting rock moves and a long section of bare rock. Nearer

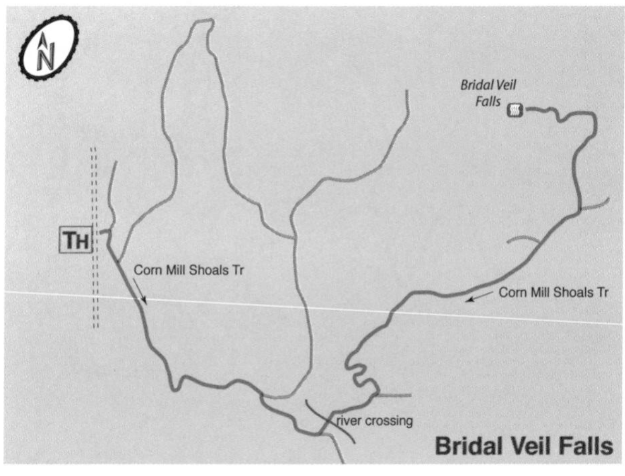

to the falls is a fun stretch through some boulders. (To read about the falls itself see p. 99.) When you're ready to go back to the trailhead, return the way you came.

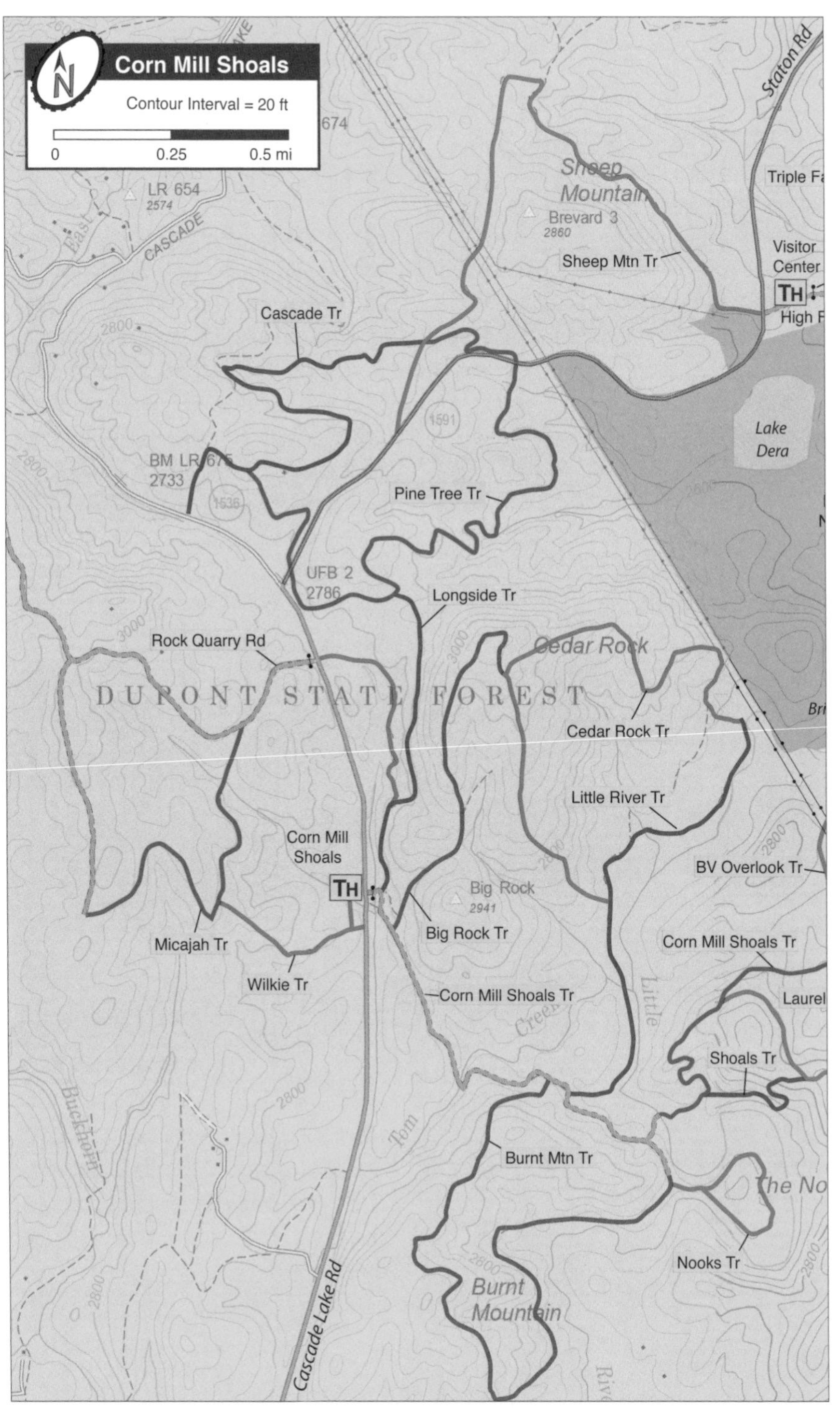

Corn Mill Shoals
Contour Interval = 20 ft
0
0.25
0.5 mi
Staton Rd
674
Sheep Mountain
Brevard 3
2860
Triple Fa
Visitor Center
TH
High F
Sheep Mtn Tr
LR 654
2574
East
CASCADE
2800
Cascade Tr
1591
Lake Dera
BM LR 675
2733
1536
Pine Tree Tr
2800
UFB 2
2786
Longside Tr
3000
Rock Quarry Rd
3000
Cedar Rock
DUPONT STATE FOREST
Cedar Rock Tr
Bri
Little River Tr
Corn Mill Shoals
TH
Big Rock
2941
BV Overlook Tr
2800
Micajah Tr
Big Rock Tr
Corn Mill Shoals Tr
Wilkie Tr
Corn Mill Shoals Tr
Laurel
Creek
Little
Shoals Tr
Buckhorn
2800
Tom
Burnt Mtn Tr
The No
Nooks Tr
2800
Burnt Mountain
Cascade Lake Rd
2800
Rive

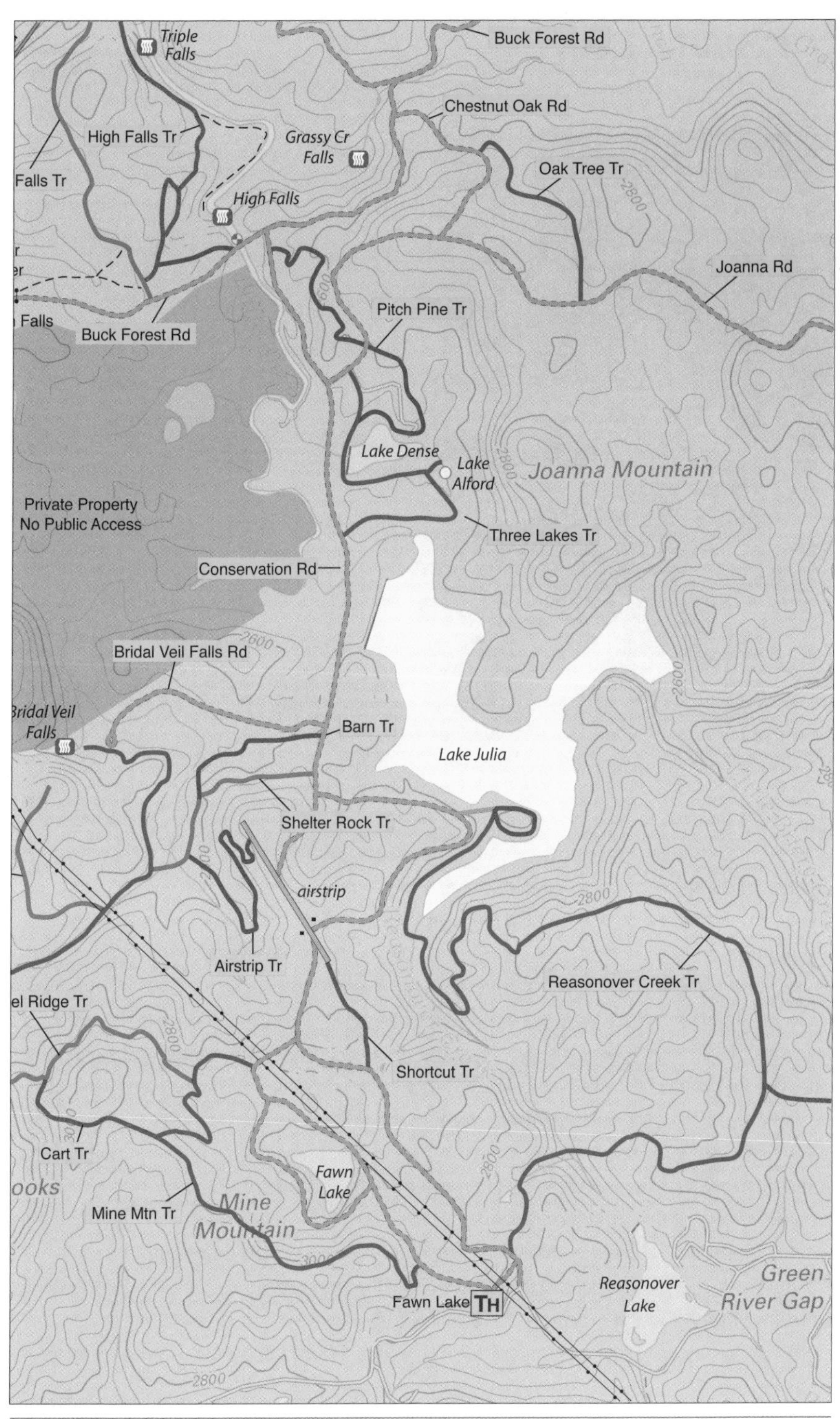
Triple Falls
Buck Forest Rd
Chestnut Oak Rd
High Falls Tr
Grassy Cr Falls
Falls Tr
Oak Tree Tr
High Falls
Joanna Rd
Falls
Buck Forest Rd
Pitch Pine Tr
Lake Dense
Lake Alford
Joanna Mountain
Private Property
No Public Access
Three Lakes Tr
Conservation Rd
Bridal Veil Falls Rd
Bridal Veil Falls
Barn Tr
Lake Julia
Shelter Rock Tr
airstrip
Airstrip Tr
Reasonover Creek Tr
Shortcut Tr
Cart Tr
Mine Mtn Tr
Mine Mountain
Fawn Lake
Fawn Lake
TH
Reasonover Lake
Green River Gap

Fawn Lake

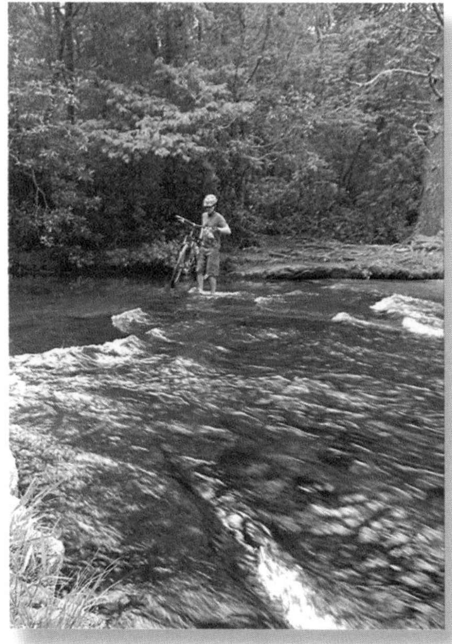
Leave your socks on when crossing the river at Corn Mill Shoals to keep from slipping.

Type	Backcountry
Parking	Plenty
Toilets	Portable
Land Manager	NC Forest Service
Fee	None
Access	Paved road
Special Rules	None

Fawn Lake is the trailhead to use when you want to access the back side of DuPont State Recreational Forest. It doesn't see quite the same volume of use as the other big trailheads, although on a fine day it too can bulge at the seams. Many folks park here and walk to nearby Fawn Lake dock to fish or swim. Mountain bikers park here because the trails are awesome.

You'll find the trails nearest the Fawn Lake trailhead to be more similar to those in Pisgah National Forest. Head one direction and you climb Mine Mountain and dabble with the trails on its flank. Head the other direction and you'll climb Reasonover Ridge or end up out in the hinterlands around Briery Fork Creek. These trails are more woodsy—lots of dirt and not so much rock. There are small streams to ford and you'll see plenty of mountain laurel and rhododendron, which is not so prevalent elsewhere in DuPont.

You can also ride from here to Bridal Veil Falls via a different sort of trail called Airstrip, which begins at the remains of an abandoned airport tucked away on a knoll in the forest. Though it's just one runway, it's a fun destination in its own right. Try lining up with your group to take off on a mad sprint down the tarmac. It's a hoot.

Getting to the Trailhead

From Pisgah Forest, go east on US 64. At the rock quarry turn right onto Crab Creek Road and continue several miles. Turn right onto DuPont Road, heading up and over the mountain as it becomes Staton Road. Pass three trailheads and the visitor center before reaching the T-intersection with Cascade Lake Road. Turn left and continue until just before Cascade Lake Road dead-ends into US 276. Turn left here on Reasonover Road and follow it out to the trailhead. You can also get there from the tiny town of Cedar Mountain on US 276 via Cascade Road, taking an immediate right onto Reasonover Road and continuing to the trailhead.

GPS Coordinates

35.160869, -82.604507

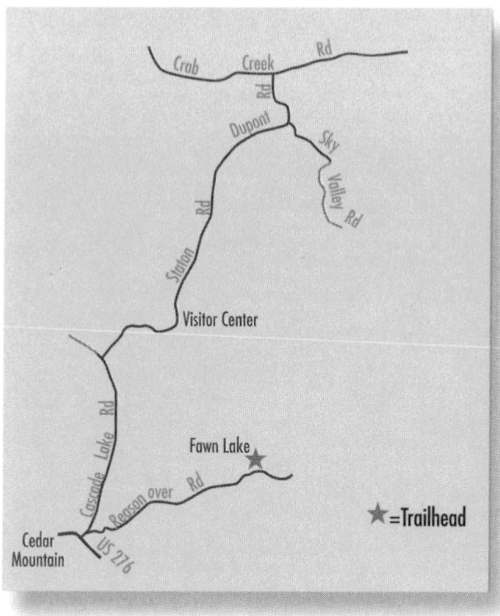

Fawn Lake Routes

Mine Mountain

Distance 4.5 miles
Difficulty Moderate
Surface Single/double track
Trailhead Fawn Lake

If you don't mind starting out with a steep climb, you'll enjoy this short route. It's a great ride in its own right and a good way to learn these trails should you want to incorporate them into a longer route.

Ride out from the trailhead on the road above the parking lot. Just up the way, turn left on Mine Mountain Trail. Long switchbacks lead you to the top of the mountain. When Mine Mountain Trail drops off the ridge to the right, continue straight onto Cart Trail. Take care on the little downhills that tend to end in right-angle turns. You'll see where riders have plunged off the trail into the woods.

Cart Trail ends at the bottom of a steep pitch on Laurel Ridge Trail. Make a mental note of this spot. Turn left, go down a little more, and then turn left on Shoals Trail to continue down through some switchbacks to Corn Mill Shoals Trail. Downhill riding is now over for a little while.

Turn right on Corn Mill Shoals Trail to ride up through some interesting boulders and past a view spot. Just as Corn Mill Shoals Trail heads down a long bare rock stretch, turn right onto Laurel Ridge Trail and continue a gradual climb. Soon you'll recognize where you

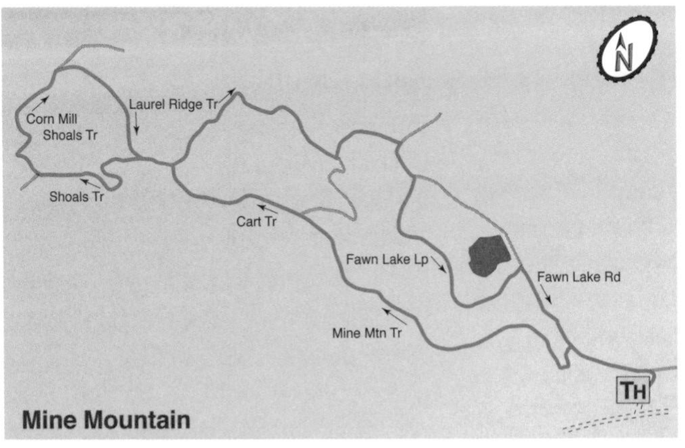

Reasonover Creek

Distance 6.2 miles
Difficulty Moderate
Surface Single track, forest road
Trailhead Fawn Lake

were earlier. When you reach the Shoals Trail intersection you'll need to bear left and ride up the steep pitch you had so much fun riding down. At the top of it is the intersection with Cart Trail. Stay on Laurel Ridge Trail here as it rolls along the contours on the flank of Mine Mountain.

When you reach the bottom of Mine Mountain Trail, turn left and continue on out to Fawn Lake Road. Here you'll take a right and then a right on Fawn Lake Loop Trail (an old road). You ride along beside the lake, but you can't see it. Reaching Fawn Lake Road again, turn left to go for a swim at the dock or right, back to the trailhead.

Reasonover Creek Trail crosses its namesake creek twice on this route, but it is hardly what you'll remember about the ride. The bulk of your experience on the trail will be climbing and then descending Reasonover Ridge. It's a big climb followed by a exhilarating descent.

On the far end of the route you'll end up on the shore of Lake Julia, a beautiful mountain lake with a picnic spot that makes a nice hangout to tell and retell stories about how you saw death staring you in the face while dropping down Reasonover.

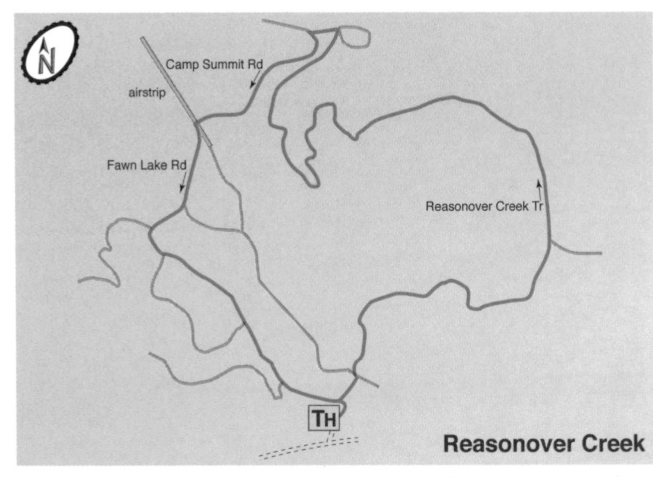

From the trailhead kiosk, ride down the road above the parking lot to Conservation Road. Cross the road onto Reasonover Creek Trail. You'll continue downhill, crossing a small stream and then Reasonover Creek. You can try your luck at riding across or take the easier way by hopping from stepping stone to stepping stone.

After the creek crossing the route begins to climb up Reasonover Ridge. Up ahead you'll arrive at the junction with Turkey Knob Trail. Just bear left and keep climbing on Reasonover Creek Trail, up and over the ridge. Up top you'll get a false start—down once, up a little more, and then begins the big downhill.

Enjoy the descent but take it easy—who knows what might be coming up? You could meet a horse. Down at the bottom, you cross the creek again. Don't make the mistake of using the horse ford; it's deep. Continue until you get to the footbridge. On the other side is Lake Julia. Now's the time to take that break.

It's easy to just follow the roads back from Lake Julia to the trailhead. Climb up Camp Summit Road to the airstrip, cross over onto Fawn Lake Road, and take it all the way to the finish.

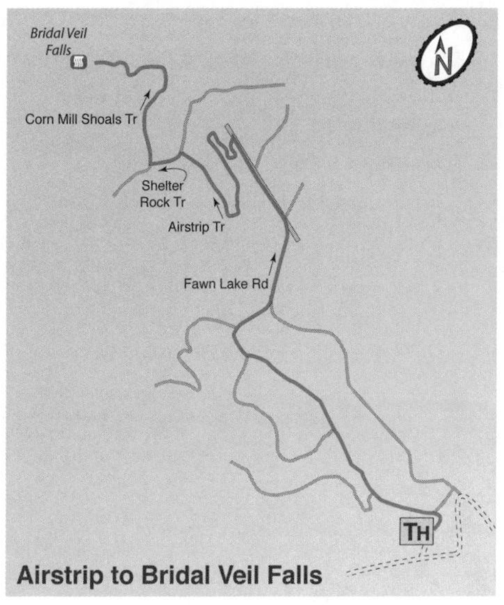

Airstrip to Bridal Veil Falls

Airstrip to Bridal Veil Falls

Distance 5+ miles
Difficulty Moderate
Surface Single track, forest road
Trailhead Fawn Lake

If you're interested in riding from Fawn Lake out to Bridal Veil Falls, this is the most direct route. Once there you can swing back by way of the gravel roads, or head out Corn Mill Shoals Trail to return via a Mine Mountain route or over Reasonover Ridge from Lake Julia (see earlier descriptions).

Begin by riding out to the airstrip on Fawn Lake Road. Once there, you'll ride right down the runway, almost to the end. Be on the lookout for the sign marking Airstrip Trail on the left.

Airstrip Trail is all downhill and there are some fun low berms and grade dips along the way. It bottoms out after about a mile on Shelter Rock Trail which is an old road. Turn left on Shelter Rock, cross two small streams, and then hop up onto Corn Mill Shoals Trail.

Turn right on Corn Mill Shoals Trail and head into a fun boulder-y stretch. There is a log ride here as well that you can try out or go around. Eventually you end at the base of Bridal Veil Falls, your destination. It really is an amazing waterfall. Park your bike here in the bike rack and take a tour on foot. There are some giant boulders at the base that the water rushes and flows against and under. They're big enough for a small group to have a large picnic, but not vice versa. Work your way over to the far left side of the falls and you can walk right up the sloped rock slab that the river slides down. Just be sure to stay on the

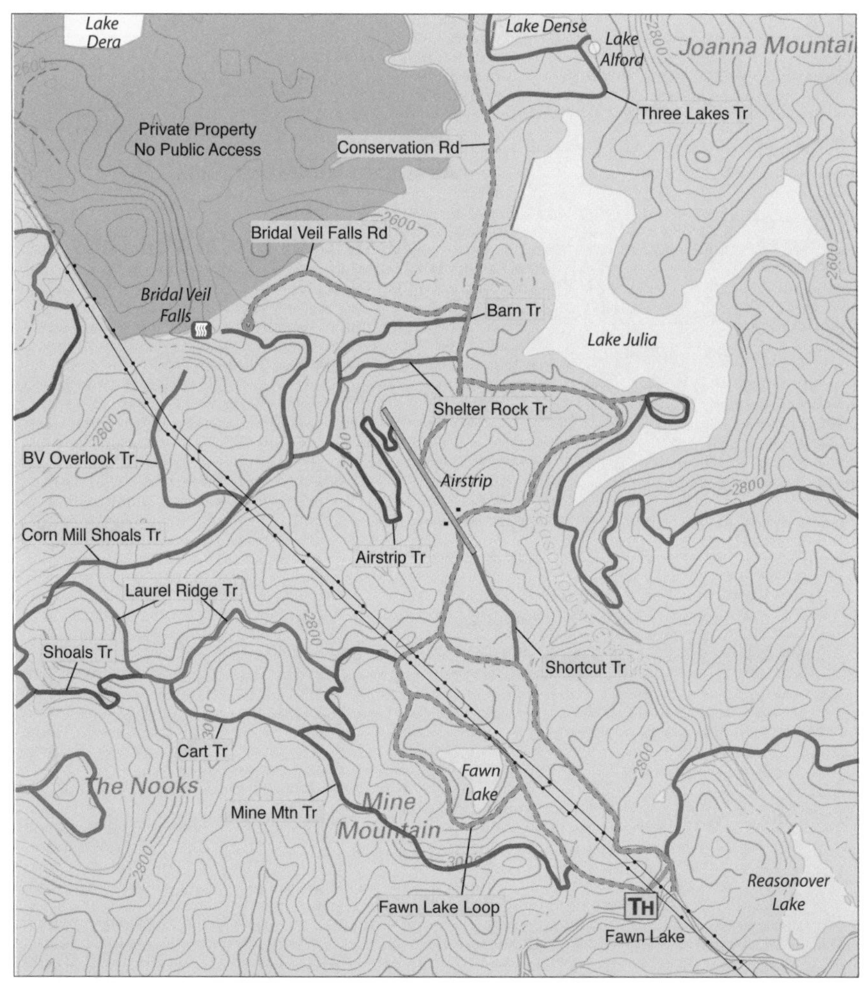

dry sections; wherever the rock is wet, it's slippery as ice. Way up at the top the river shoots over a wide lip forming a "veil"—thus the name. With care, you can walk up under the overhang and cross to the other side, right under the falls! It is just about the coolest thing since sliced bread. The curtain of water roars right by while you remain largely dry.

As stated above, you can return from here any number of ways. The quickest way is via the gravel roads. But if you've got the time and want to get in some hill climbing and some technical single track, go by way of Mine Mountain or out past Lake Julia and on over Reasonover Ridge.

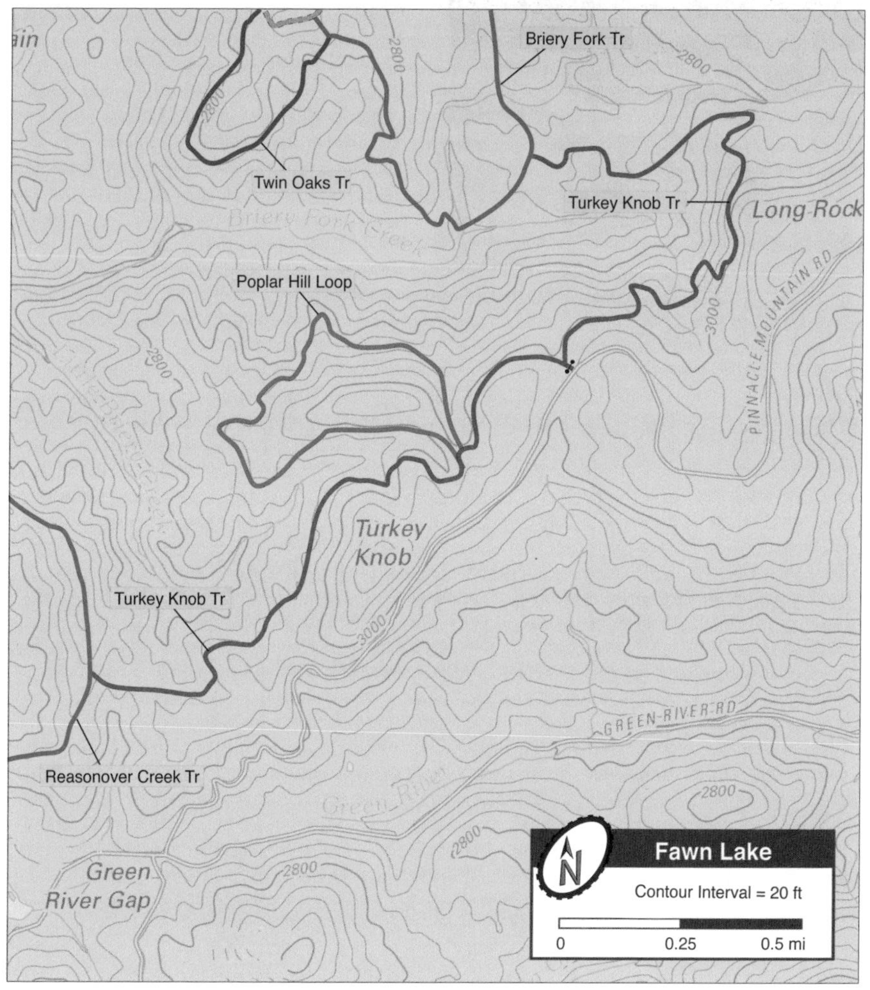

Hendersonville Bike Park

Little kids go for big air off the jumps at Hendersonville's Bike Park.

Type	Bike park
Parking	Plenty
Toilets	Nearby
Land Manager	Jackson Park
Fee	None
Access	Paved road
Special Rules	*Yes

* The park is closed during wet weather.

Kids love riding at Jackson Park's bike park in downtown Hendersonville. Most nice days after school you're bound to see groups of children circling through the obstacles, pumping up and down on the pump track, and most of all soaring through the air off the jumps. More often than not there's a group of parents hanging at the picnic tables chatting and watching the fun. Here's a secret: this bike park is good fun for grownup kids, too. You'll just want to pick those times when the swarms of kids are in school or elsewhere.

The folks who built this park did their homework. You'll find areas to practice just about everything you might encounter on a backcountry ride in the mountains. There are balance beams to simulate precarious riding, rock jumbles to fine-tune your rough terrain skills, tire humps and banked turns for confidence building, and of course the jumps. You can progress from easy little humps to big high-fliers.

To preserve the dirt features, the park is open during dry weather only. If it's raining or has been raining a lot you'll find the gate locked. It is also closed in late winter/early spring when the ground is going through a freeze-thaw cycle.

Getting to the Trailhead

From exit 49 on I-26, travel west on US 64 (Martin Luther King Jr. Drive) and turn left onto Harris Road just before US 64 splits, following signs for Jackson Park. At East 4th Street turn left into Jackson Park and wind down the hill to take the first right along the creek. Follow this gravel road out to the bike park.

GPS Coordinates

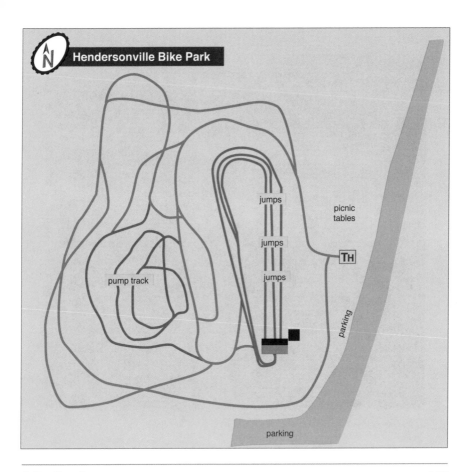

35.315, -82.450

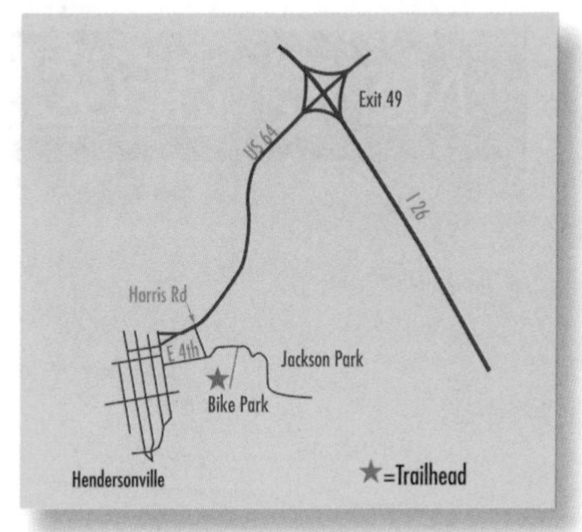

Hendersonville Bike Park

jumps
jumps
jumps
picnic tables
TH
pump track
parking
parking

Nantahala & The Far West

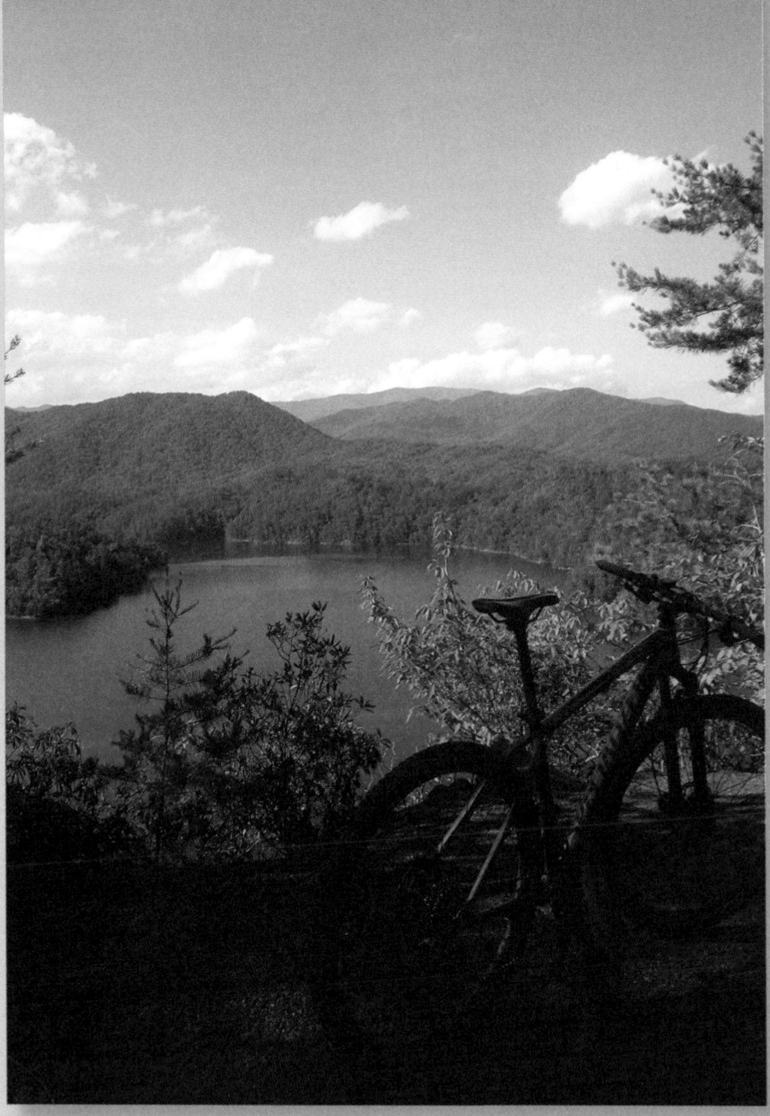

The clifftop view from Tsali's Left Loop looks across Fontana Lake to Great Smoky Mountains National Park.

The far western part of North Carolina has many small networks of mountain bike trails spread throughout the region. Although most of these are located in Nantahala National Forest, there are couple of trails inside Great Smoky Mountains National Park open to bikes, and there's also a trail system on the campus of Western Carolina University. In the national forest, the trail areas are typically located along the shore of a lake. The exception is Panthertown, in a high valley on the Highlands Plateau near Cashiers. The most well-known trails in the region are at Tsali Recreation Area on Lake Fontana near Bryson City, but the trails of the newer area at Jackrabbit on Lake Chatuge are quickly gaining deserved recognition.

When it comes to difficulty, most all the trails of the far west fall into the moderate category. None have terribly long climbs, they're mostly well maintained, and obstacles such as rocks and roots are rare. If you are looking for an easy ride, head for Deep Creek in Great Smoky Mountains National Park or pick a short loop at Jackrabbit. For the most dramatic scenery, cruise up to Panthertown. With all its cliff faces and waterfalls, it has been called the Yosemite of the East. And for a real roller-coaster workout, don't miss the trails at Western Carolina University in Cullowhee.

A few bike shops service the region. You'll find them in Sylva, Bryson City, Franklin, and Waynesville (see p. 205). Some have rentals available and all offer repairs and merchandise.

Options for where to stay depend mostly on where you want to ride. Many folks base out of Bryson City or due to its proximity to Great Smoky Mountains National Park, Tsali, and Nantahala Gorge. Others will choose to stay in the higher altitude resort towns of Highlands or Cashiers. But it hardly matters; with the 4-lanes of US 74, US 64, and US 441, getting around quickly is pretty easy. Heavy traffic is rarely an issue this far west.

Campers will find beautiful developed public sites at Deep Creek, Tsali, and Jackrabbit, where you can ride straight out onto the trails.

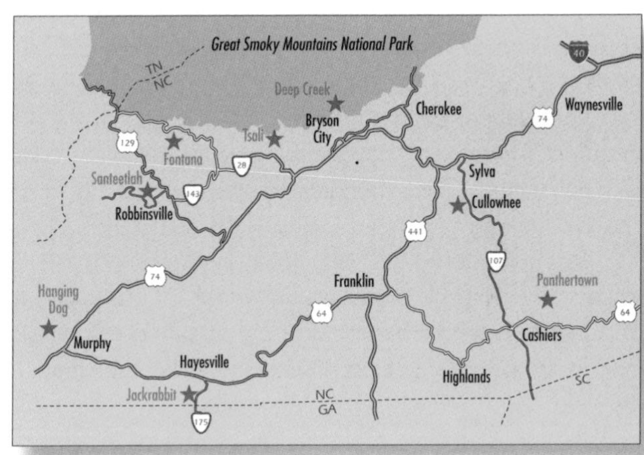

Panthertown Valley

Start early enough, and you'll get a great sunrise over the valley.

Type	Backcountry
Parking	Moderate
Toilets	None
Land Manager	USFS
Fee	None
Access	Paved road
Special Rules	None

It seems odd to travel uphill for miles in order to get to a valley, but such is the case for Panthertown. This valley sits so high up that even at its lowest point you are still above the 3,000-foot mark. Forming a bowl-shaped area northeast of Cashiers, Panthertown Valley is remote and beautiful. Barefaced cliffs hang like curtains from the mountainsides and gushing streams alternately meander and cascade through the woods. For the intrepid, there are 14 waterfalls to explore.

For many years this area was owned by an electric power company. Maybe they had plans to build a reservoir here. Fortunately they never did. Better still, they kept it from being developed. Ride off National Forest land and you'll quickly see that much of the area immediately surrounding the valley is home to new upscale housing.

Mountain biking in Panthertown at its most basic is a down-and-up experience. The trailheads are all on the rim of the valley and the trails are within it. This means that no matter how you do your ride, you'll start with a big descent and finish with a big climb. Within the valley itself there are hills to contend with as well.

Take Panthertown's elevation into consideration, especially if you're planning a ride during the winter months. Rain down low may mean snow up high, so check the weather forecast closely. Likewise, if you're looking for somewhere to cool off in the heat of summer, Panthertown is the place to go.

The routes described here begin and end at the Salt Rock Gap trailhead. You can just as easily ride them from Cold Mountain Gap trailhead; only the start and finish would be different.

Getting to the Trailhead

Salt Rock Gap On the western end, take US 64 from Cashiers for 2 miles. Turn left on Cedar Creek Road and go 2.3 miles to Breedlove Road. Turn right and go 3.5 miles to the trailhead.

Cold Mountain Gap Take NC 281 from Lake Toxaway. Just beyond the lake, turn left onto Cold Mountain Road and follow it to its end as it winds and twists up the mountain.

GPS Coordinates

Salt Rock Gap 35.169, -83.041
Cold Mtn Gap 35.160, -83.002

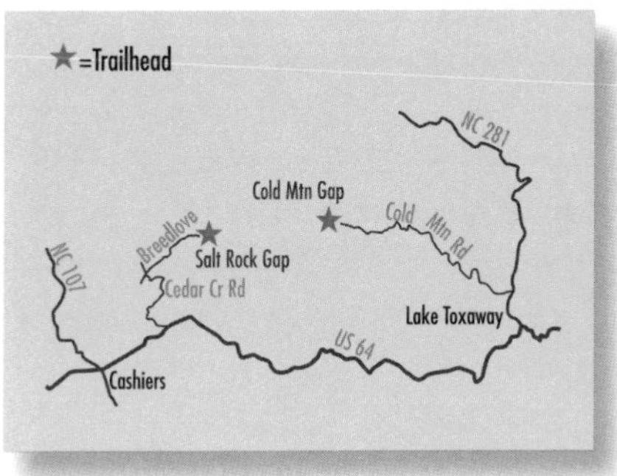

Panthertown Valley Routes

Blackrock Mountain

Distance 8 miles
Difficulty Moderate
Surface Single/double track
Trailhead Salt Rock Gap

You'll stay up high a while on this route before dropping down in fits and starts into the valley. Blackrock Trail takes you up over Blackrock Mountain before heading north where you'll circle Sassafras Mountain through Sassafras Gap.

Once down at river level, pass between two impressive waterfalls and then farther along pass near another as well before circling back and climbing out of the valley the way most folks go down.

Begin by riding a very short distance out from the trailhead the way you drove in. Turn right on Blackrock Trail to ride up and over Blackrock Mountain and all the way down to Powerline Trail. Turn right onto this trail, which is more road than trail and was originally built to access the powerlines you'll soon see. At Sassafras Gap where Rattlesnake Knob Trail exits to the left, bear right and continue along the old roadbed.

A mile or so farther you'll reach a junction with Riding Ford Trail. Turn left here and roll on down to ford the river at Riding Ford. It gets pretty steep just before the ford. At normal flows this is a shallow crossing, but don't just cross over and keep riding. Immediately downstream is Riding Ford Falls. You'll want to scramble down there along the right bank to have a look. To get to another waterfall, head up the trail about 100 feet and look for a small foot trail on your right. Walk down to the worn campsite and then through the rhodo to the river to a large lakelike pool below impressive Jawbone Falls. It's a great place to take a break, have a snack, or go for a swim.

After you've had enough of waterfalls, continue on up the trail which climbs not too steeply up the ridge and then drops back down to meet Panthertown Valley Trail. Turn right and ride down to cross the bridge over Greenland Creek. If you want to see Schoolhouse Falls, park your bike here and walk 0.2 mile up Little Green Trail. This waterfall also has a big plunge pool and you can work your way around to stand behind the curtain of water crashing over the cliff and into the pool.

Continue the route by riding along the rocky washed section to the bridge over the river. Cross over and turn right on Powerline Trail, pass through the large campsite, and then turn left on North Road Trail. Follow North Road up the valley to intersect Panthertown Valley Trail again, then follow it up and out of the valley.

Mac's Gap

Distance 7.8 miles
Difficulty Moderate
Surface Single/double track
Trailhead Salt Rock Gap

This has always been one of Panthertown's more popular rides. It takes you straight down into the valley to where Panthertown Creek and Greenland Creek come together to form the Tuckaseigee River. You then climb to the Cold Mountain Gap trailhead before dropping back down again to ford Greenland Creek. Another climb leads over Mac's Gap and back down to the valley floor through a quiet white pine forest.

The directions are pretty simple. To start, ride down Panthertown Valley Trail into the valley, through the valley on North Road Trail, and then up the other side all the way to Cold Mountain Gap trailhead on Panthertown Valley Trail again. It's a little over 3 miles. At the eastern trailhead, turn onto Mac's Gap Trail and take it down to ford Greenland Creek, up through Mac's Gap, and down again to a junction with the Panthertown Valley Trail. You then just ride up what you rode down to start with.

Along the way, as you can see on the map, you pass a number of waterfalls. All of them are accessed by foot-travel-only trails, but most are just short walks. Explore as many as you like; each one is unique.

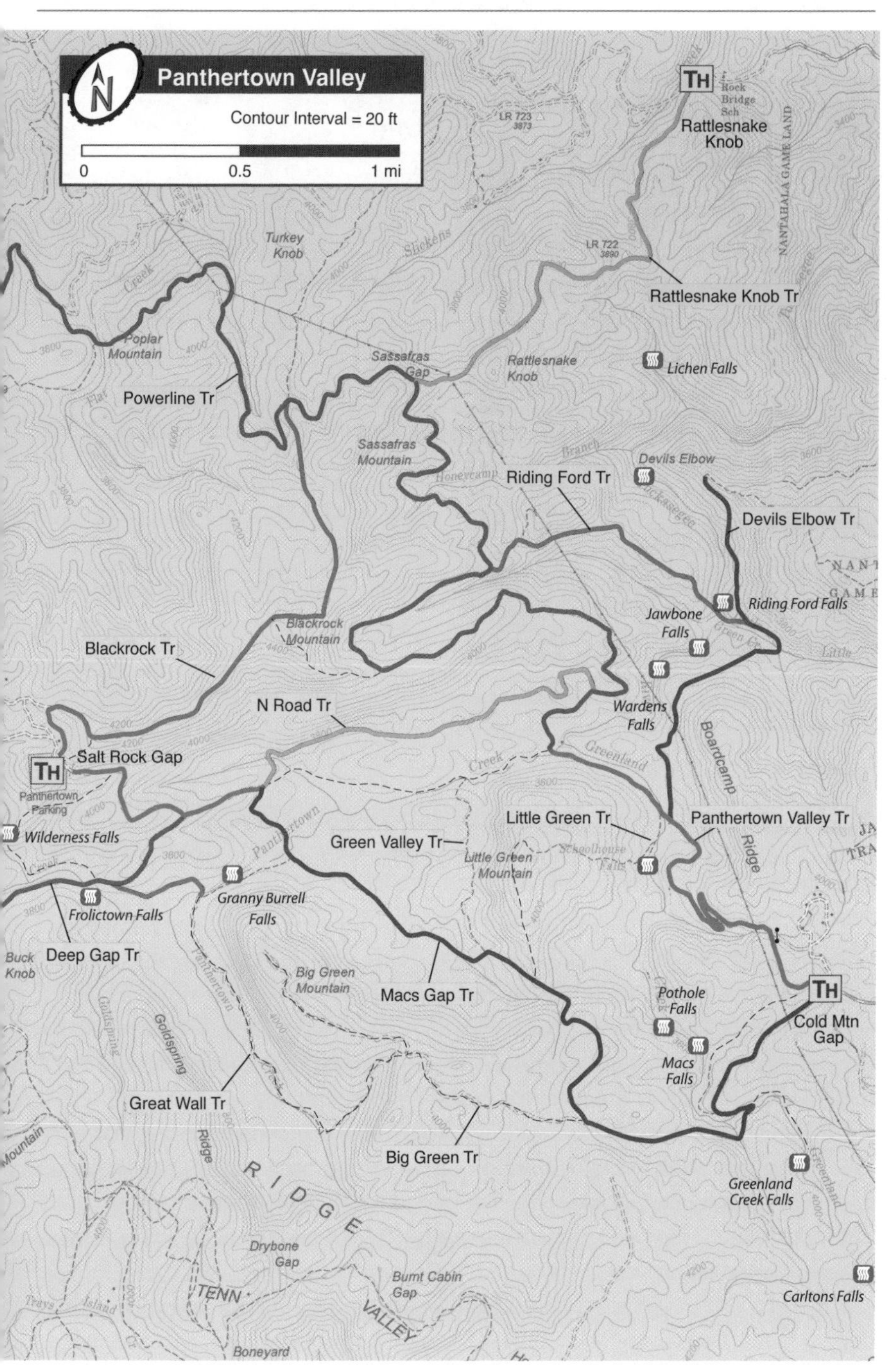
Panthertown Valley
Contour Interval = 20 ft
0
0.5
1 mi
TH
Rattlesnake Knob
Rattlesnake Knob Tr
Lichen Falls
Turkey Knob
Poplar Mountain
Powerline Tr
Sassafras Gap
Rattlesnake Knob
Sassafras Mountain
Devils Elbow
Riding Ford Tr
Devils Elbow Tr
Riding Ford Falls
Jawbone Falls
Blackrock Mountain
Blackrock Tr
Wardens Falls
N Road Tr
Boardcamp Ridge
TH
Salt Rock Gap
Panthertown Parking
Wilderness Falls
Little Green Tr
Panthertown Valley Tr
Green Valley Tr
Little Green Mountain
Granny Burrell Falls
Frolictown Falls
Buck Knob
Deep Gap Tr
Big Green Mountain
Macs Gap Tr
Pothole Falls
TH
Cold Mtn Gap
Macs Falls
Goldspring
Great Wall Tr
Big Green Tr
RIDGE
Greenland Creek Falls
Drybone Gap
Burnt Cabin Gap
TENN
VALLEY
Boneyard
Carltons Falls

WCU Trail System

Banked turns make the trails at WCU easy to negotiate.

Type	Urban
Parking	Moderate
Toilets	None
Land Manager	Western Carolina University
Fee	None
Access	Paved road
Special Rules	None
Distance	3 to 8.5 miles
Difficulty	Moderate
Surface	Single track

Get ready for a roller-coaster ride! Western Carolina University has created some of the most fun trails in the region on a wooded mountainside above the college's main campus. For almost every foot of trail there is something to grab your attention. Coming at you randomly are whoops, dips, small jumps, banked turns, big wall rides, tight turns, switchbacks, and more. The trails are smooth and fast with few rocks and roots. Just keep in mind there may be other users coming up the same hill you're flying down.

You have two trailheads to choose from to start your ride and both require a bit of a grunt climb to get up to the loops. For a longer ride (and longer initial climb), start out on Cullowhee Connector Trail. Once you connect to the first loop, circle around counterclockwise on Upper Long Branch Trail. If you decide to connect over to the Gribble Gap Trail loop, circle it in the same direction. The two loops plus Cullowhee Connector make an 8.5-mile ride with the last 2 miles almost all downhill.

If start at the HHS trailhead you'll shorten the ride by at least 3.4 miles. The ride up to the loops is not so long as coming up from Cullowhee, but it is somewhat steeper. Again, ride both loops counterclockwise for the best experience.

Getting to the Trailhead

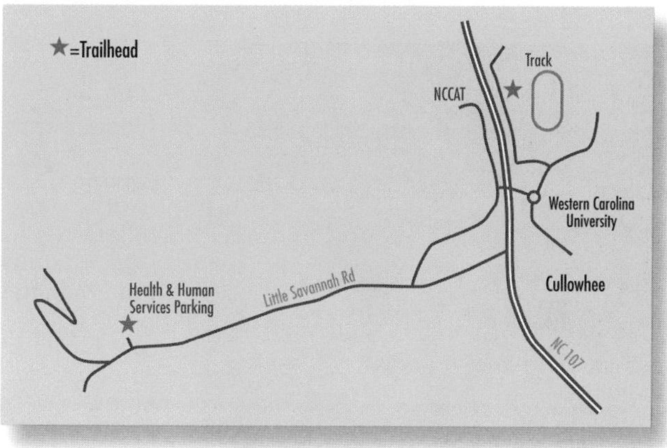

Cullowhee (closest to the main campus) Go north from the university entrance traffic circle. Take the first left and drive around behind the track. The trailhead is located at the end of the road. Look for a trail info kiosk and a tunnel leading under NC 107.

HHS Take Little Savannah Road from the traffic light on NC 107 (at the pedestrian overpass) for 1 mile. Turn into the entrance for the Health & Human Sciences complex. Look for the trail info kiosk on the left, just up the road.

GPS Coordinates

Cullowhee 35.313, -83.188
HHS 35.305, -83.204

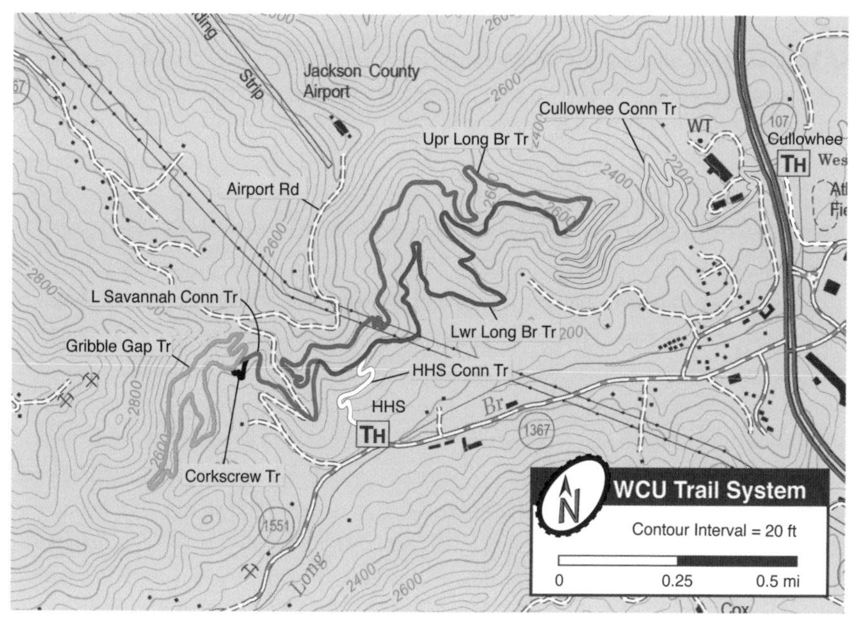

Deep Creek

Wide bridges take you over idyllic Deep Creek.

Type	Backcountry
Parking	Plenty
Toilets	Yes
Land Manager	GSMNP
Fee	None
Access	Paved road
Special Rules	None

Within the Great Smoky Mountains National Park bicycles are allowed on trails in only one place: Deep Creek, just outside Bryson City. It needs to be said right up front that the two trails, Deep Creek Trail and Indian Creek Trail, are actually gated dirt roads. Nevertheless, they are both ideal places for a mountain bike ride. Each follows a beautiful mountain stream and it's fun to ride along with your friends, side by side as you watch the tubers floating the creek or anglers casting for trout.

Maybe this is your first time on a mountain bike. You'll want to spend some time figuring out how to change the gears, how high to adjust your saddle, how your brakes work, and other things like that. The wide, relatively flat roads at Deep Creek are ideal for someone just starting out. There is a huge picnic area on the banks of the creek just before you reach the backcountry trailhead. Park here for a picnic before you ride. There's a big paved loop where you can circle round and round to get everything all figured out. If you've got young riders, this is an ideal spot to get them used to the bikes before hitting the dirt.

Typically the trailhead at Deep Creek is a busy, happening place. Folks come here year-round to walk out to the waterfalls or try their luck fishing. Day hikers start from here for several popular loop hikes, while backpackers will be heading out for extended treks in the backcountry. Local runners show up daily for their workouts. But in the hot summer months these numbers are dwarfed by the multitude of tourists who come to float down the creek on tubes. On days when tubers are out in force, you'll have to slowly weave in and around them for the first half-mile of your ride.

Getting to the Trailhead

From Bryson City, follow the brown directional signs strategically placed throughout town to Deep Creek Campground.

GPS Coordinates

35.464, -83.434

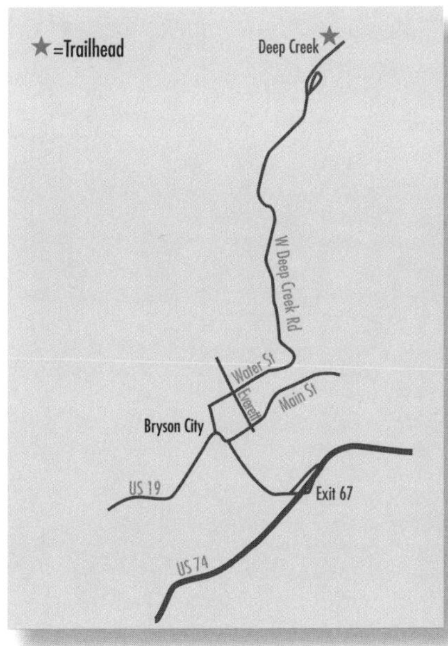

Deep Creek Routes

Deep Creek

Distance 4.5 miles
Difficulty Easy
Surface Double track
Trailhead Deep Creek

This is the easier of the two rides at Deep Creek. Except for a couple of gentle hills going and coming, it's pretty much flat. The trail is a little rocky in places, but nothing that bike of yours can't handle.

Directions are easy. Ride around the gate and onto Deep Creek Trail (a road). Stay on Deep Creek Trail all the way out past the fourth bridge. Here it becomes a little more trail-like for another 0.4 mile until you reach a turnaround. Deep Creek Trail continues on from here as single track, but bikes are allowed no further. Retrace your route to the trailhead.

Indian Creek

Distance 6.6 miles
Difficulty Easy
Surface Double track
Trailhead Deep Creek

While still on the easier side, Indian Creek Trail is the more difficult route from the Deep Creek trailhead. It's longer, there's more climbing, and it's just as beautiful. You'll pass several old homesites, but don't expect to see any structures. All that is left are the shrubs and flowers planted by the early settlers; if you look closely you might see the outlines of a foundation. You'll pass Tom Branch Falls early on and Indian Creek Falls farther along. And you know you're passing through a mini-gorge when you hear the creek roaring off to your right. Hold your speed down on the downhill return; you are likely to meet hikers, bikers, runners, or horses coming straight at you.

The route starts out just like the Deep Creek ride. Head up Deep Creek Trail, passing the first bridge. Just before the second one, turn right on Indian Creek Trail. Follow this trail uphill past Indian Creek Falls and all the way to the junction with Deep Low Gap Trail. Turn around when you see the "No Bikes Beyond This Point" sign. As you return the way you came, enjoy the long downhill coast.

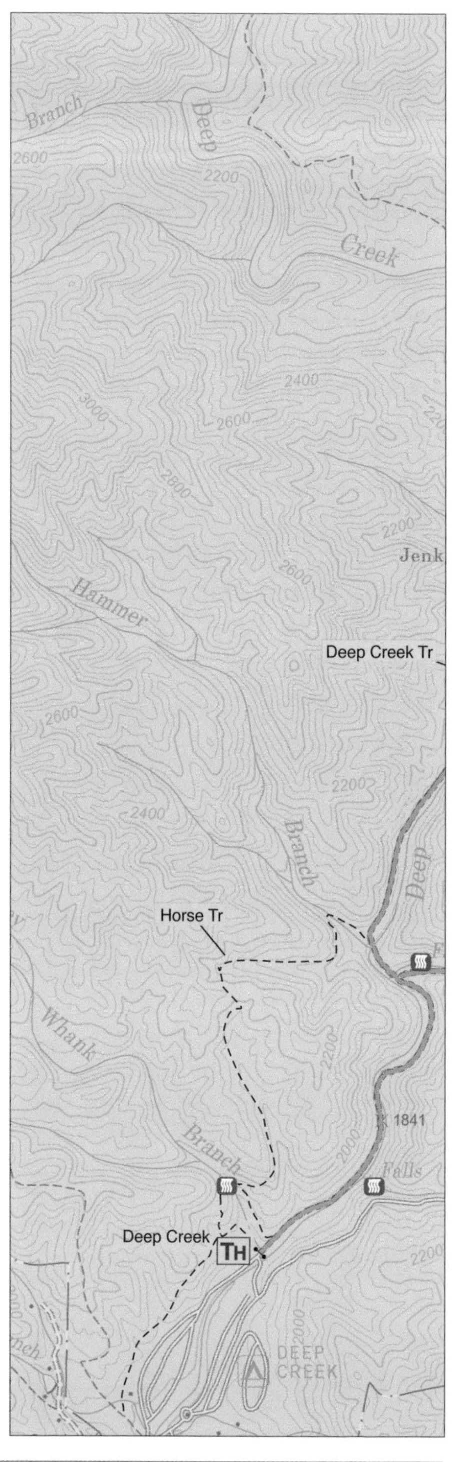

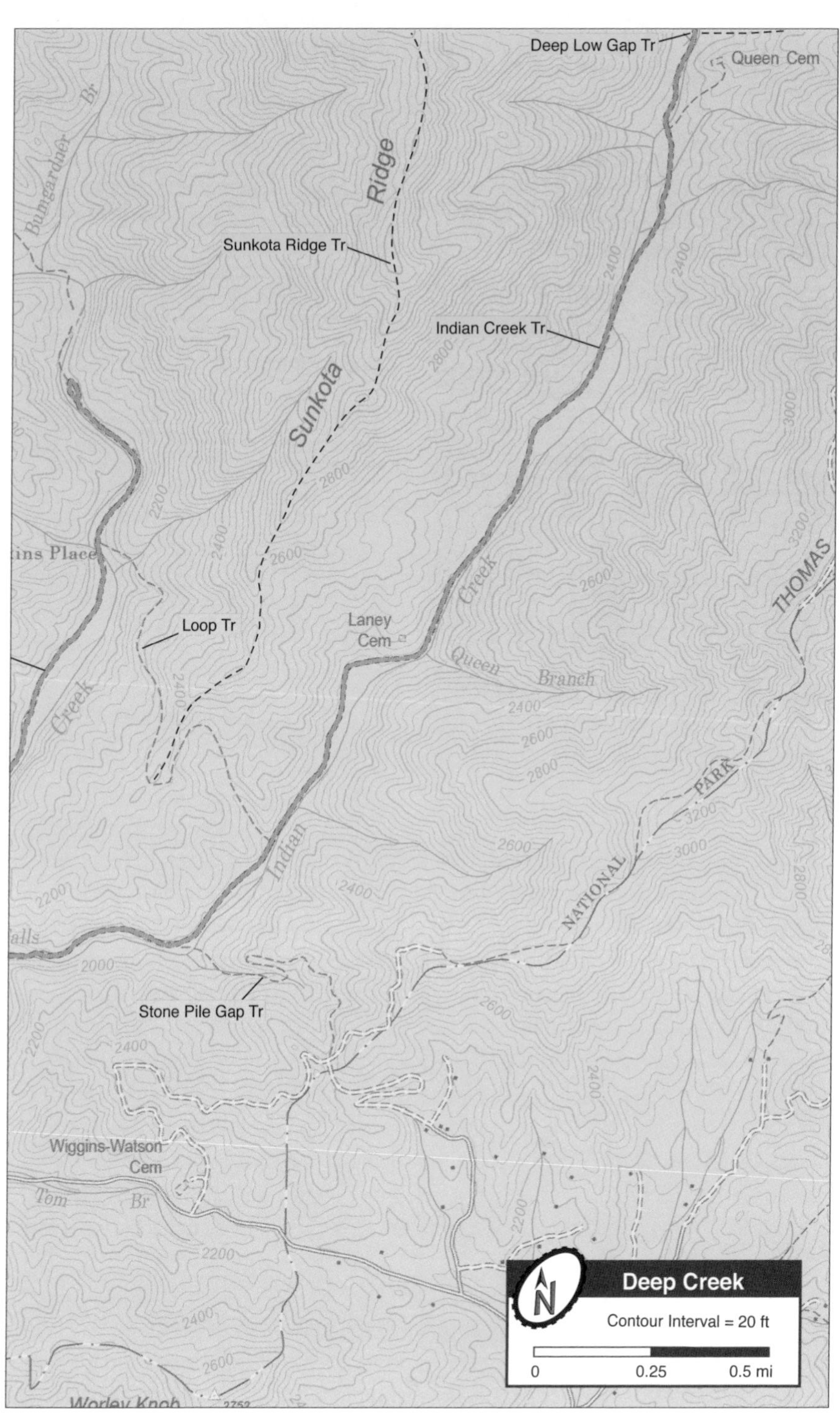
Deep Low Gap Tr
Queen Cem
Bumgardner Br
Ridge
Sunkota Ridge Tr
Indian Creek Tr
Sunkota
Loop Tr
Laney Cem
Creek
Queen Branch
THOMAS
PARK
NATIONAL
Indian
Creek
Stone Pile Gap Tr
Wiggins-Watson Cem
Tom Br
Deep Creek
Contour Interval = 20 ft
0
0.25
0.5 mi

Tsali Recreation Area

You'll pass an old homesite on the left loop.

Type	Backcountry
Parking	Plentiful
Toilets	Yes
Land Manager	USFS
Fee	$2 pp
Access	Paved road
Special Rules	*Yes

* Check the kiosk at the trailhead for directions that alternate on different days. Generally, when the Left and Right Loops are open to bikes, the Thompson and Mouse Branch Loops are not, and vice versa.

Tsali Recreation Area, part of Nantahala National Forest, in the early years was one of the most popular mountain biking destinations in the eastern United States. With over 40 miles of single track trails to choose from, it's no wonder. The trails here wind their way over rolling terrain along the shore of Lake Fontana, and for the most part they are not difficult. There are no extremely long continuous climbs, rocks and roots are scarce, and sharp turns are few. This means that in many places you can shift up to those big gears and push the pace as hard as your legs and lungs can stand. But not everyone riding at Tsali is a testosterone-pumping race mode. Most folks just enjoy spinning along, stopping occasionally to take in a nice view. Just across the lake is Great Smoky Mountains National Park, and it's not uncommon to see bald eagles soaring over the water in search of fish. You can ride loops from 4 to 20 miles in length, and when you combine loops with various connector trails, the possibilities seem endless.

Once you arrive at Tsali (pronounced *SAH-lee*) you'll find lots of amenities. A large parking lot is bordered on one side by picnic tables and at the far end an information kiosk is posted with the latest trail updates. There are toilet facilities and even a bike-washing station so you can clean your bike at the end of a ride. Right next door is a 42-unit campground with level sites and showers open seasonally, spring through fall.

Tsali has four main loops. The traditional Right and Left Loops were built for horses in the early 1980s and are connected in the middle by gated County Line Road. The Thompson and Mouse Branch Loops were built in the mid-1990s for (and for the most part by) mountain bikers. You could describe them all as similar, but each loop has its own characteristics. Typically when Thompson and Mouse are open, Left and Right are closed to bikes and vice versa. Be sure to check the kiosk for any changes.

Getting to the Trailhead

Take NC 28 north from US 74 west of Bryson City for a few miles. At the Swain–Graham County line turn right onto the paved Tsali entrance road. The trailhead parking lot is at the bottom of the hill, just past the entrance to the campground. You can't miss it, it's huge.

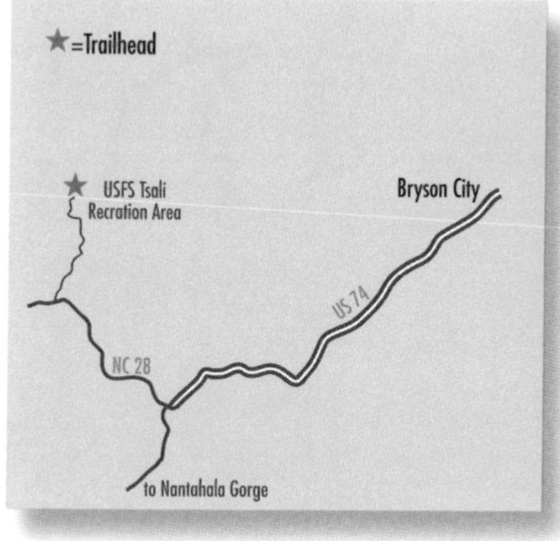

GPS Coordinates

35.406, -83.585

Tsali Routes

Right Loop

Distance 13.4 miles
Difficulty Moderate
Surface Single/double track
Trailhead Tsali

Rolling along the contour lines, this is a fast loop. It has fewer creek crossings than Left Loop and several climbs of note. Sections of berms add to the excitement, but beware—they've sent more than one cyclist to the hospital with a broken collarbone or worse. Be sure to take Windy Gap Loop for a fine overlook high above the lake. If you skip it, the loop is 11.2 miles long. The suggested direction of travel is counterclockwise.

Left Loop

Distance 12.3 miles
Difficulty Moderate
Surface Single/double track
Trailhead Tsali

On this loop you'll cross several small creeks. They can be a challenge, but are definitely ridable. In other places it feels as if you might teeter right off the trail and into the lake. You'll find climbs on this side of the peninsula as well, with one tricky one right out near the overlook. The highlight of the ride is the clifftop view looking out over Lake Fontana onto Great Smoky Mountains

National Park; you'll find that on Cliff Overlook Trail. The suggested travel direction for Left Loop is clockwise.

Mouse Branch Loop

Distance 9.8 miles
Difficulty Moderate
Surface Single/double track
Trailhead Tsali

This loop is a blast to ride as it rolls out to a one-way loop trail and a nice overlook. The return is very twisty with lots of short ups and downs that seem to go on forever. The suggested travel direction for this loop is clockwise. The Mouse Branch Overlook Loop is counterclockwise, one-way only.

Thompson Loop

Distance 7.4 miles
Difficulty Moderate
Surface Single/double track
Trailhead Tsali

Though this is Tsali's shortest loop, it has the longest continuous climbs and takes about as long as any of the others to complete. You'll enjoy winding through rhododendron tunnels and laurel thickets along the lakeshore. It all ends with a heart-stopping descent back to the trailhead. The suggested travel direction for this loop is counterclockwise.

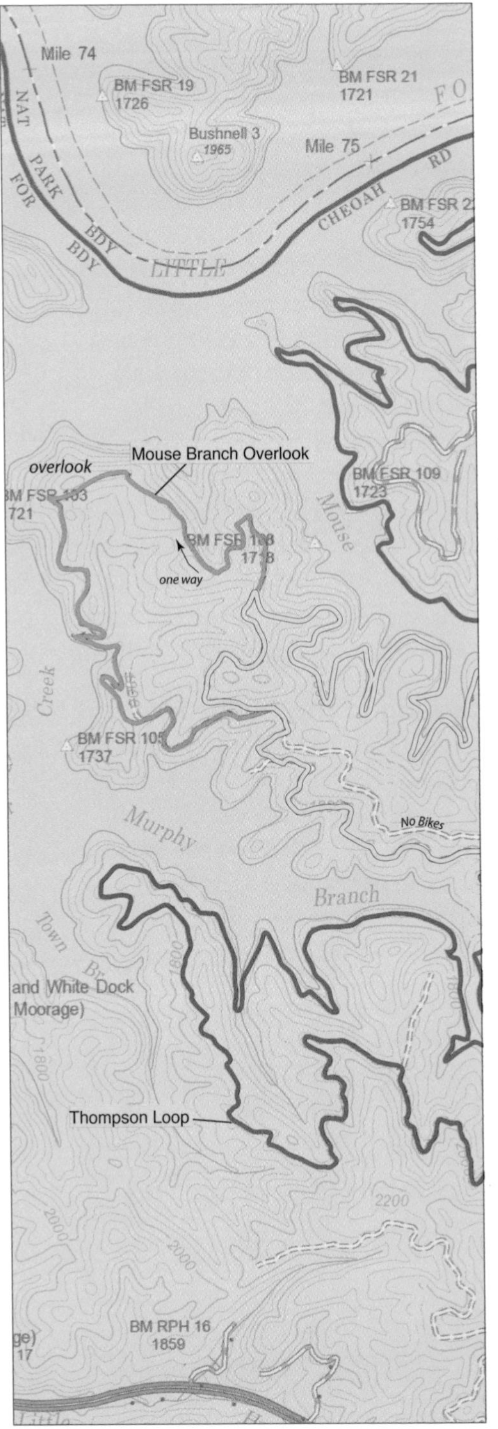

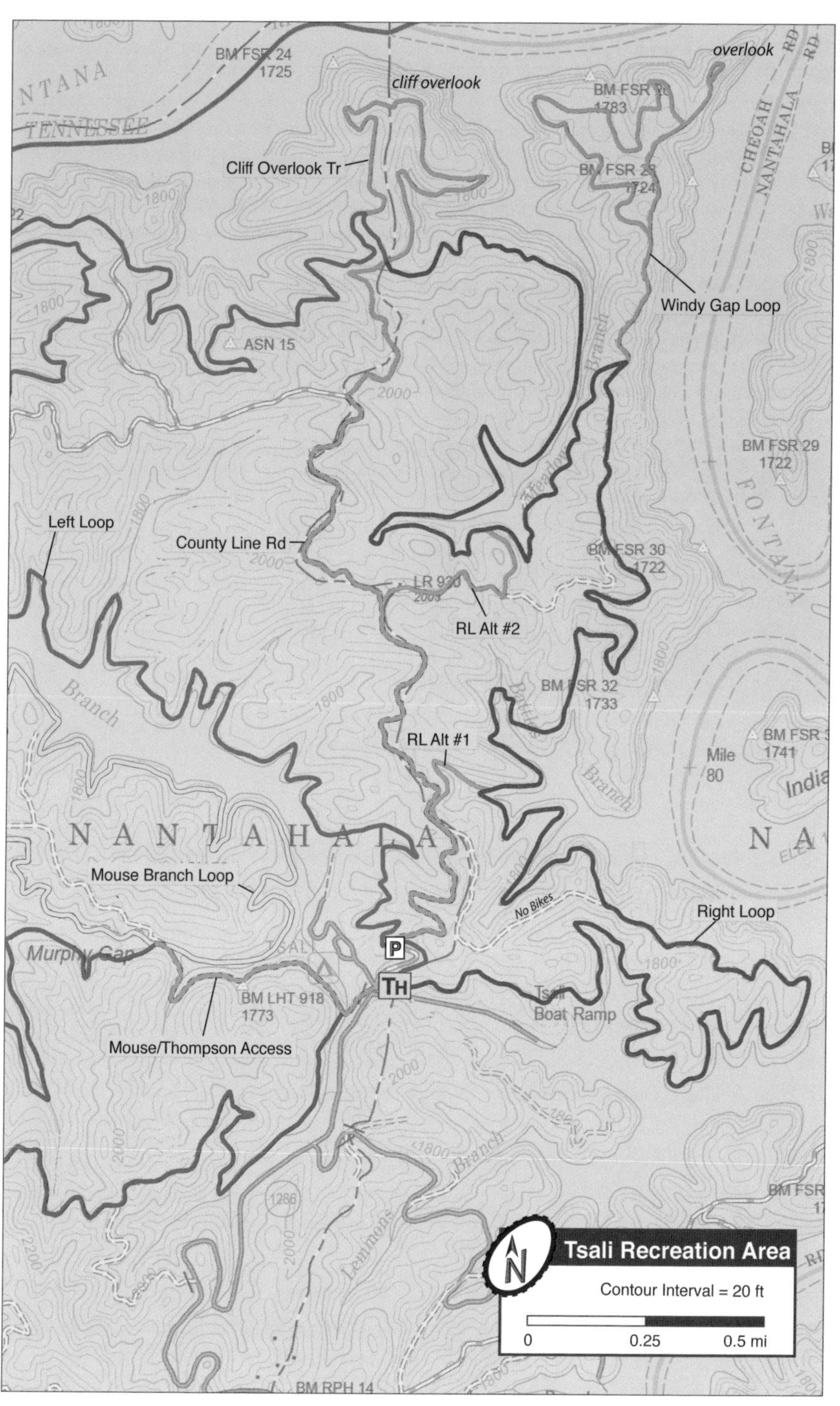
overlook
cliff overlook
BM FSR 24
1725
Cliff Overlook Tr
Windy Gap Loop
ASN 15
Left Loop
County Line Rd
LR 930
RL Alt #2
BM FSR 29
1722
BM FSR 30
1722
BM FSR 32
1733
RL Alt #1
Mile
80
NANTAHALA
Mouse Branch Loop
No Bikes
Right Loop
Murphy Gap
BM LHT 918
1773
Tsali
Boat Ramp
Mouse/Thompson Access
TENNESSEE
CHEOAH
NANTAHALA
FONTANA
Tsali Recreation Area
Contour Interval = 20 ft
0
0.25
0.5 mi
BM RPH 14

Fontana

Great views of Fontana Dam and the Smokies beyond pop up on the trail.

Type	Backcountry
Parking	Moderate
Toilets	None
Land Manager	USFS
Fee	None
Access	Paved road
Special Rules	None
Distance	5.6 miles
Difficulty	Moderate
Surface	Single track, forest road

You'll find the area around Fontana Dam to be some to be some of the wildest country in western North Carolina. Every bit of the geography seems to funnel down to where the lake meets the dam. To the north side is Great Smoky Mountains National Park, its high ridges marking the boundary between Tennessee and North Carolina. The Appalachian Trail crosses right over the top of the dam as it leaves the Nantahala Mountains and heads into the Park. Adjacent to Fontana Village Resort, on Nantahala National Forest land, are a couple of loop trails that connect to the privately-owned trails within the resort.

Llewellyn Cove Trail winds through a beautiful wildflower-filled hollow where small waterfalls crash beneath narrow bridges and the woods are brilliantly green. On the far end of Llewellyn Cove is Gold Branch Loop, which snakes close to the Appalachian Trail and then makes use of a gated forest road to finish the loop. From this route you'll have open views of the lake, the face of Fontana Dam, and the ridgeline of the Smokies. It's best to ride the Lewellyn Cove loop by taking the upper trail (the one to the right) first and then ride Gold Branch counterclockwise; that way you'll ride up FS 2624. Finish by riding the lower portion of Lewellyn Cove. It all makes a big 5.6-mile, figure-8 loop.

Fontana Village Resort has its own network of trails, and some were built with mountain bikers in mind. You can check in at the outdoor programs building to see what they currently have open.

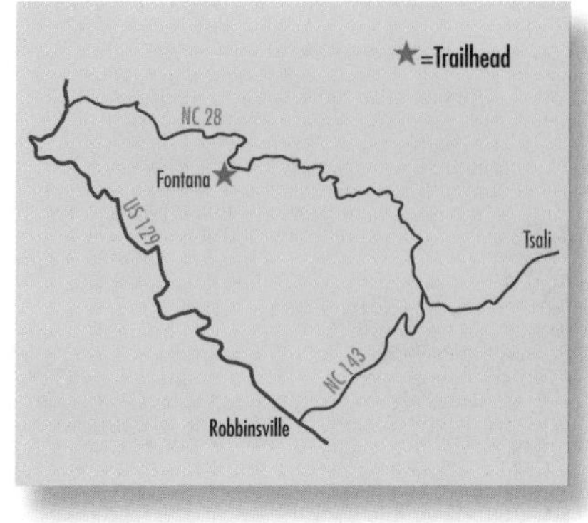

Getting to the Trailhead

Park at Fontana Village Resort off NC 28 to access these trails. It's a big place; you might even want to rent a cabin. The best parking area is near the outdoor programs building, just up the road from the general store; the actual trailhead for Lewellyn Cove Trail is located right off NC 28 at the hilltop of its twisty section on the southern end of the resort property.

GPS Coordinates

35.433, -83.824

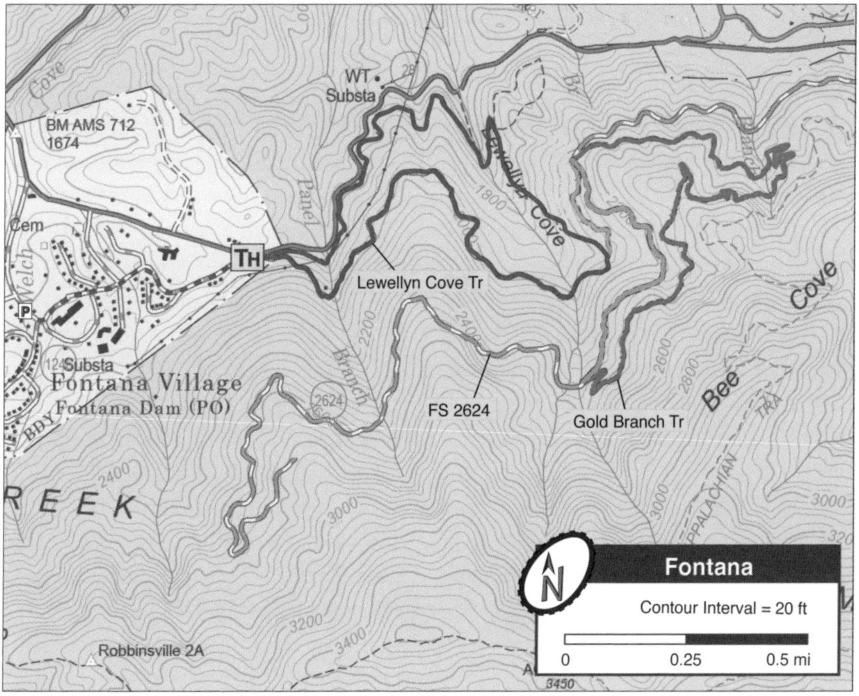

Santeetlah Lake Trail

No brown ring. Santeetlah Lake is always full and you ride right beside it.

Type	Backcountry
Parking	Moderate
Toilets	None
Land Manager	USFS
Fee	None
Access	Paved road
Special Rules	None
Distance	4 to 15 miles
Difficulty	Easy/Moderate
Surface	Single track, forest road

You have some options here. For a great beginner ride, start at West Buffalo Cemetery and ride the Long Hungry Loop. It's a combination of forest road and single track that follows along the shore of Santeetlah Lake. You'll pass a number of dispersed-use campsites along Long Hungry Road; they are right on the lake and can make a fine base if you're in the area for a while. The loop is about 4 miles long.

For the big 15-mile ride, you'll want to do all of Santeetlah Lake Trail, which includes the Long Hungry Loop. Starting down at Snowbird Road, the route begins with a steep (with tennis-ball-sized-gravel) pitch before settling into the contours around the lake. This trail needs to be ridden. It's beautiful, but you can expect brambles reaching out to grab you in some places, and don't be surprised if you have to hop some downfalls. Chances are you'll have it to yourself.

The trail is well marked and easy to follow, as it was once a forest road. Mileage is marked on posts every half-mile and there are signs at intersections. Once you've completed the trail and circled Long Hungry, either return the way you came (15-miler) or take your chances along a quick 2-mile stretch of NC 143.

Getting to the Trailhead

From the intersection of US 129 and NC 143 in Robbinsville, go north on US 129/NC 143. Just out of town, turn left on NC 143. Seven miles from the intersection in Robbinsville you'll reach the Santeetlah Lake trailhead. It's just across from Snowbird Road. Continue another 2 miles to get to the trailhead on Long Hungry Road. Follow Long Hungry Road out to West Buffalo Cemetery to park.

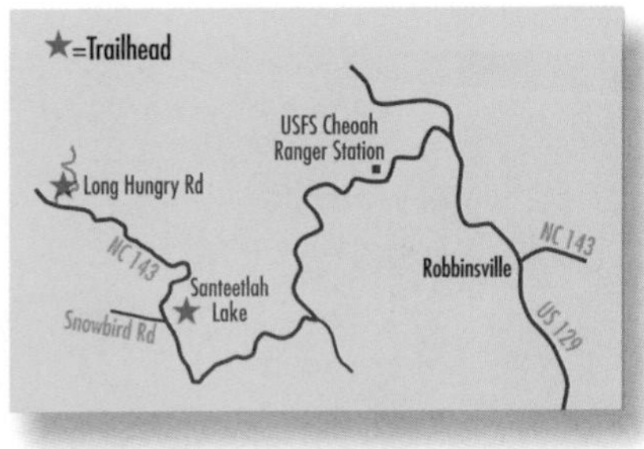

GPS Coordinates

Santeetlah Lake 35.316, -83.861
Long Hungry 35.328, -83.868

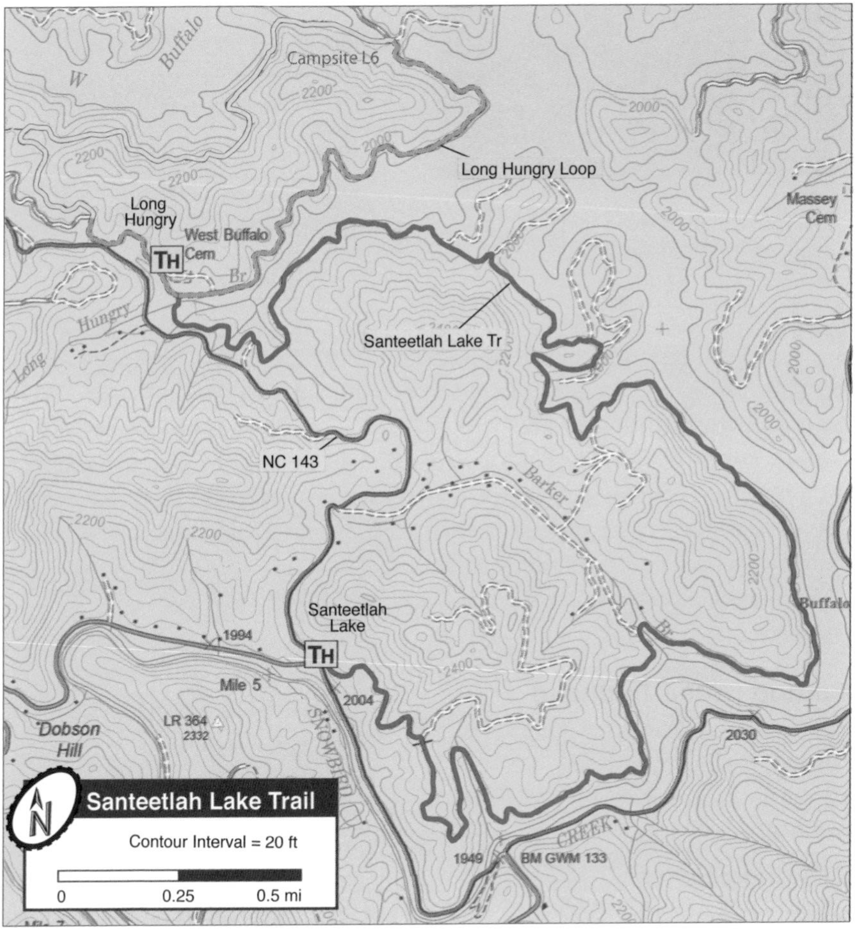

Santeetlah Lake Trail
Contour Interval = 20 ft
0 0.25 0.5 mi
Campsite L6
Long Hungry Loop
Long Hungry
West Buffalo Cem
TH
Santeetlah Lake Tr
NC 143
Massey Cem
Santeetlah Lake
TH
Mile 5
2004
1994
Dobson Hill
LR 364 2332
1949
BM GWM 133
2030

Hanging Dog Recreation Area

Trails at Hanging Dog are marked with signs and blazes.

Type	Backcountry
Parking	Plenty
Toilets	None
Land Manager	USFS
Fee	None
Access	Paved road
Special Rules	None
Distance	8 miles
Difficulty	Moderate
Surface	Single track

Hanging Dog is way more appealing than it sounds. You're not likely to find any dogs being hung. You *will* find a network of good trails on a peninsula jutting out into Hiwassee Lake. Look for lots of variety in both the trails and the scenery. But beware, there are a lot of trail junctions and it can get confusing, especially since a recent timber harvest. Trails are marked by number and sometimes it looks like the same trail is going in multiple directions. If you ride the entire outside loop, it's all single track and covers close to 8 miles. These trails see little use, so you could even have the place to yourself.

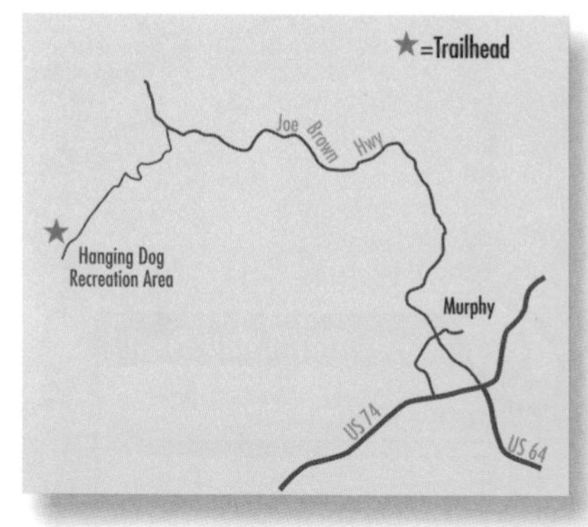

Getting to the Trailhead

Take Tennessee Street out of Murphy which becomes Joe Brown Highway. After 4 miles turn left into Hanging Dog Recreation Area. Park at the boat ramp.

GPS Coordinates

35.098157, -84.090529

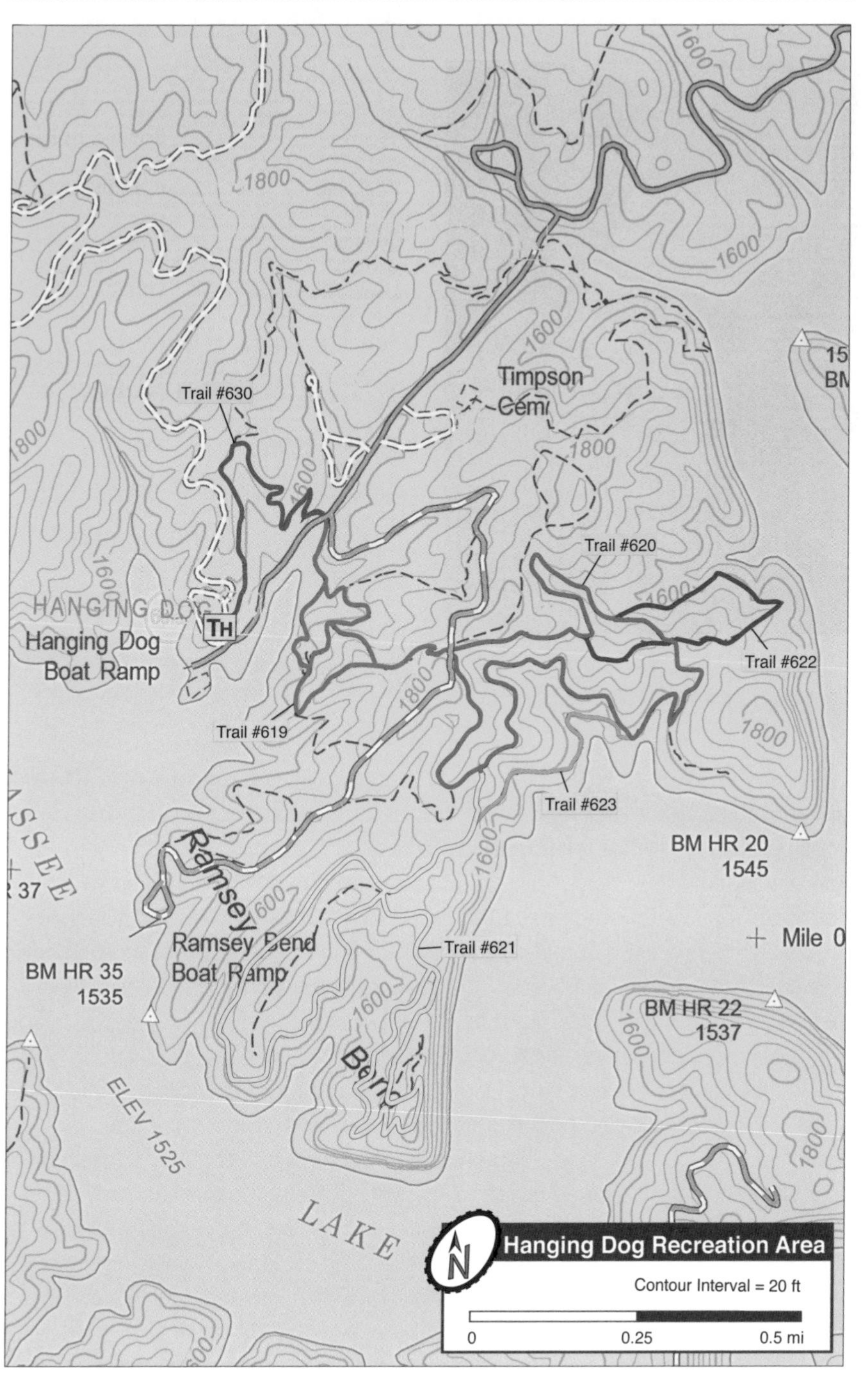

Hanging Dog Recreation Area
Contour Interval = 20 ft
0
0.25
0.5 mi
Trail #630
Timpson Cem
Trail #620
Trail #622
Trail #619
Trail #623
Trail #621
HANGING DOG
Hanging Dog Boat Ramp
Ramsey Bend Boat Ramp
Ramsey Bend
BM HR 20 1545
BM HR 35 1535
BM HR 22 1537
Mile 0
ELEV 1525
LAKE
1800
1600

Jackrabbit Recreation Area

The best view looking out over Lake Chatuge is from High Point Trail.

Type	Backcountry
Parking	Plentiful
Toilets	Yes
Land Manager	USFS
Fee	None
Access	Paved road
Special Rules	No

Jackrabbit is a trail area done right. On the peninsula jutting out into Lake Chatuge are some of the finest mountain bike trails in the area—especially for less than advanced riders. These trails are almost always in perfect condition; with their many swoops and dips they drain water fast and avoid erosion. With their frequent twists and turns, speeds are easily kept in check. Sometimes it's even hard to remember you're in the mountains. The few climbs are short and relatively easy. All in all, it's just a really nice place to ride a mountain bike.

There are eight different trails at Jackrabbit varying in length from 1 to 3 miles, and the theme here is loops branching off of one central loop. Picking a ride is just a matter of deciding how many loops you want to add to your ride. The central loop is 3.1 miles long. If you added every loop to create the longest ride possible without backtracking or repeating parts of trails, you'd ride a total of just over 13 miles. Since each trail has its own characteristics, a brief description of each follows so you can put together whatever type of ride you want. And getting around is easy, since every junction is marked with a numbered post that includes a trail map and a "you are here" location symbol.

Just down the road from the trailhead is a 100-unit forest service campground with a sandy swimming beach. This makes a great place to stay for a weekend of cycling.

Getting to the Trailhead

From Hayesville NC on US 64, take NC 175 south for 3.5 miles and turn right onto Jackrabbit Road. The trailhead is 0.5 mile on the left. From Hiawassee, GA on US 76, take GA 75 north. About a mile into North Carolina, turn left on Jackrabbit Road. The trailhead is 0.5 mile on the left.

GPS Coordinates

35.000, -83.762

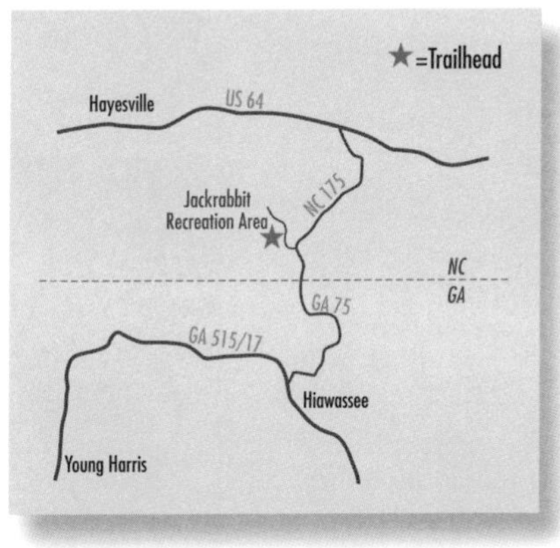

Jackrabbit Trails

Central Loop

Distance 3.1 miles
Difficulty Easy
Surface Single track

This is the loop from which all the other loops branch. It's wide and marked with white blazes. For the most part it follows the contour line about 40 feet above the lake. Look for the signs identifying the various trees and plants, including the rare American Columbo which blooms in late May.

Burnt Tree Peninsula

Distance 1 mile
Difficulty Easy
Surface Single track

On this short loop you'll find the closest access to the lake from the trail-head. The trail is twisty and somewhat narrower than Central Loop. Look for easy short ups and downs and lots of ferns. Burnt Tree Peninsula Trail is blazed green.

Yotee's Run

Distance 1.5 miles
Difficulty Easy
Surface Single track

Yotee was a dog—just in case you were wondering. You can read all about Yotee on the trail sign where Yotee's Run begins. Blazed blue, Yotee's Run has a bit more climbing than Central Loop, is narrower, and has lots of swoops. It's also higher above the lake. You can cut this loop in half by taking the more difficult High Point Trail.

High Point Trail

Distance 1 mile
Difficulty Moderate
Surface Single track

This is the most difficult trail at

Jackrabbit, but as the rating indicates, it is not too hard. Basically it climbs up onto the ridge and circles above Yotee's Run. There is one stretch that is short but steep. Up top you'll find a very nice view of Lake Chatuge and the surrounding mountains. The route is blazed orange.

Burrell Cove Trail

Distance 1.7 miles
Difficulty Easy
Surface Single track

Burrell Cove has lots of twists and turns with some really fun berms and whoops. Blazed red, it's the route to take if you want to go to SABA Beach.

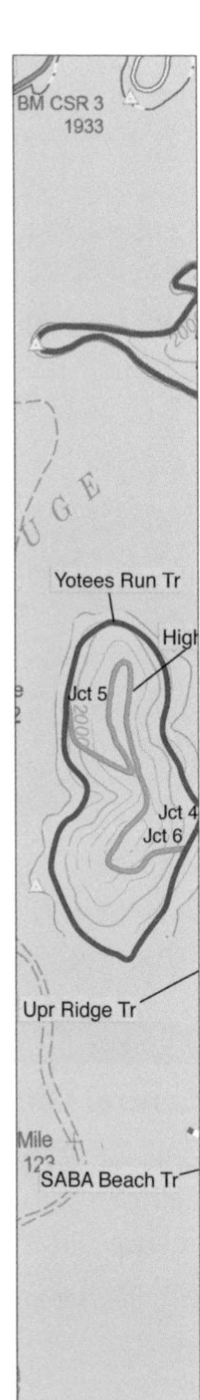

SABA Beach Trail

Distance 0.7 mile
Difficulty Easy
Surface Single track

This short loop takes you out to a great swimming beach. SABA stands for Southern Appalachian Bicycle Association, which maintains these trails. Look for the red and white blaze.

Sneaking Creek Trail

Distance 3.2 miles
Difficulty Easy
Surface Single track

Sneaking Creek has a somewhat different feel than the rest of the trails here. It twists and swoops pretty much like all the rest, but it also comes in close proximity to private property. In places you might feel you are riding through someone's back yard. Still, it's fun and adds considerable distance. The route is blazed brown.

Upper Ridge Trail

Distance 1.5 miles
Difficulty Moderate
Surface Single track

Upper Ridge consists of a long climb (for Jackrabbit) followed by a relatively long downhill with a short up-and-down thrown in for good measure. The up is not too hard and the down is a real blast, with just enough twisty turns to check your speed. Those who love climbing will definitely want to add this trail, along with High Point, to any ride they do here.

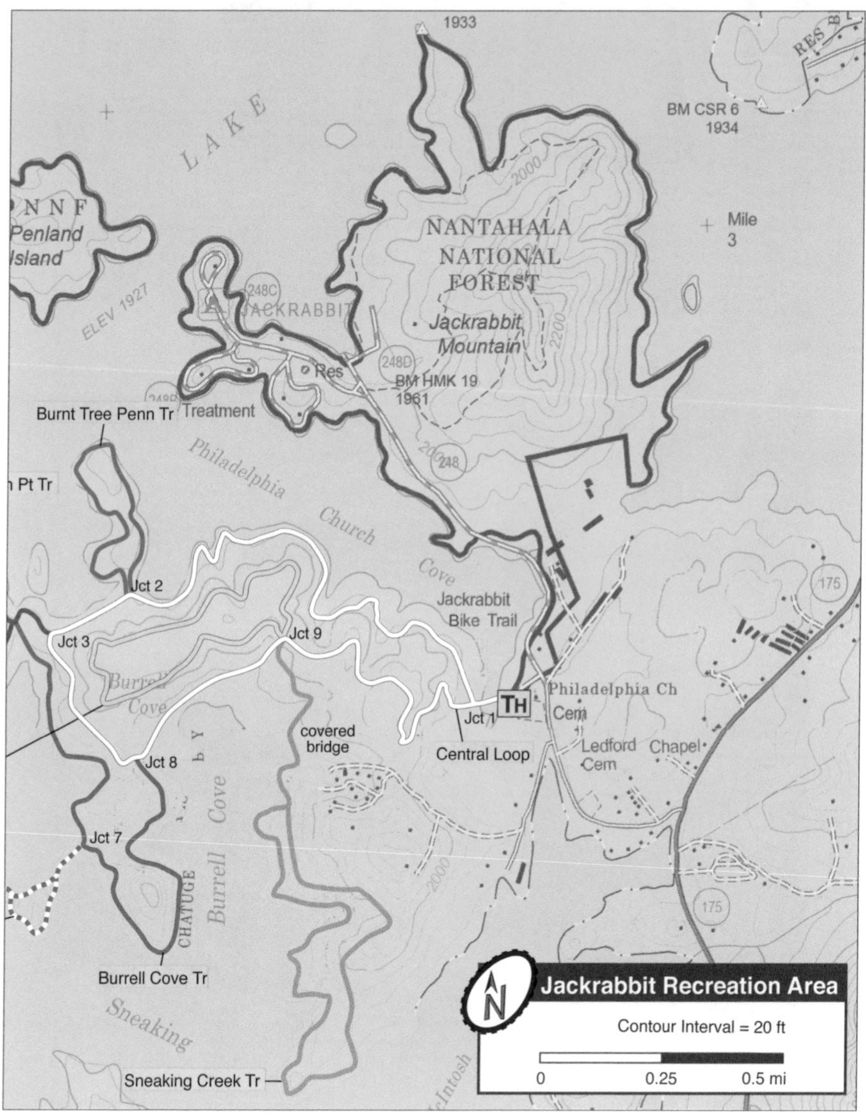

Greenville–Spartanburg

The trail at Pleasant Ridge is awesome—like riding an oversized pump track that's five miles long.

Greenville and Spartanburg have got to be the most bike-friendly and cycle-centric towns in the Carolina mountains. You'll see folks on bikes most anywhere you go. There are bicycle lanes in town and Greenville county boasts the Swamp Rabbit Trail, a paved route that runs from Travelers Rest to South Greenville. This area is one of the few places in the South you can walk into a convenience store with your cycling togs on and not have people look at you sideways.

Many of the trails here were built specifically for mountain bikers, and all but two are in small county or city parks. They've turned out to be great resources for locals as well as for people visiting on business. Duncan Park is right downtown in Spartanburg and just down the street from a bike shop. Lake Conestee is a nature park on the Reedy River south of Greenville which connects to the Swamp Rabbit Trail. Pleasant Ridge, up near the state line, has the biggest climb and fastest descent around.

Each town has a state park nearby with excellent trails. Croft State Park, just south of Spartanburg, has a beautiful network built with cyclists in mind. Those looking for longer, easier, and fast routes should head here. Paris Mountain State Park's trail network was built long before mountain bikes came on the scene. Its routes are a little more rugged and involve some climbing—perfect for the seasoned cyclist. And if you are looking for a bike park, Travelers Rest has one right downtown. Grab the kids and head out on the jumps or practice your skills on logs, roots, and rocks.

There are a number of bike shops in Greenville, Spartanburg, and Travelers Rest (see p. 206). These guys all know their stuff and can get you on a new bike or a rental, or service your own if it needs attention. Bike vacationers to the Upstate can choose from a multitude of lodging options. Campers, of course, will want to head to the state parks where developed campgrounds await.

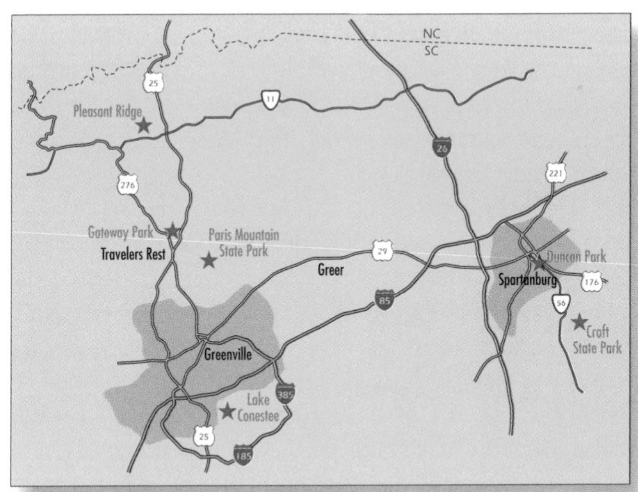

Croft State Park

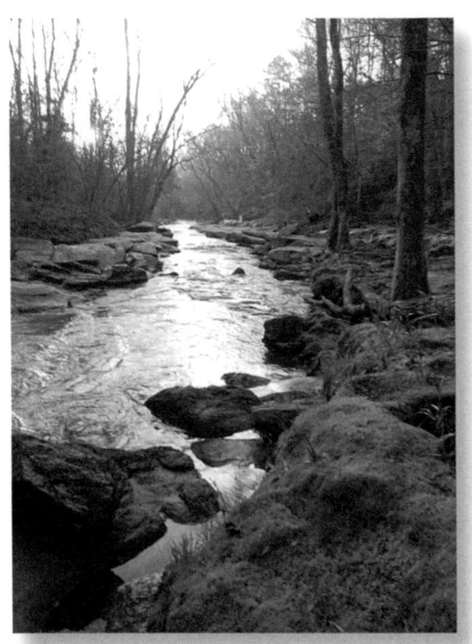

Half of the Southside Loop Trail follows along Fairforest Creek.

Type	Backcountry
Parking	Plenty
Toilets	Yes
Land Manager	SC State Parks
Fee	$2 pp
Access	Paved road
Special Rules	None

Croft State Park's Southside Loop Trail could very well be known as the Tsali of the Upstate. Tsali Recreation Area, located across Fontana Lake from Great Smoky Mountains National Park in North Carolina, became world famous back in the 1990s, mostly due to its buffed trails along the lakeshore. Southside has the same feel. Parts of the trail are incredibly smooth and fast, but there are plenty of roots, rocks, and short steep hills to get your attention. One way to describe it would be nicely worn-in, but not worn out. It's a really nice trail system with nearly 20 miles worth of riding options.

Originally a military camp, Croft State Park was where thousands of soldiers prepared for battle during World War II. The US Army transformed what was once a series of cotton and tobacco farms into a training ground. Soldiers came through here before shipping out to Europe and the Pacific. They learned to fire rifles at various rifle ranges, chuck grenades, and deal with poisonous gases. Luckily you won't have to do any of that, but you can ride your bike past areas that once were used for those purposes. Imagine what it must have been like for those guys. They were probably having fun and getting in shape just like you, but unlike you they didn't get to go home at the end of the day; they were heading to a place where people were trying to kill them.

A highlight of these trails is Fairforest Creek, which is your riding companion for miles. You can hear it gurgling over small rapids much of the time and it's fun to stop and check out the little sandy beaches just off the trail. You might see a kingfisher swooping out across the creek searching for fish, or spot deer and other animal tracks leading down to the water. Ride early or late in the day and you'll have a good chance of seeing some of the animals themselves.

The Southside Trails should be enough to sate your biking appetite, but if for some reason you want to check out even more trails in or near the state park, the Croft Passage of the Palmetto Trail heads north from here and the Glenn Springs Passage heads south. Both of these are out-and-back-style rides, but you might find them interesting. To go north, ride from the Palmetto Trail trailhead toward the headquarters building and then turn left onto the multipurpose Craig Trail. To go south, follow the Southside Loop Trail out to Fosters Mill Circle Road.

Getting to the Trailhead

There are two trailheads. Palmetto Trail is located within the state park itself and the other is at Southside Park, managed by Spartanburg County. Pay your use fee at the entrance to Croft State Park or at the payment station at the county park trailhead. Each charges $2 per person.

Palmetto Trail From Spartanburg, travel south on SC 56. After passing the South Carolina School for the Deaf and Blind, look for the Croft State Park sign. Turn left off SC 56 and then turn right to enter the park. From the gate it's about 3 miles out to the trailhead, just past the campground entrance and the park store and headquarters.

Southside Park Follow the directions from Spartanburg as above. Stay on SC 56 as you pass the entrance to Croft State Park and continue another 3 miles or so. Turn left on Groce Road and follow it to the park. The trail starts behind the kiosk.

GPS Coordinates

Palmetto Trail 34.862, -81.839
Southside Park 34.855, -81.855

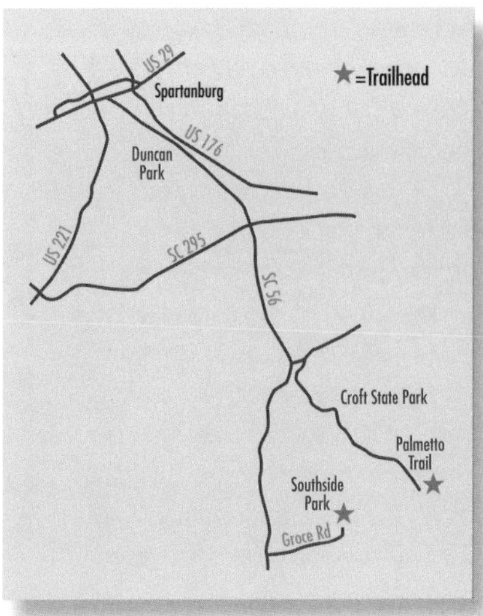

Croft State Park Routes

Southside Loop

Distance 9.7 miles
Difficulty Moderate
Surface Single track
Trailhead Palmetto Trail or Southside Park

This is the big outside loop at Croft State Park. It's easy to follow, since all the trails are marked so well. Just look for the white diamond blazes saying Southside Loop. To ride more mileage means making connections with the internal trails and then repeating parts of this one. You can ride it in either direction and if you ride here often, you'll want to change directions every now and then to keep things interesting.

Much of the route you can crank along in your bigger gears, just be ready to shift down at a moment's notice to twist through some trees or—more likely—to dip down across a tiny creek and make a steep but short climb up the other side.

If you start at the Palmetto Trail trailhead, you'll coast down to a narrow bridge across Fairforest Creek. Once on the other side you'll need to decide to go right (counterclockwise) or left (clockwise). If it's your first time, go right. That way you'll get the easy riding along the creek first and finish with a tricky downhill. The same goes for starting at Southside Park. Go counterclockwise the first time and you'll start with a good downhill.

Generally the most difficult portions of the loop are found on the outer ends. If you want to skip a difficult climb and some major roots, take Flat Pass Trail on the west end.

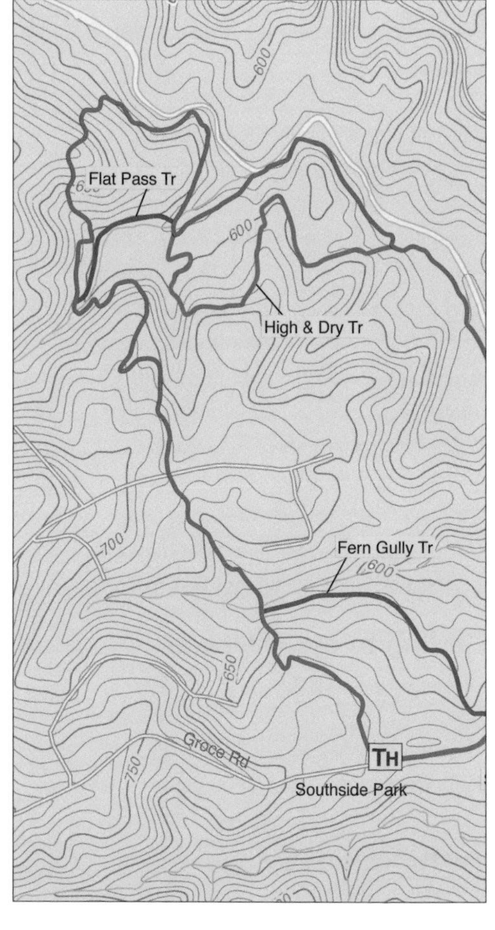

Short Loop

Distance 5 miles
Difficulty Moderate
Surface Single track
Trailhead Southside Park

Try this for a shorter and somewhat easier loop ride. You can ride it in either direction, but if it's your first time, ride it counterclockwise.

From the trailhead, begin on Southside Loop Trail. It's straight and fast here, so be ready for trail junctions. Turn left on Centerline Trail to cut the loop roughly in half. When you reach Southside Loop Trail again, go left and follow the trail along Fairforest Creek. When you reach Flat Pass Trail, turn left again. Back on Southside, go left once more and follow the loop trail all the way back to the parking lot.

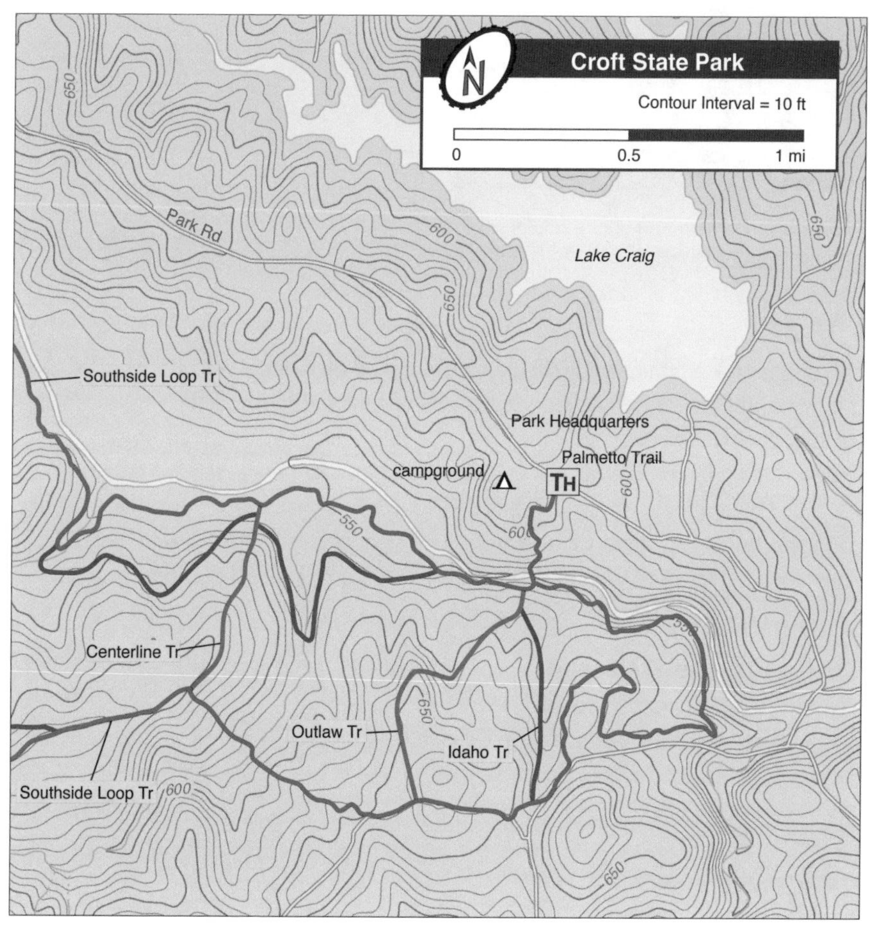

Duncan Park

The trails in Duncan Park circle a lake and sometimes parallel neighborhood streets.

Type	Urban
Parking	Plenty
Toilets	Yes
Land Manager	Town of Spartanburg
Fee	None
Access	Paved road
Special Rules	None
Distance	1 to 5 miles
Difficulty	Easy
Surface	Single track

With about 5 miles of trail all told, Duncan Park gives you lots of choices. For a good start try circling the park on the outer Northern and Southern Trails, leaving out super-twisty Monorail Trail; then you can head into the interior of the park. Trolley Trail under the powerlines is great fun if you like berms and banked turns—you don't even need to pedal on this one. Beginners wanting to improve their skills can jump on circular blue Thomas Trail. It's also a blast to coast down Central Trail from the top. Monorail with all its tree roots is more advanced and has so many twists it's confusing, but give it try as well.

Getting to the Trailhead

From downtown Spartanburg take Dean and then Union Street, which becomes SC 56. Duncan Park is on your right on Duncan Park Drive as you head out of town. You'll see the trail kiosk in the upper part of the stadium parking lot.

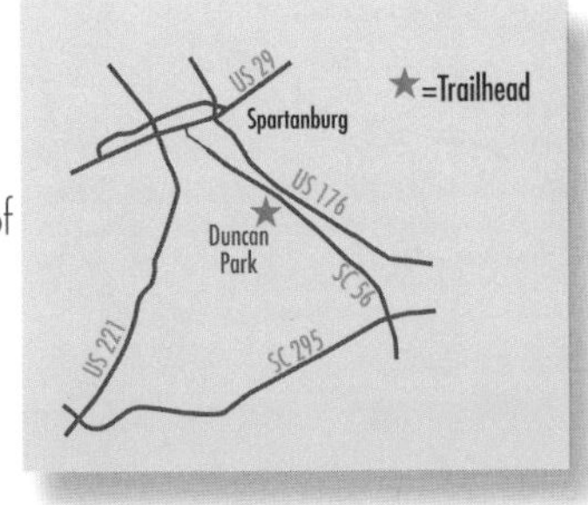

GPS Coordinates

Stadium Parking 34.937, -81.912

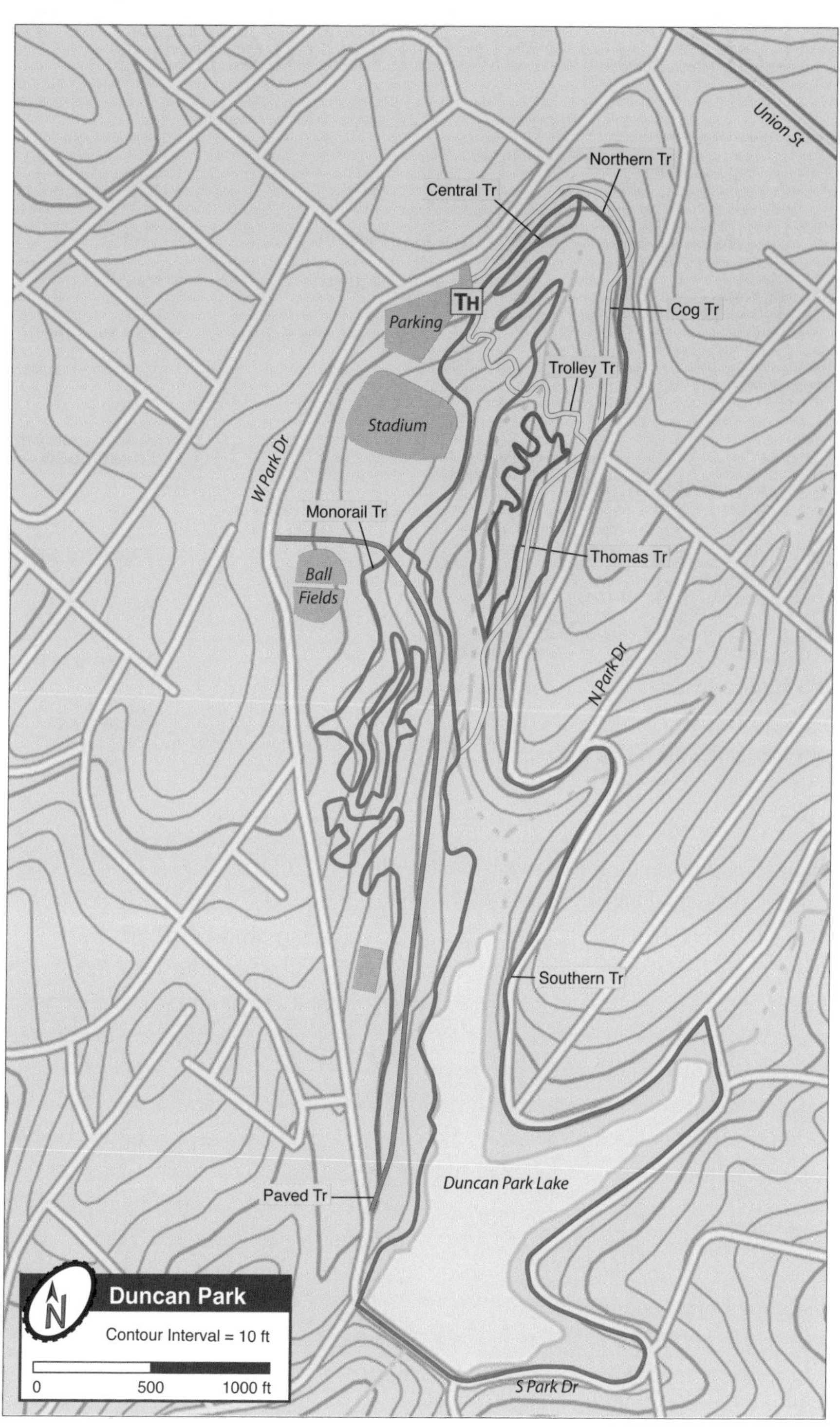
Union St
Northern Tr
Central Tr
Cog Tr
TH
Parking
Trolley Tr
Stadium
W Park Dr
Monorail Tr
Thomas Tr
Ball Fields
N Park Dr
Southern Tr
Duncan Park Lake
Paved Tr
Duncan Park
Contour Interval = 10 ft
0
500
1000 ft
S Park Dr

Lake Conestee Nature Park

White Tail Trail circles a huge field with big oak tree and some picnic tables.

Type	Urban
Parking	Plenty
Toilets	Yes
Land Manager	Greenville County Parks
Fee	None
Access	Paved road
Special Rules	*Yes
Distance	1 to 5 miles
Difficulty	Easy
Surface	Single track

* Signage at various bridges asks that you dismount and walk your bike across.

Conestee is an urban ride with the feel of a backcountry route. No, you don't head out into the hinterlands, but unlike many urban parks, the trails are not so twisty and curvy. You'll find them to be wide, swooping, and lots of fun. It's a great place for beginner riders. The trails are well marked and easy to follow. An additional benefit is that the paved Swamp Rabbit Trail goes right through the park. You can use it to extend your ride if you want, or you might want to ride it to get to Conestee from elsewhere in town.

For a good 5-mile route, start out by riding from the trailhead around the edge of the field, under the big arch, and then down and across the high bridge over the Reedy River. Once across, bear right at the first few trail junctions, then go left when you reach Flat Tail Trail. Stay on Flat Tail until you reach the first junction with White Tail Trail, where you'll take a right and almost immediately cross over paved Swamp Rabbit Trail. The next section is really pleasant. You'll circle a huge meadow before reaching Swamp Rabbit Trail again. Turn left onto it briefly and then angle off right onto White Tail Trail. It's just a short hop down to Flat Tail Trail where you'll again take a left just before a boardwalk bridge.

At Woodie Walk Trail, turn right across a boardwalk bridge to Possum Run again and follow the trail up and over the big bridge. You could end here, but for more great riding turn right on Raccoon Run Trail just before the arch. Follow it out to Dragonfly Way Trail where you'll get a great view of Conestee Lake. Circle back on Dragonfly Way, eventually returning to the trailhead via Raccoon Run the way you came.

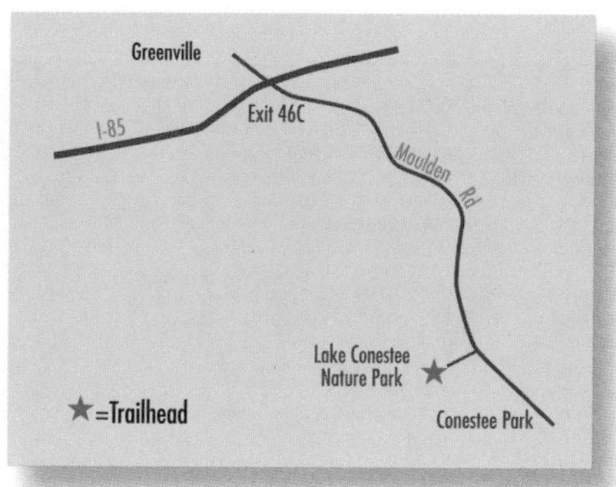

Getting to the Trailhead

From I-85 just south of Greenville, take exit 46C and travel south on Mauldin Road. In not so many miles you'll come to Conestee Park on your right. Turn into the main park entrance, then pass the dog park and huge parking lot for the play area. Trailhead parking for Lake Conestee Nature Park is the last lot you come to. Look for the trailhead kiosk with a big map and other information.

GPS Coordinates

Nature Park 34.779, -82.352

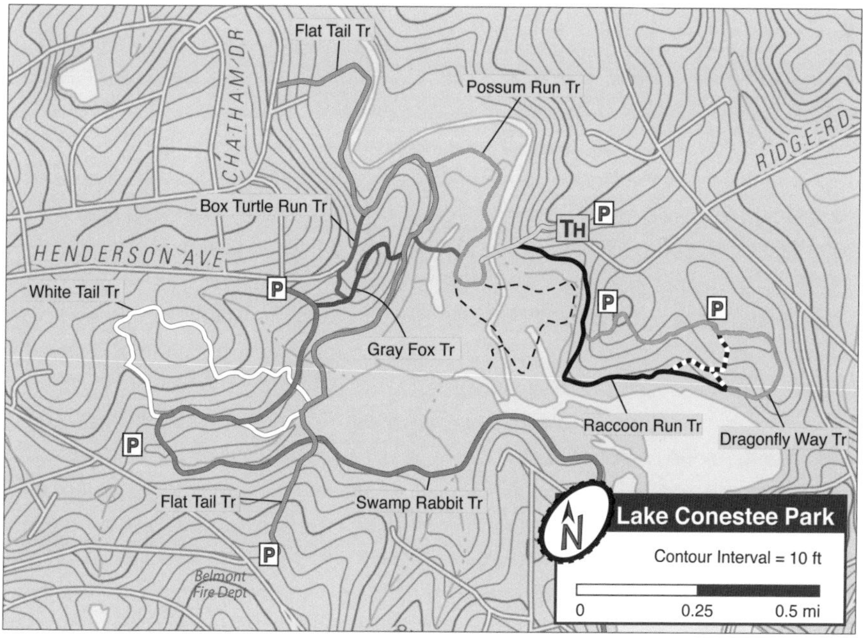

Paris Mountain State Park

The entrance sign at Paris Mountain State Park welcomes you on every visit.

Type	Backcountry
Parking	Plentiful
Toilets	At lower trailheads
Land Manager	SC State Parks
Fee	$2 per adult
Access	Paved road
Special Rules	*Yes

* No bikes allowed on trails on Saturdays.

If you live in Greenville, sooner or later you're going to end up mountain biking at Paris Mountain State Park. It's a great place to ride! There are a number of routes to choose from and there's something for every ability level.

On this end of the Upstate it's not hard to spot Paris Mountain. Sticking up all by itself just to the north of Greenville, you can't miss it. At 1,800 feet it may not seem like much compared to its big sisters to the north, but given that it stands a good 1,000 feet higher than its immediate surroundings, it really stands out. The state park takes up only a small percentage of the entire mountain. You'll see housing developments surrounding it and up top are enough cell, radio, and TV towers to send communications to Mars. Once in the woods, though, you'll hardly know it. Paris Mountain State Park has done a wonderful job of preserving this area. In fact, it's one of the oldest protected public spaces in South Carolina, with sections of old-growth forests and a number of lakes originally built to provide drinking water for Greenville. Amenities for visitors include a swimming lake and picnic shelters with flush toilets.

For the most part riding here involves climbing and descending Paris Mountain. You can start low and ride up or start at the top and begin by riding down.

For easier rides, stick to the trails that circle the top of the mountain. Riding up from the bottom certainly adds difficulty, and so does dropping off the back side where you'll have to ride back up.

Getting to the Trailhead

From downtown Greenville and the south Take US 276 north and turn onto SC 253 (State Park Road). Follow it for several miles. At the state park sign, turn left and head into the park.

From Travelers Rest and the north Take the other end of State Park Road east for 8 miles. Turn right at the state park sign and head into the park.

GPS Coordinates

Lower 34.927, -82.369
Upper 34.940, -82.390

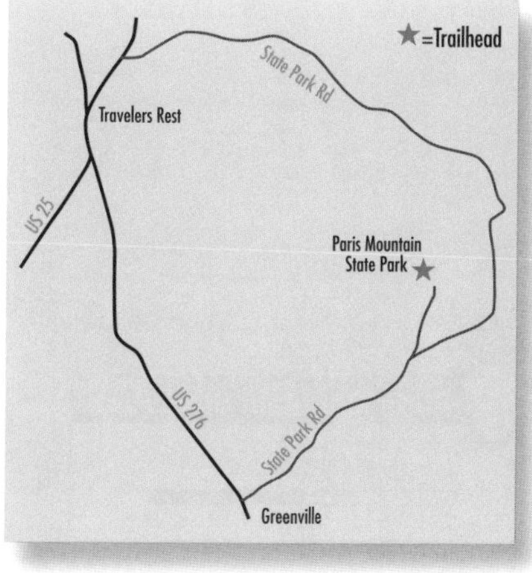

Paris Mountain Routes

Mountaintop Loop

Distance 3 miles
Difficulty Easy
Surface Single track
Trailhead Upper Lot

This all-single track loop is one of the easier rides at Paris Mountain. Since you start at the top of the mountain and never drop down, there is very little climbing on the route.

Begin at the upper trailhead parking lot. When you drive up the mountain, as soon as you crest the top you'll notice a small parking area in front of a gate. Don't park here, but continue to the right along the ridge to the much larger parking lot on the left.

From the trailhead, follow the road back to the gate you passed in your car. Continue past this gate onto Sulphur Springs Trail. It's an old roadbed at this point. After about a mile, bear right onto Fire Tower Trail and continue up the small hill to the next junction. Turn right on the connector trail and then right on Kanuga Trail. Follow Kanuga Trail as it rises and falls along the contour line until it meets Brissy Ridge Trail. Turn right on Brissy Ridge and follow it back to the trailhead.

North Lake Loop

Distance 5 miles
Difficulty Moderate
Surface Single track
Trailhead Upper Lot

On this ride you'll explore the trails

on the back side of Paris Mountain. Going down to the reservoir is fast and furious; just remember you may meet someone coming up. The ride back up is where you pay for the great downhill.

Begin at the upper trailhead parking lot and for the first part of the ride follow the directions in the previous route. When you reach Kanuga Trail after the connector trail, turn left down the mountain. For the most part the trail heading down is fairly smooth, but there are some places where roots bump things up a bit and you'll splash through some small rocky streams.

Once down by the reservoir, circle it clockwise by turning left on North Lake Trail at your first opportunity. If you want a slightly shorter ride don't circle it; bear right along the southern shore. Either way you'll eventually reach Pipsissewa Trail and follow it back up the mountain. It's a grunt, but except for a couple of difficult moves, all ridable. When you reach Brissy Ridge Trail, turn right and follow it back to the trailhead.

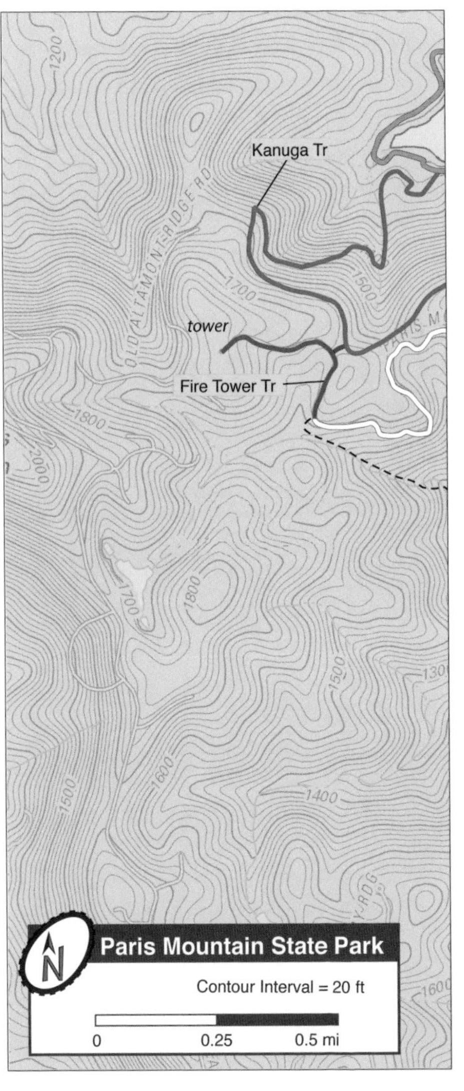

The Big Downhill

Distance 2.5 miles
Difficulty Moderate
Surface Single track
Trailhead Upper Lot

This is one of those rides you do at the end of the day as a treat. Think of it as an extension of or addition to any other ride at Paris Mountain. It's the big downhill—2.5 miles of single track from the top of the mountain all the way back to the bottom at Lake Placid.

There are a couple of different ways to do it. Start at Lake Placid and ride up the road to the top, catch your breath, and then come back down the trail—or have someone run your shuttle and just start at the top.

To start the downhill, hop onto Sulphur Springs Trail at top of the hill; it's across the road from the upper trailhead kiosk. Tight switchbacks lead down for almost a mile, then things open up a bit after passing the first parking lot. Keep it under control and watch for Mountain Creek Trail on your left; it takes you down the rest of the way. You know you've missed it if you reach the road too soon.

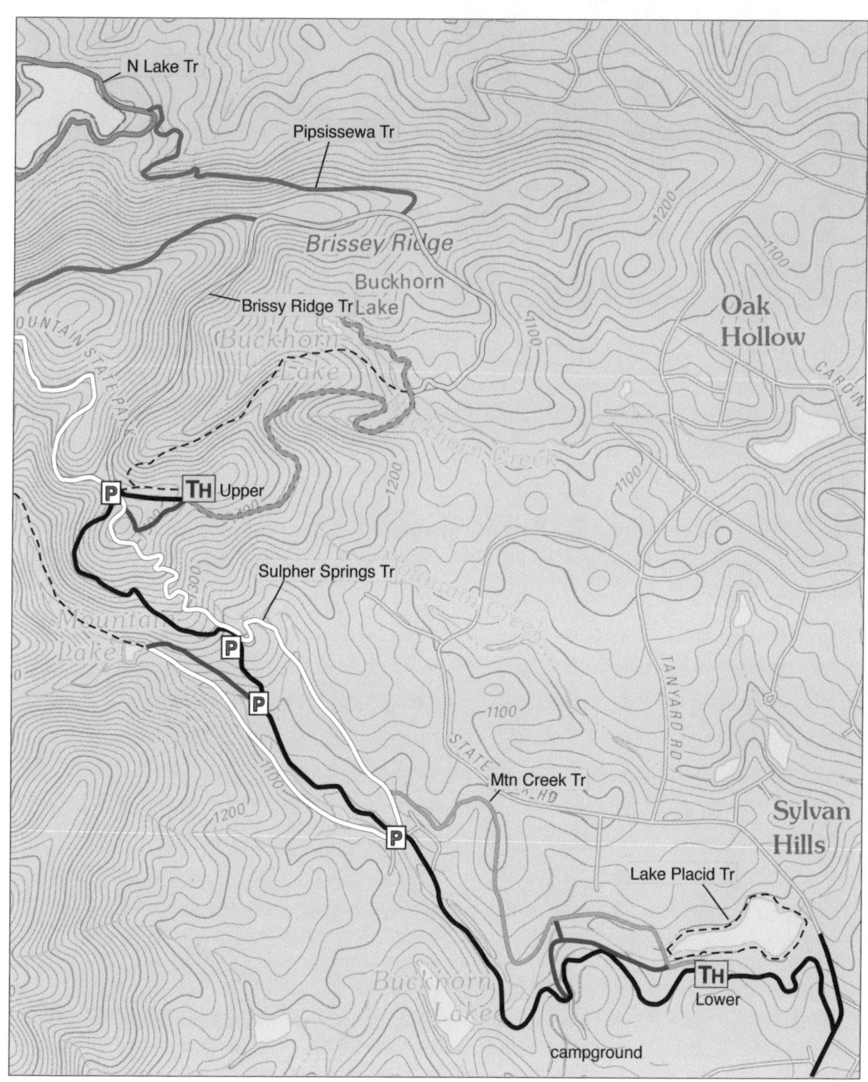

Gateway Mountain Bike Park

Banked boardwalks are a prominent feature in bike skills flow park.

Type	Bike park
Parking	Plenty
Toilets	Yes
Land Manager	Greenville County Parks
Fee	None
Access	Paved road
Special Rules	*Yes

* Pump track and jumps are closed when wet.

Gateway Park in Travelers Rest has a very interesting and fun mountain bike park. Here you'll find a pump track, log jumps, rock gardens, angled boardwalks, dirt jumps, berms, banked turns, log-ride balance beams, and more—all in short order. Think of it as a condensed version of a extraordinary backcountry ride. All the elements are here, only you'll encounter them one right after the other, without having to drive miles and ride long distances to get to each one. Expect to find riders of all abilities here, lots of kids, and plenty of folks without helmets—go figure. Just be sure to wear yours and set a good example.

One of the great things about Gateway is that it's located right behind Sunrift Adventures, which has a full-service bike shop where you can get a tune-up before hitting the park (or a fix-up after taking that big crash!). It's also right next to Swamp Rabbit Trail. Go for a ride on the Swamp Rabbit and finish up with a couple of loops around Gateway.

Basically the course consists of a big outer loop that's trail only, and several inner loops with all the special features. The outer loop itself is pretty easy to ride, but expect a bumpy circuit; the trail is constructed of broken-up concrete for durability and it is rough stuff.

After a warm-up spin around the loop you'll certainly be drawn to the jumps. These are a lot of fun and, since this feature is located on the side of a hill, you won't have any trouble getting up enough speed to go for the big air. You can do endless loops here.

Head into the maze of log obstacles, tilted boardwalks, and rock gardens when you've had enough air time. This is the best place in the park to fine-tune those trail-riding skills you'll use the most. Take a spin around the outer loop one more time before calling it a day.

Getting to the Trailhead

Head north on US 276 from the main traffic light in Travelers Rest at the junction with Poinsett Highway. Just past Sunrift

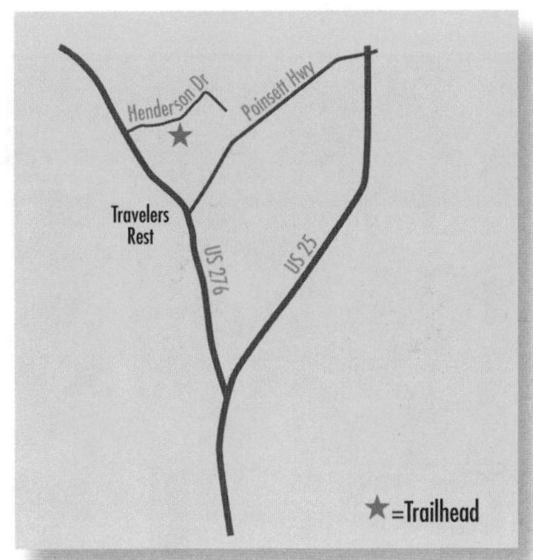

Adventures turn right on Henderson Drive, cross the Swamp Rabbit Trail, and follow the signs into Gateway Park. You'll see the trail kiosk on the left.

GPS Coordinates

Gateway Park 34.970, -82.443

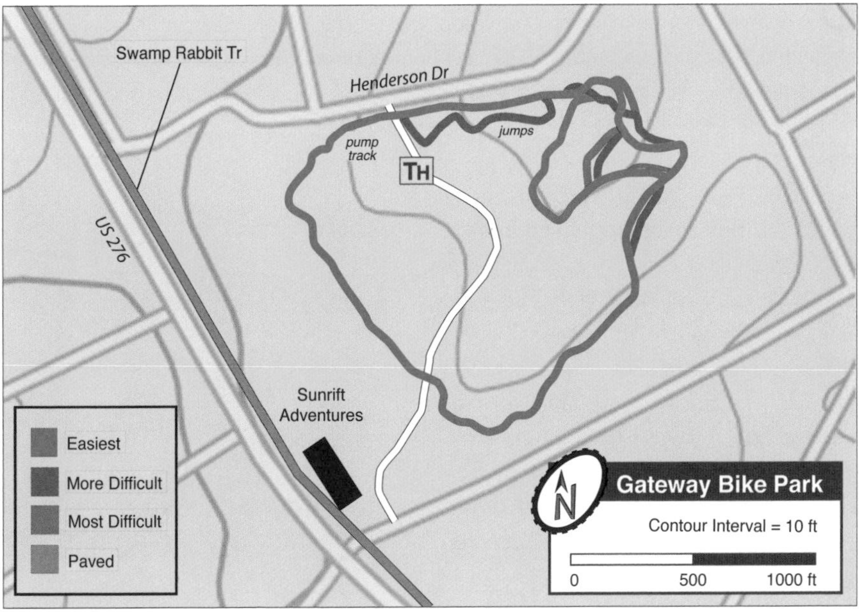

Pleasant Ridge Park

There's no doubt which direction to ride at Pleasant Ridge. Check the sign at the start.

Type	Backcountry
Parking	Plenty
Toilets	Yes
Land Manager	Greenville County Parks
Fee	None
Access	Paved road
Special Rules	*Yes
Distance	5.2 miles
Difficulty	Moderate
Surface	Single track

* Trail is directional and alternates with hikers.

Sometimes this feels like a long, giant pumptrack, albeit one on the side of a mountain. There are so many dips and humps on this trail, you'll lose count within the first mile. There are also plenty of roots and rocks to get your attention.

The direction of travel for cyclists changes periodically, so there's no point describing a turn-by-turn route. It's just one big loop with only intersections; it would be near impossible to get lost. Just check the sign at the beginning to see which way to start the loop and then go. The trailhead is at the bottom of the loop, so no matter which way you go you'll be riding generally uphill for the first half of the ride and generally downhill for the second half. The uphill portions are a grind, but all are definitely ridable. The downhill portions are a blast. All those humps and dips and banked turns are incredible.

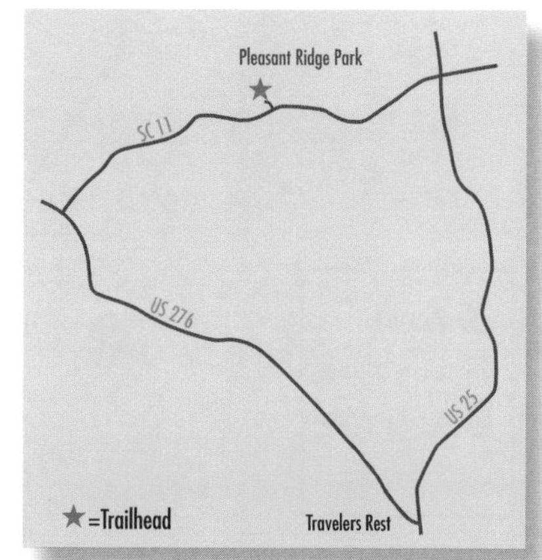

Getting to the Trailhead

Head north from Travelers Rest on US 25 and turn east (left) onto SC 11. Pleasant Ridge Park is just a few miles down the road on the right.

GPS Coordinates

Pleasant Ridge 35.086, -82.479

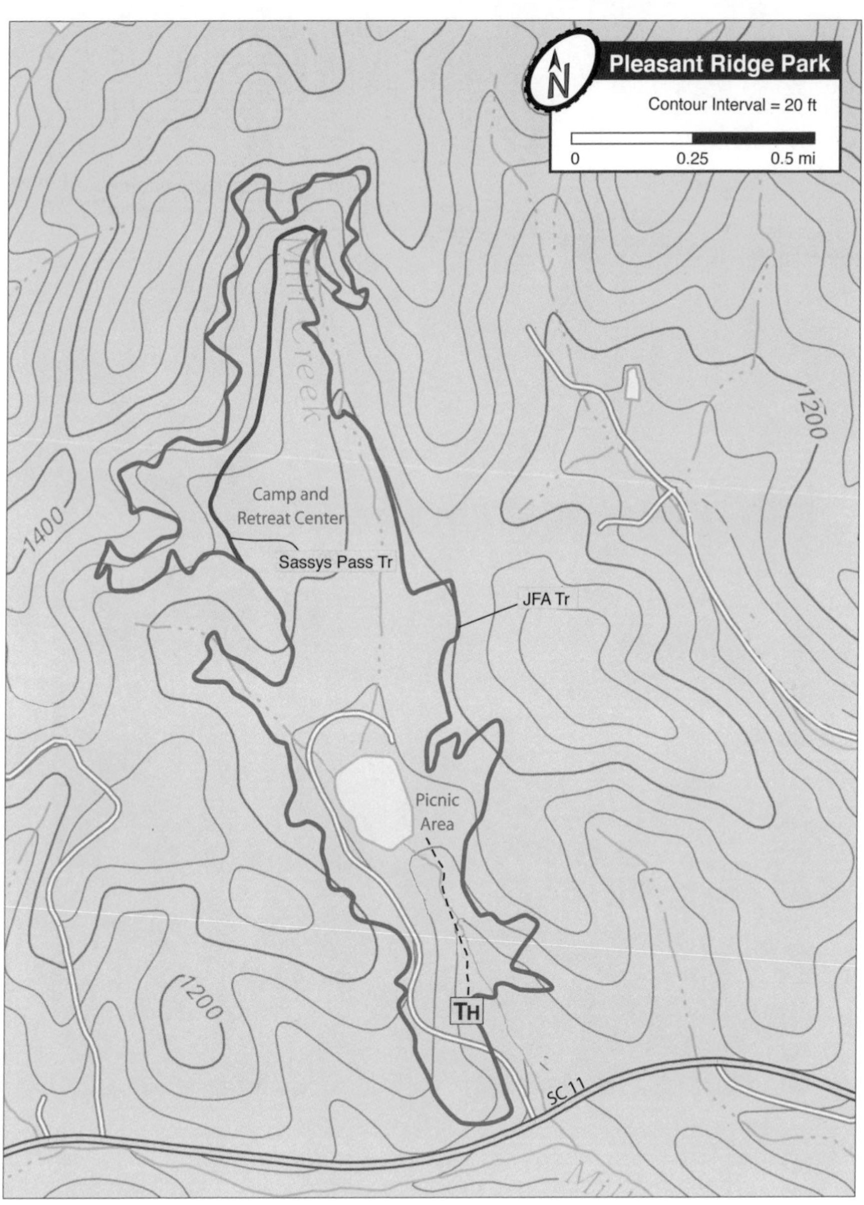

The Western Upstate

The trails of both Issaqueena Lake and Fant's Grove circle the shores of Lake Hartwell. Look closely; the mountains are far in the distance.

Most of the mountain biking opportunities in the western Upstate are concentrated around the college town of Clemson. Here you'll find two big trail networks—one south of town (Fant's Grove) and one just north (Isaqueena Lake). Both of these huge networks are on property managed by Clemson University, and a lot of time and energy has gone into making them what they are today. Fant's Grove has four big loops with plenty of connecting trails. It's all fairly flat, but don't assume it's easy terrain. Head there on a cool, dry day and watch out for horses. Issaqueena Lake is amazing. It's as if someone said, Here's a big piece of land on the lake; create as many miles of mountain bike trails as you can. Trails just go everywhere—enough to keep you busy for a while.

In the far west you'll find the best downhill in all of the Upstate. The northern terminus of the Palmetto Trail is at Oconee Station near Walhalla. Between Station Cove Falls and Oconee State Park the trail climbs over Station Mountain. When you head north to south on the trail, you'll drop like a rocket for 3 full miles over berms and around turns.

Pickens is just a tiny town, but its bike park is better than any other in the Upstate or the North Carolina Mountains, constructed with giant wooden walls, steep jumps, and bermed turns to draw cyclists to the town. It's working; folks come from all over to test their skills.

If you are coming to the area to ride and will be around overnight, finding a place to stay should be a snap. Just don't go looking for a hotel room in Clemson when there's a football game going on. Camping is a little tougher, but Oconee State Park isn't far.

Looking for a bike shop? Clemson is the town for that (see Appendix D).

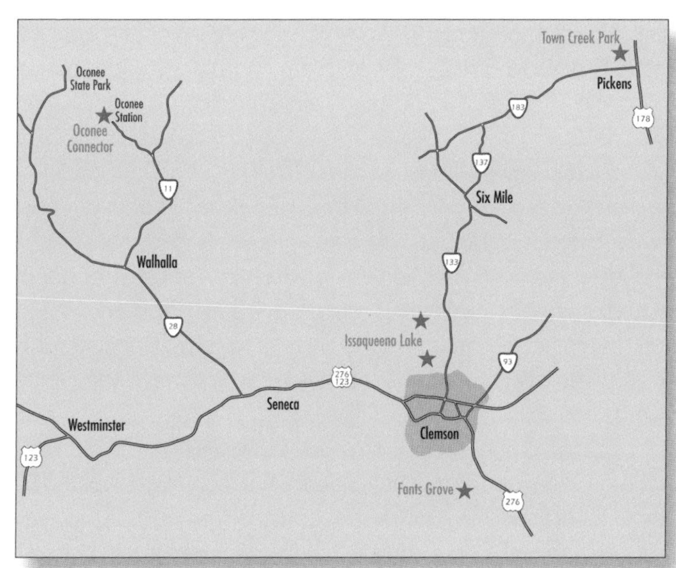

Fant's Grove

Marker posts make finding your location on the map a little easier.

Type	Backcountry
Parking	Moderate
Toilets	None
Land Manager	Clemson University
Fee	None
Access	Paved road
Special Rules	*Yes

* Some trails are closed during special hunt days in the fall.

Just south of Clemson and adjacent to Lake Hartwell is Fant's Grove. Here you'll find a section of Clemson University's experimental forest containing over 40 miles of trails open to bike use. It's an interesting place to ride, but you'll want to take a couple of factors into account before loading up your bike and heading for the woods.

Factor number one is weather. This part of South Carolina sees relatively mild winters, awesome springs and falls, and brutally hot and humid summers. Think twice before deciding to ride here in July or August; some of the experiments in the forest involve timber harvesting which leaves behind bare areas that will suck you dry. Equally important is rainfall. If Clemson has endured periods of wet, rainy weather, regardless of the time of the year steer clear of Fant's Grove. Those nice pinestraw-covered trails turn into a sloppy mess with mud that sticks like glue, turning an easy spin into a difficult slog.

Factor number two is horse use. Given that you pass Clemson's huge equestrian arena en route to your trailhead, you can guess that this is horse country. You may not actually meet any horseback riders on the trail (no big deal if you do), but you will certainly see evidence that they've been there. During the wet seasons, the trails take on a Jekyll and Hyde personality. You can be cruising along nicely on a buffed trail one moment, only to round a turn and go flailing into a hundred-foot stretch of churned-up, muddy, sloppy, horsed-up nastiness the next.

Now that those caveats are out of the way, this really can be a good place to ride a mountain bike. There are four big loops from which to choose, plus a number of connecting and ancillary trails. Your best bet is to take it in small doses. Though it is possible to piece together an epic ride, it would get monotonous after a while since the scenery and character of the trails doesn't change much. The four loops are marked with green, gray, red, and blue blazes. You'll also see a number of yellow-blazed trails. These seem to be all over the place, but most indicate cutoffs that often head back toward the trailhead for a shorter loop.

Most every trail junction or road crossing will also have a post with a number on it, for example, B27. These are great for helping you locate where you are on the map. Without those and the blazes, it would be an easy place to get turned around because everything looks so similar.

The sections of single track are linked together with gated forest roads, which are wide and relatively straight with little elevation gain or loss. Once on the single track, you'll find some of it is smooth and flowing while other sections are quite twisty. Crossing streams involves dipping steeply down to the water briefly and then climbing steeply back up. The major obstacles are roots, and some sections can be quite rooty while others are root-free.

Getting to the Trailhead

Fant's Grove has four different trailheads. Seed Orchard is closest to Clemson and is accessible from Cherry Road, south of the Botanical Gardens. Take State Road 39-115 south just before crossing the lake. For the other three trailheads, go south on US 76 and turn onto Twin Lakes Road. Butch Kennedy is just behind the arena on Woodburn Road. Fant's Grove Road and Big Oaks are both on Fant's Grove Road.

GPS Coordinates

Seed Orchard 34.645, -82.822
Butch Kennedy 34.635, -82.813
Fant's Grove Rd 34.625, -82.828
Big Oaks 34.613, -82.824

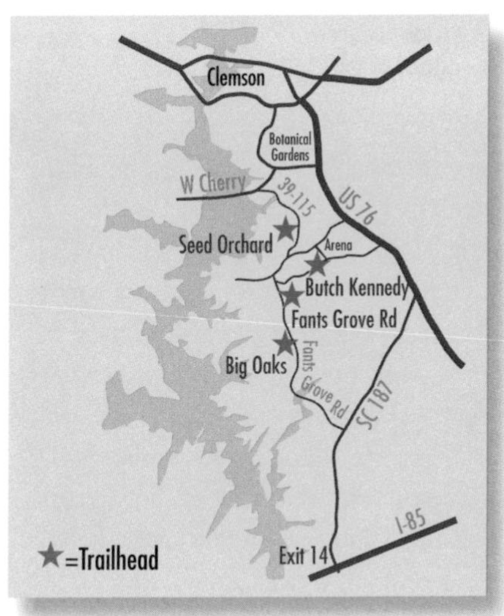

Fant's Grove Routes

Seed Orchard Road

Distance 4 miles
Difficulty Easy
Surface Double track
Trailhead Seed Orchard

Closest to Clemson, Seed Orchard is a popular trailhead, especially with the after work crowd. It allows an easy spin with quick access to the lake; you can ride out and back on gated Seed Orchard Road to some covered picnic tables overlooking Lake Hartwell (A10 on the map.) There is a nice beach here as well. Return the way you came or, for a slightly more difficult ride, loop around on Green Trail to A8 and take Yellow Trail back to Seed Orchard Road and the trailhead.

Green Trail Loop

Distance 7 miles
Difficulty Moderate
Surface Single/double track
Trailhead Butch Kennedy or Seed Orchard

Half single track and half double track, this is the best biking loop in Fant's Grove. You'll see a lot of the lake and have access to a number of sandy beaches. The single track here sees somewhat less horse use; there are fewer sections of trail obliterated by hoof action and manure. Crossing the drainages and dodging roots is always a challenge, but you'll find some really fun sections of smooth, pine straw-covered trail.

From Butch Kennedy, follow the combined Grey and Green Loops out to B2, then A15. Then it's Green all the way—first by the lake on single track and then circling the pig farm clockwise on old roads and trail.

Grey, Red, Blue Loops

Distance each approx. 7 miles
Difficulty Moderate
Surface Single/double track
Trailhead Butch Kennedy, Fant's Grove Road, or Big Oaks

Although all these loops are similar, each travels to a different part of the forest. You can ride each one in its entirety simply by following the blazes, or you can select parts of each and make up your own route. There is no best way, just pick a section and go. All have good bailout options to shorten the loop; for instance, if you're riding Grey Loop from Fant's Grove Road trailhead in a clockwise direction, you might want to bail at B2 and ride Red Trail back in.

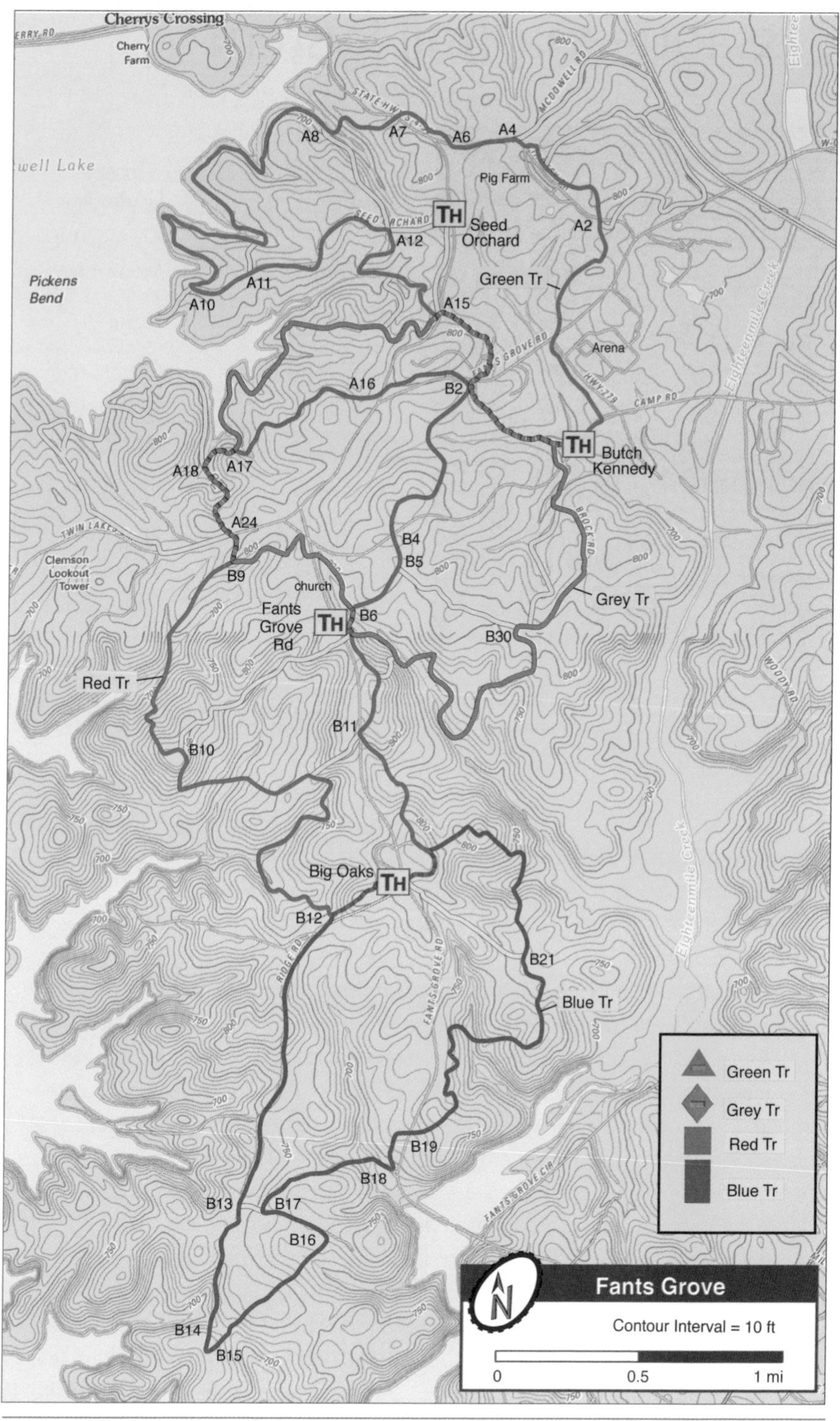

Cherrys Crossing
Cherry Farm
Pickens Bend
Pig Farm
Seed Orchard
Green Tr
Arena
Butch Kennedy
Clemson Lookout Tower
church
Fants Grove Rd
Grey Tr
Red Tr
Big Oaks
Blue Tr
Green Tr
Grey Tr
Red Tr
Blue Tr
Fants Grove
Contour Interval = 10 ft
0
0.5
1 mi

Issaqueena Trail System

Trails at Isaqueena Lake have interesting artsy signs, benches, and sculptures.

Type	Urban & Backcountry
Parking	Moderate
Toilets	None
Land Manager	Clemson University
Fee	None
Access	Paved road
Special Rules	None

Issaqueena Lake is Clemson's flagship mountain biking area, where miles and miles of single track trails and old logging roads to explore, create endless loop potentials. These trails, so close to Clemson, are for the most part well marked and superbly maintained.

Like Fant's Grove to the south of Clemson, Issaqueena Lake is a multi-use area. You'll see hikers, bikers, runners, and horseback riders. The kiosk at the main trailhead has a big map of the area where several routes are outlined for the various users. Hikers and walkers are directed toward the old roads, equestrians to the northern trails, and mountain bikers to the southern trails. People tend to follow these suggestions; many more horse users head to the old roads and trails in the northern section while mountain bikers go south. Pretty much everyone uses the trails in the middle, although no horses are allowed on Issaqueena Lake Trail.

This is an active trail-building area. Don't be surprised to find new woods trails not shown on the map, or reroutes or trails that no longer exist. It's called fine-tuning and it's why the trails stay in such good shape.

Four routes are listed here to get you started; any of them can be done in a few hours or less. If you're a beginner just trying out your wheels, you might want to ride down to Issaqueena Lake and back on Dam Road. It'll give you a chance to get used to the bike and get a hill climb in as well. Experts can go pretty much anywhere they want; epic, all-day rides are possible by hooking together a number of the loops. If you're new to the area, carry a map or take a picture of the big one at the trailhead with your phone. You might even want to swing over to the western part of the system and give the downhill or dual slalom race course a try.

Getting to the Trailhead

Issaqueena Lake Take SC 133 out of Clemson about 4 miles and turn left on Old Six Mile Road. The trailhead is just down the road on the right. There are also numerous pulloff spots along the roads in the area. Most riders park at the main lot and just ride to the trails they want to explore. **Hunting Arrow** (closest to Clemson) has a good pullout right at the start. Take SC 133 out of Clemson and turn left on Old Six Mile Road after the second lake crossing. Park at the first gated dirt road on the left.

GPS Coordinates

Issaqueena Lake 34.738, -82.841
Hunting Arrow 34.717, -82.839

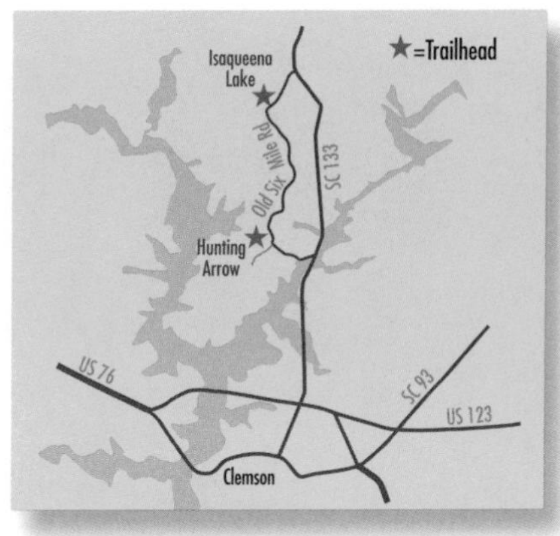

Issaqueena Routes

Hunting Arrow

Distance 6.5 miles
Difficulty Moderate
Surface Single track, forest road
Trailhead Hunting Arrow

This is the closest loop to Clemson and offers not only a really nice ride, but a history lesson as well.

The ride starts out with a short uphill on Doyle Bottom Road before hitting the single track. After the road fork, turn left onto Hunting Arrow Trail and start twisting and turning through the young pine trees. It's tight stuff with a fair number of roots on the trail. Chances are you'll spend a lot of time in your smaller gears, it's hard to open up with all the turning.

After a couple of miles the trail connects back to the road. This is your first bailout option. Hang in there though, the next bit gets you down along the lake. A mile and a half later, you'll connect with the road again for another chance to bail. Don't do it! There are some fun ditch crossings still to go and more lake.

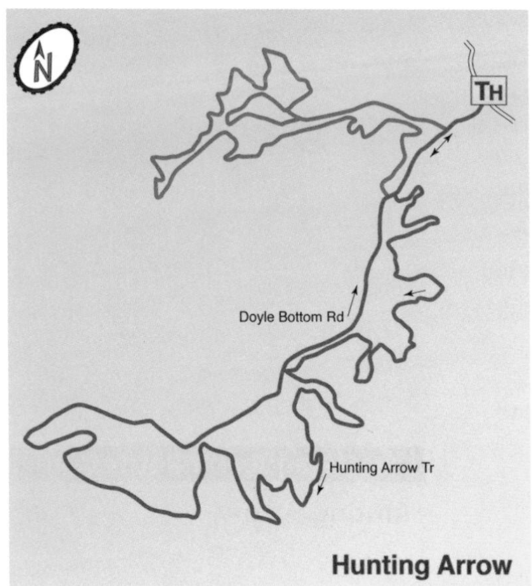

the trail itself is very nice. On this ride you'll head out to Issaqueena Lake right off the bat and then loop back around some of the most popular trails in the area. Expect to see lots of other users here.

At the trailhead you have a choice. You can zip on down to the lake quickly on Dam Road or twist and turn and hop over roots on Dam Road Trail—one parallels the other. Whichever you choose, when you get to the lake you'll turn onto Issaqueena Lake Trail.

Once you start along the eastern shore of the lake you'll see why horses are not allowed here—there's no room. The trail is cut into a steep slope, leaving you little space to maneuver. Take care not to careen into the lake by mistake.

Eventually you'll loop around the point by the lake and hop back up on the road for the ride back. You can crank it up the hill if you want, but don't miss a stop at the historic cemetery. You'd never guess it, but the founder of Clemson University is buried here.

Follow the road back to your car.

Issaqueena Lake Loop

Distance 6 miles
Difficulty Moderate
Surface Single track, forest road
Trailhead Issaqueena Lake

If you only go on one ride at Issaqueena, make sure to head out to the trail by the lake. It's a beautiful spot and

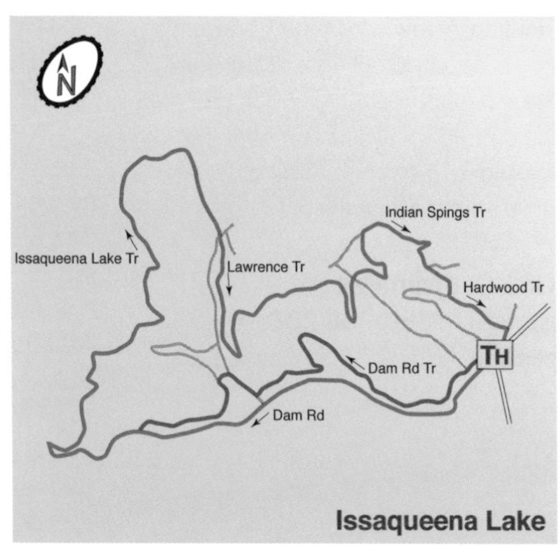

At the far end, you'll come to a confusing intersection with Rocky Road. Head straight onto Lawrence Trail and stay on it for 1.5 miles until you run into Indian Springs Trail; take Indian Springs to Hardwood Trail. Just keep taking right turns, then follow Hardwood Trail back to the trailhead.

Double Logging Road

Distance 4 miles
Difficulty Moderate
Surface Single track, forest road
Trailhead Issaqueena Lake

If you want a somewhat easier option, give this ride a try. It's not easy, but it is easier than a lot of the other rides in this network. You can probably guess how it got its name: two logging roads are connected on the end by a 1.5-mile section of single track down by the lake.

This first part of the ride goes by quickly. You can either ride down Dam Road to the first gated road on the left (the easier route) or take the single track connector that begins at the stop sign. A quick climb soon brings you to the top of the hill where the Southern Connector Trail heads south. Stay on the logging road and scream down the hill until it ends.

At the end of the road, head into the woods and bear right at the fork on Double Logging Road Trail. This trail can be a little technical, but it's a great place to practice riding over roots and swooping through ditches.

After a tour along the shore of the lake, the trail turns back into a logging road again. Thus begins a grinding climb back up the hill you so effortlessly flew down earlier. Well before you pass out from exertion, you'll top out—and then it's an easy spin back to the trailhead. Just be sure to turn right past the gate onto Dam Road.

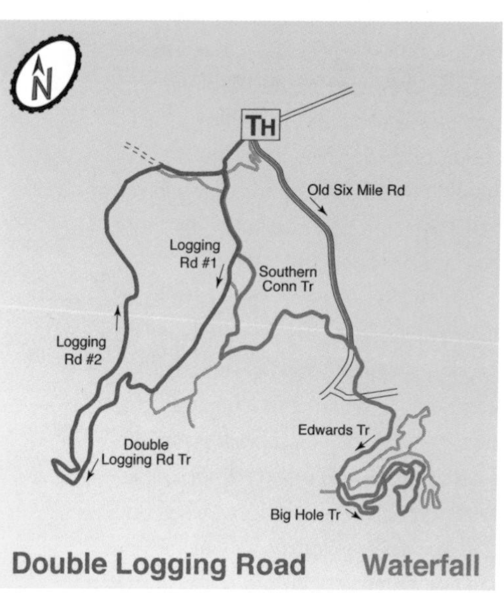

Big Hole and a Waterfall

Distance 6 miles
Difficulty Moderate
Surface Single track, forest/paved road
Trailhead Issaqueena Lake

This variation of the suggested bike route listed on the big map at the trailhead kiosk takes you down into the southern part of the trail system. Once you get down there, there's plenty to explore: a waterfall, a big hole, and a lot of trail that looks like spaghetti noodles flung onto a map.

Begin by coasting down the paved Old Six Mile Road. Yes, it's pavement, but it goes by quick. At 0.8 mile, turn left onto RC Edwards Trail. This will cut a corner, cross another road, and then drop you down beside a creek leading into the lake. Cross over the small bridge and turn right on Big Hole Trail. You'll understand later why it got this name. Almost immediately after making the turn, you'll see a small waterfall on the right. It's a pretty spot.

Continue along the trail as it leads down to the lake. You're now heading into the spaghetti noodle section. The trail twists and turns back on itself, back and forth as you climb back up the hill. After a while, you'll come to an unmistakable huge hole. It's right by the trail and big enough for a VW Beetle—thus the trail name. Just before getting back to the little bridge, you'll arrive at a junction with Twelvemile Loop Trail. Take it for another serving of spaghetti (don't worry, it's not 12 miles long, it's named after Twelvemile Creek) or drop on back down to the bridge.

From the bridge, retrace your route on RC Edwards Trail back to Old Six Mile Road. This time, cross the road to continue on RC Edwards Trail. Soon you'll reach the junction with Triple Creek Trail. Turn right to continue on RC Edwards, which leads up a challenging hill to connect with Logging Road #1. Then turn right again on the old road to return to the trailhead via Dam Road.

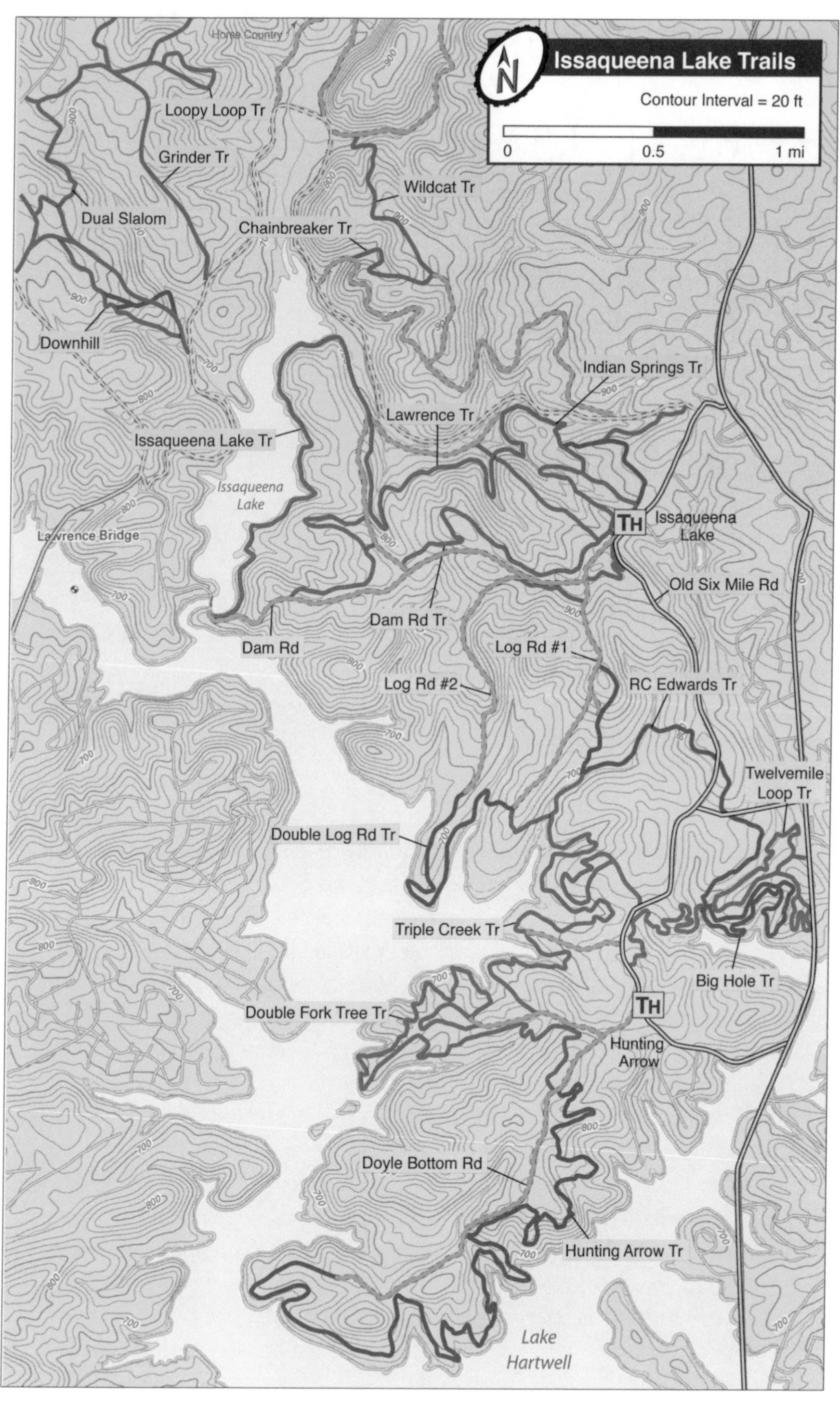
Issaqueena Lake Trails
Contour Interval = 20 ft
0
0.5
1 mi
Horse Country
Loopy Loop Tr
Grinder Tr
Wildcat Tr
Dual Slalom
Chainbreaker Tr
Downhill
Indian Springs Tr
Lawrence Tr
Issaqueena Lake Tr
Issaqueena
Lake
Lawrence Bridge
Issaqueena
Lake
Old Six Mile Rd
Dam Rd Tr
Dam Rd
Log Rd #1
Log Rd #2
RC Edwards Tr
Twelvemile
Loop Tr
Double Log Rd Tr
Triple Creek Tr
Big Hole Tr
Double Fork Tree Tr
Hunting
Arrow
Doyle Bottom Rd
Hunting Arrow Tr
Lake
Hartwell

Oconee Passage

Once you get on top of the ridge, the trail follows the path of an old road.

Type	Backcountry
Parking	*Limited
Toilets	*None
Land Managers	SC State Parks & USFS
Fee	*None
Access	Paved Road
Special Rules	None
Distance	3.2 /7.4 miles
Difficulty	Moderate
Surface	Single track

* $2 per person fee if you park at either Oconee State Park or Oconee Station, both of which have toilets and more parking.

Starting high in the Upstate, the Palmetto Trail will eventually traverse the entire state, from the mountains all the way to the sea. It is South Carolina's cross-state trail, one of only 16 cross-state trails in the United States. This section begins at its northern terminus and is called the Oconee Passage. The southern terminus is in Charleston, over 500 miles away. Not all sections are open to bicycles, so don't get your hopes up for riding all the way to the beach. However, you *can* ride from Oconee Station to Oconee State Park and it's an awesome ride, with one of the best downhills in the Upstate.

One option for this route would be to set a shuttle and just ride from the state park to Oconee Station. It skips the big uphill, but it's also a lot of driving while you could be riding. If you do it as an out-and-back you can survey the downhill as you slowly grind up it on your way to the top. As you ride up those big berms it's fun to imagine all the big air you're going to get when you ride down them. Just try to keep your lungs and heart down in your chest. And if you make the 1.5-mile, 1,000-foot climb to the top without stopping, you can claim "king of the hill." No matter how out of breath you are, don't pass up the short walk to the waterfall at the end.

Getting to the Trailhead

Oconee Station From Walhalla drive north on SC 11 for 6.3 miles and turn left on Oconee Station Road. Continue another 2.5 miles to the trailhead on the left. Look for the Palmetto Trail kiosk.

Oconee State Park From Walhalla drive north on SC 28 for 8.4 miles and turn right on SC 107. Continue another 2.5 miles to Oconee State Park on the right. The trailhead is on the road to the left, after the fee station.

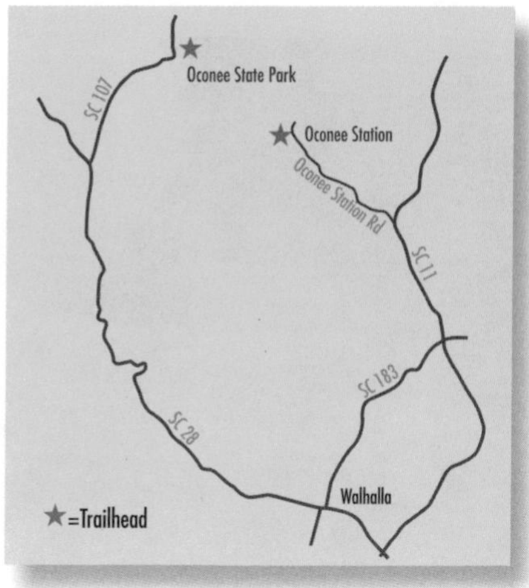

GPS Coordinates

Oconee Station 34.849, -83.074

Oconee State Park 34.872, -83.106

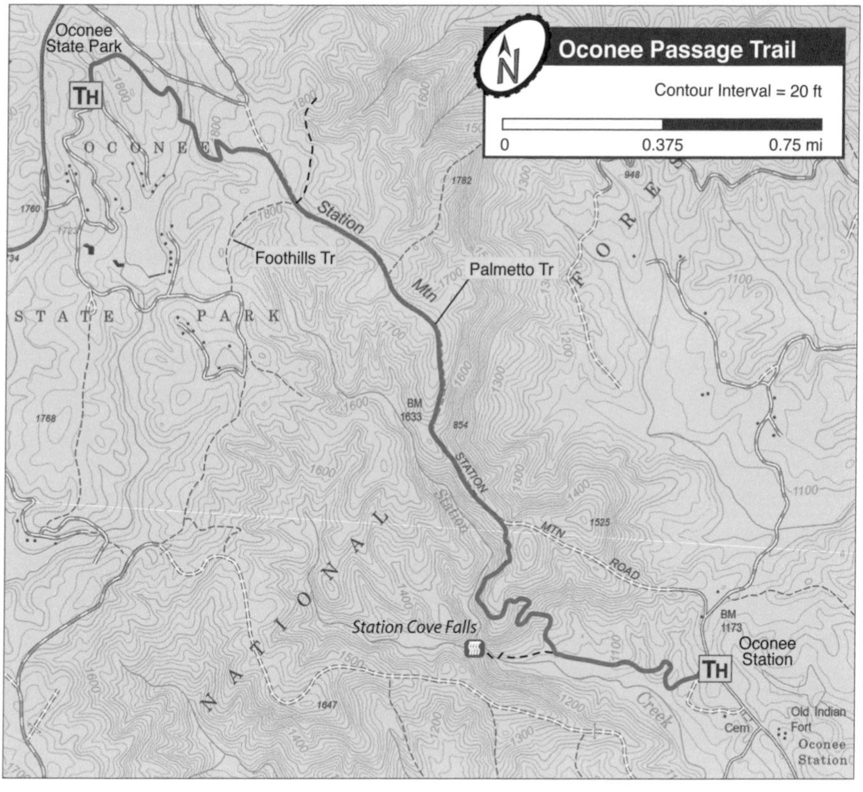

Town Creek Bike Park

Ramps lead into giant wall rides at Pickens's Town Creek Bike Park.

Type	Bike park
Parking	Plenty
Toilets	Yes
Land Manager	City of Pickens
Fee	None
Access	Paved road
Special Rules	*Yes

* Users must sign a waiver at the kiosk. Use of elbow and knee pads (as well as neck braces!) is recommended by the park.

Bike parks are great places to improve your mountain biking skills and Town Creek is one of the best around. It certainly has the greatest variety of elements. Located on a knoll, the trail makes use of the slight elevation changes in the topography to enhance your experience. You can expect a pump track, two big walls, lots of jumps, log rides, angled boardwalks, steep wooden humps, and more.

The town of Pickens takes its bike park seriously. Before entering the park, you'll need to fill out and sign a waiver at the self-service kiosk. Helmets are required (a no-brainer) and the waiver also recommends you wear knee pads, elbow pads, and even a neck brace. They really do not want you to get hurt—and given the height of the wall rides and some of the jumps, it's no wonder.

Once you get to the park, spend a little time studying the big map posted at the entrance kiosk. It'll help you get a feel for what will come up quickly once you are on the course. Basically it shows you which segments are of which difficulty and what direction you're supposed to ride through the various sections. Out on the trail the information signs become little more than a blur as you're whizzing by. More than once you're going to say, "I have no idea which direction I'm supposed to be going." No matter—you'll figure it out, and everyone else is in the same boat. Look around—people are laughing and smiling and saying things like "uh-oh" or "aiyeeeee!"

Bring the kids and strap on your gear. You're going to love it.

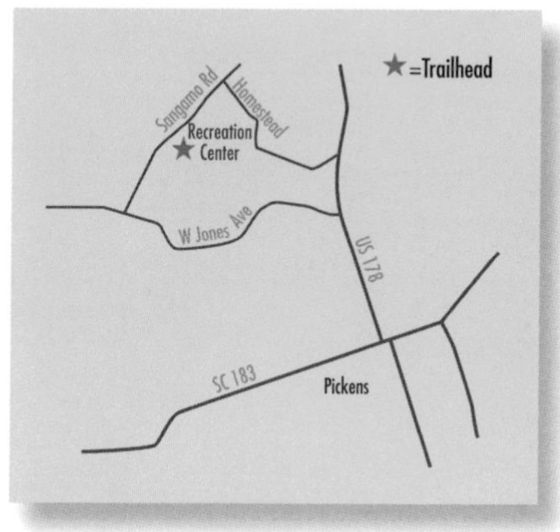

Getting to the Trailhead

From downtown Pickens, take US 178 north. After crossing Town Creek, turn left on Homestead Road. Continue out past Town Creek Park and then turn left on Sangamo Road. The bike park is located behind the town recreation center.

★=Trailhead
Sangamo Rd
Homestead
Recreation Center
W Jones Ave
US 178
SC 183
Pickens

GPS Coordinates

Recreation Center 34.893, -82.720

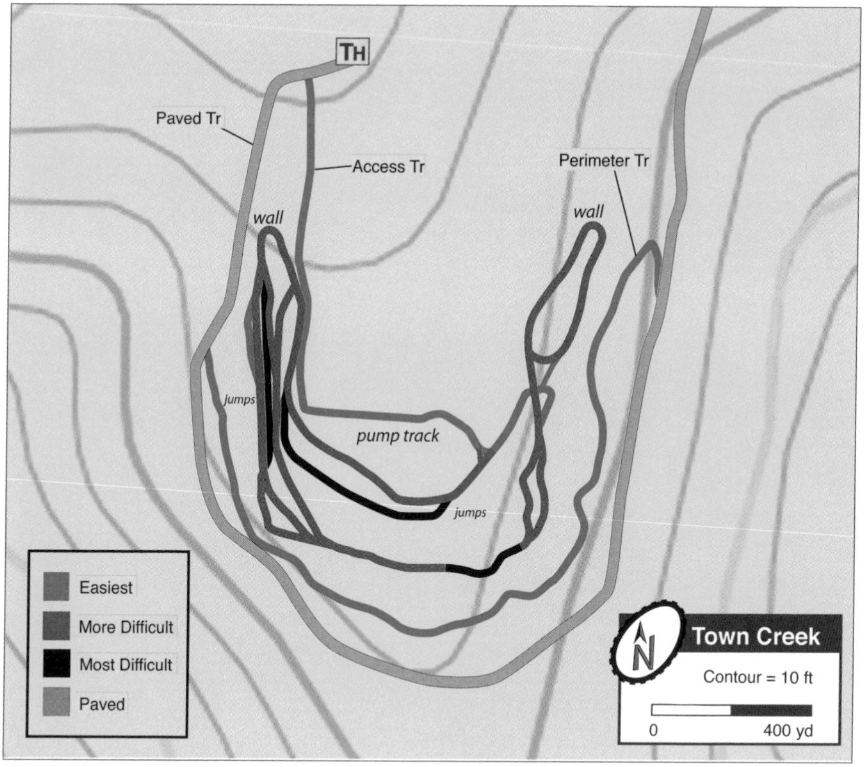

TH
Paved Tr
Access Tr
Perimeter Tr
wall
wall
jumps
pump track
jumps
Easiest
More Difficult
Most Difficult
Paved
N
Town Creek
Contour = 10 ft
0
400 yd

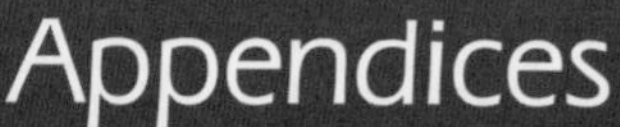
Appendices

Appendix A: Epic Rides

What's an epic mountain bike ride? Most of the routes suggested earlier in this book can be done in a morning or an afternoon. That's great, and on most days that's plenty—you've got something else to do with your day or you just don't have that kind of energy. There are times, though, when you'll want to pack up your gear—bring a lunch, snacks, maybe a water filter—and head out for an all-day adventure. But simply riding all day does not necessarily qualify as an epic. To meet that definition, you need to add some pizazz to the trip. That could mean climbing and descending several thousand feet on rugged trails or visiting six different waterfalls. You might decide to circle an entire forest or do some huge point-to-point that finishes sometime after dark. You might even try something really crazy, like riding every single trail in DuPont. Potential epics abound.

Both Pisgah and DuPont have vast networks of trails and broad ranges of topography that lend themselves well to epic rides. Several ideas are listed here to get your thinker ticking. In far western North Carolina and the South Carolina Upstate, working out a mostly trail and/or gravel road epic is not so easy. You either have to get really creative or start adding a lot of pavement to link things together.

Sometimes the actual planning of the ride and then talking (*read*: bragging) about it later is more fun than the actual thing itself. When you're out there on the trail—cold, hungry, worn out, and on the edge of being ticked off at yourself—it might not seem so fun. Usually at that point you're referring to it as a death march. But hey, if you're not suffering, it's not an epic, right? Take a look at these suggested routes. Give one a try or flip through the book and dream one up for yourself.

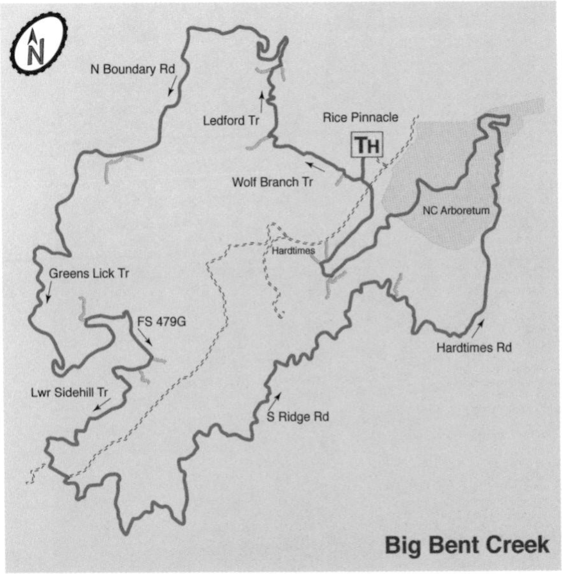

Big Bent Creek

Asheville Area Epics

Big Bent Creek

Distance 24 miles
Difficulty Strenuous
Surface Single track, forest roads
Trailhead Rice Pinnacle

Basically this is a circumnavigation of Bent Creek. There are plenty of ways to mix it up and bail out if necessary. Begin at Rice Pinnacle and head out on Deer Lake Lodge Trail. Take the first turn up Wolf Branch and work your way up the mountain onto Ledford Trail and then Ledford Road and finally onto North Boundary Road. You'll stay on North Boundary all the way to Green's Lick Trail.

Scream down Green's Lick, then down FS 479G to Lower Sidehill Trail. Turn right and ride Lower Sidehill all the way to Bent Creek Gap Road. Turn down the mountain again and take the first gated road you come to on the right. This is FS 479M (South Ridge Road).

Initially you'll climb up South Ridge Road, then it's a good long gradual descent. When you connect with Hardtimes Road, turn right and follow it all the way to the Arboretum. Now you can mellow out for a while. Circle back through the Arboretum on Old Bent Creek Gap Road, eventually turning right to head toward Hardtimes trailhead. Finally, jump on Hardtimes Connector to make your way back to Rice Pinnacle.

Heartbreak Ridge–Kitsuma

Distance 29 miles
Difficulty Extreme
Surface Single track, forest/paved road
Trailhead Old Fort

This route has an insane amount of climbing and two righteous downhills, It's basically a combination of the *Heartbreak Ridge* ride (p. 26) and *Kitsuma* (p. 25).

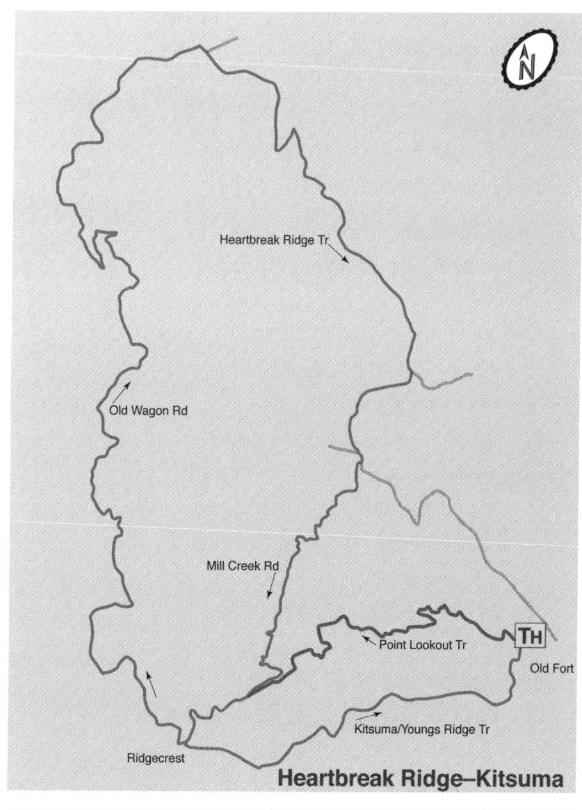

Heartbreak Ridge–Kitsuma

It's pretty straightforward. Begin down at the USFS Old Fort picnic area so you'll finish with a big downhill. Ride up the paved and gated Point Lookout Trail and continue up to Ridgecrest on Mill Creek Road. Once you reach Ridgecrest, follow the directions for the entire Heartbreak Ridge route. When you arrive back at the Ridgecrest trailhead on Royal Gorge Road, follow Kitsuma/Young's Ridge Trail back to Old Fort. Simple directions for an extremely strenuous ride.

Pisgah Epics

Black Mountain Epic

Distance 20+ miles
Difficulty Extreme
Surface Single track, forest/paved road
Trailhead Ranger Station

Black Mountain T rail follows the high ridge that separates the Davidson River from the South Mills River, crossing over the tops of Rich Mountain, Clawhammer Mountain, Black Mountain, and Hickory Knob as it goes. On this ride you'll work your way up to the Pink Beds before turning back south and finishing along Black Mountain Trail. Depending on the season there are slight variations to this route.

Begin at Black Mountain trailhead just south of the ranger station. Ride the short stretch of US 276 to Forest Service Route 477 where you'll go right. Between October 15 and April 15, follow FS 477 until you get to Bennett Gap Trail, then take that trail up and over Coontree Mountain to Bennett Gap. April 16 through October 14, stay on FS 477 to Bennett Gap. At the gap turn onto Buckwheat Knob Trail, following it over the steep knob and down again to Club Gap, where you turn left onto Club Gap Trail. This takes you back down to FS 477. Turn right and ride up to US 276,then continue to the Pink Beds.

At the Pink Beds the route varies again according to season. Between October 15 and April 15, turn onto the northern side of the Pink Beds Loop Trail and follow it all the way to the South Mills River gauging station at the end of FS 476. The rest of the year, loop around the Pink Beds on FS 1206 to FS 476 and follow it out to its end at the gauging station.

From the gauging station, ride onto the South Mills River Trail along the river. After a while you'll cross the river on a bridge and then start climbing the mountain. Partway up, the trail splits. Bear right here onto Buckhorn Gap Trail and ride it on up to the gap.

When you reach Buckhorn Gap you'll finally get on Black Mountain Trail. Now all you have to do is ride/hike-a-bike up over Clawhammer and then Black Mountain. There are some incredible clifftop views here. From Black Mountain to Pressley Gap is a monster downhill that will work your shocks to their limits. From there it's up and over the hump of Hickory Knob and then a rip-snorting downhill all the way back to the trailhead.

Four Gaps–Four Waterfalls

Distance 23+ miles
Difficulty Extreme
Surface Single track, forest roads
Trailhead Fish Hatchery

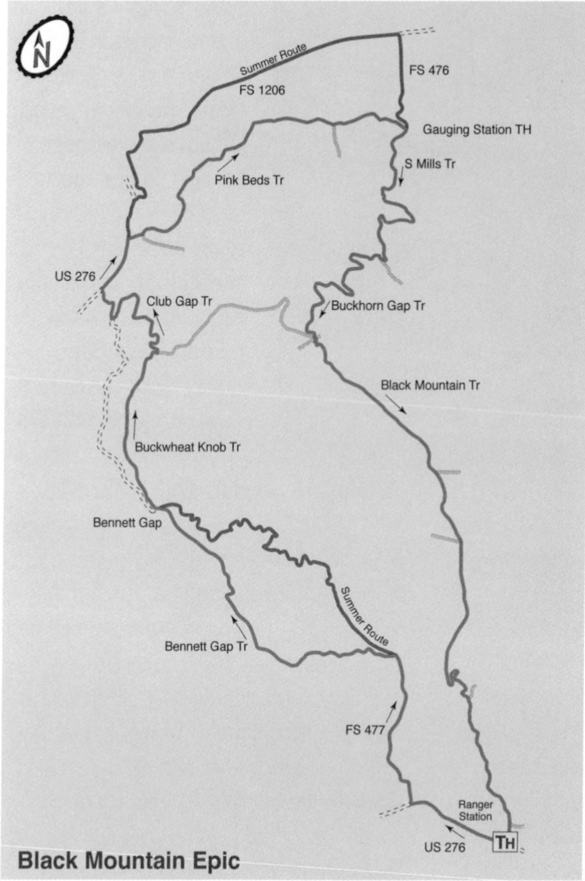

Black Mountain Epic

This ride is best done between October 15 and April 15 when the Cat Gap Loop Trail portion is open to bikes. To do it in the warmer season, you'll need to make an extra jog via Long Branch Trail to make it work. In all, you'll pass through four gaps (Butter, Gloucester, Deep, and Farlow), pass by four waterfalls, and see some incredible scenery.

Begin at the fish hatchery. In the cooler season, ride out the back of the parking lot (near the wildlife center), past the gate to FS 475C and then turn immediately right onto the Cat Gap Trail. Follow it up the mountain to where it meets Butter Gap Trail, turn right and follow Butter Gap Trail up the steep climb to Butter Gap.

In the warmer season (April 15 to October 15), leave the fish hatchery and ride west on FS 475. After a short distance bear left onto Davidson River Trail to bypass the hill on FS 475. At the entrance to Cove Creek Group Camp, turn left onto FS 475 again and follow it up past the Daniel Ridge trailhead and then to a gated road on the left, FS 5095. Turn left on this road. It eventually connects with Long Branch Trail, onto which you'll turn left again. Ride Long Branch across the creek and over the hill to where it connects with Butter Gap Trail.

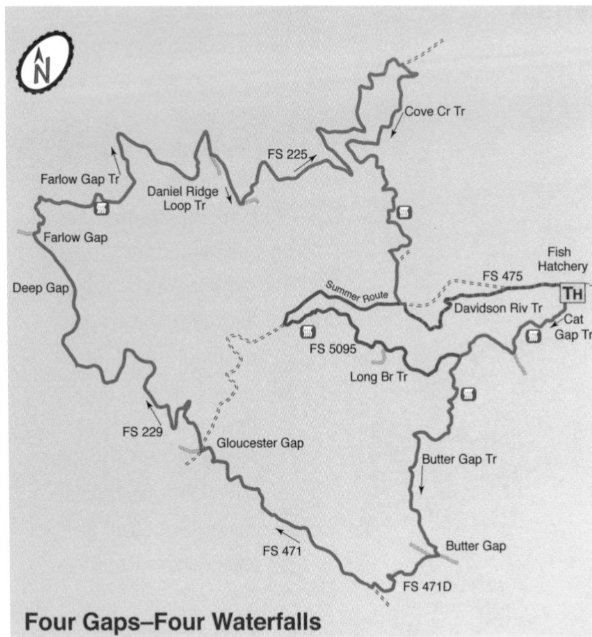

the barricade to the upper (left) road and continue on what is now a rocky old roadbed. Not far up ahead is Deep Gap (gap #3). You'll recognize it by a camping spot on the right and a small stream crossing under the road. Just up in the woods to the left is a trail shelter. Continue on the old road. Soon you'll cross the Art Loeb Trail and then circle around to a beautiful wooded, grassy gap. This is Farlow Gap (gap #4). Off to your right you should

Now you can turn right and head up to Butter Gap.

At Butter Gap (gap #1), you'll come to a 5-way intersection. Bear extreme right—not on the Art Loeb Trail—and circle around to another part of the gap where you do cross the Art Loeb Trail. At this point you are on an old woods road that will become FS 471D. Follow it down the mountain to a gate where you'll turn right on FS 471, a major forest road. Ride back up the ridge on FS 471 to Gloucester Gap (gap #2).

At Gloucester Gap cross FS 475 and turn up FS 229 (sometimes the gate here is open, other times it's closed) to climb the flank of Pilot Mountain. You'll ride uphill for a long time, so settle in.

FS 229 finally ends at a turnout with dirt barriers blocking two roads. Go over

see the trail wand for Farlow Gap Trail. Take this trail and get ready for a heinous downhill. It's very steep and there's a fair amount of loose rock. Hang on for the next half-mile or so until the trail becomes more sane.

Stay on Farlow Gap Trail all the way to where it meets Daniel Ridge Loop Trail. Turn left on Daniel Ridge and head back up the hillside. As you top out, look for an unmarked trail on your left. You'll know you missed it if you ride down a big hill. Turn left and follow this trail up the hill to its connection with the far end of FS 225, where you'll bear right. Now you get to go downhill again. Follow FS 225 all the way down to a gate; go around it and continue a little farther to look for a gated road on your right. This is FS 225B and just past the gate should be a sign for Cove Creek Trail. Follow this road, which becomes Cove Creek Trail, through a pretty, white pine-filled campsite. You'll then stay on Cove Creek Trail all the way back to Cove Creek Group Camp and finally to FS 475. Jump on Davidson River Trail here and continue to the Fish Hatchery to end your ride.

Pilot & Chestnut Mountain Loops

Distance 21 miles
Difficulty Strenuous
Surface Single track, forest roads
Trailhead Daniel Ridge

On this route you'll completely circle Pilot Mountain on some old forest roads which have reverted to trails. It involves a lot of climbing just to get up to the old roads; once there you'll keep to the higher altitudes for a while. After looping around Pilot, you'll swing down and then up and over the flank of Chestnut Mountain as you circle it.

Begin at the Daniel Ridge Trailhead and start the route by riding up to Gloucester Gap on FS 475. This is only the first leg of a very long climb, so pace yourself. At the gap, turn right around the gate and onto FS 229. The gate may or may not be open. Keep on climbing.

Eventually the road ends at a turnout with dirt barriers blocking two roads. Go over the barricade to the upper (left) road and continue on the rocky old roadbed. You'll soon pass through Deep Gap and then a mile father along you'll reach Farlow Gap, just after crossing Art Loeb Trail. Stay on the old roadbed as it begins to descend the west side of the gap. Pay attention—the road will make two big switchbacks. In the middle of the second one, bear left over a dirt barricade onto an unmarked trail. You don't want to miss this turn! But don't worry too much, it's ridden-in fairly well and you should be able to see where other bikers have come this way.

You'll follow this old roadbed-turned-trail for the next 3 miles as it goes up and down the contour lines, dropping abruptly

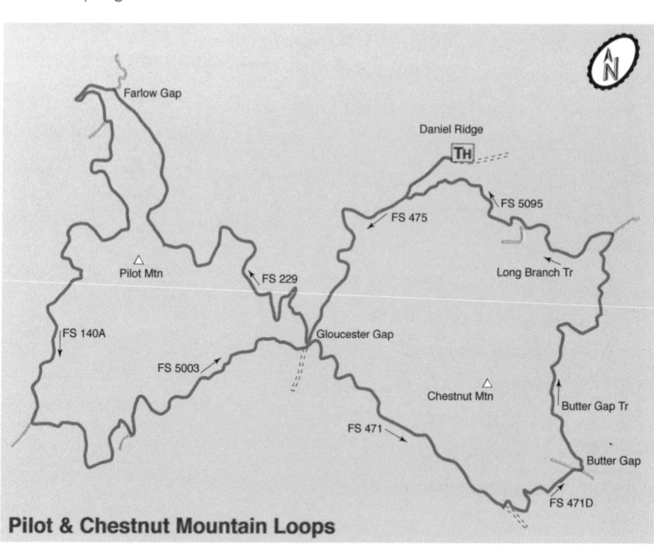

Pilot & Chestnut Mountain Loops

now and then to cross a stream. Eventually it dumps you at a 5-way junction of unmarked trails/roads. Take the road farthest to the left. This is FS 5003 (Indian Creek Road). You'll follow it—mostly downhill—all the way back to Gloucester Gap.

At this point you've ridden about 13 tough miles and you could certainly bail. But why do that? Go straight across the gap onto FS 471. Initially it climbs a bit to get away from the gap, then it drops quickly down into the Cathey's Creek watershed. Enjoy the big downhill, but be on the lookout for the second gated road on your left after crossing the Art Loeb Trail, near the top of the big downhill. It should be marked FS 471D.

Ride up FS 471D. Almost from the beginning it resembles a trail more than a road. You'll follow it all the way up to Butter Gap where you cross the Art Loeb Trail. It, too, is pretty ridden-in, but if in doubt at a junction, turn right. Once at the gap, cross Art Loeb Trail and then circle around to where you meet Art Loeb again. You are still in the gap at this point. Turn down the mountain here on Butter Gap Trail. Take care; there are some pretty big erosion drops in the first mile or so. After that it begins to settle down as you continue to descend.

Your next turn will be a left onto Long Branch Trail. Follow it over a steep knoll and then down across a creek. When you reach the far end of FS 5095 in a grassy clearing, turn right. Follow FS 5095 all the way down to FS 475, turn right, and in no time you're done.

South Mills River Tour

Distance 24 miles
Difficulty Strenuous
Surface Single track, forest roads
Trailhead South Mills Gauging Station

This is most definitely a warm- season ride and one you will not soon forget. The number of stream and river crossings is crazy; there are something like 30 of them, but it's hard to keep count after a while. Just know that you will get really wet.

You'll see this loop has several trailheads where you can begin it, because you'll pass them as you ride. The South Mills Gauging Station is a good place to start; it's a nice spot to leave a car and there are a couple of campsites right there.

From the gauging station, ride back out FS 476, the way you drove in. Turn right on FS 1206 and ride down into Bradley Creek area. Just as FS 1206 starts to climb back away from the creek, turn right on Bradley Creek Trail. It takes you (steeply at first)down along Bradley Creek and it won't be too long before your first creek crossing. Don't even think about taking off your shoes to keep them dry. That will get really old, really fast. Just wade on out and get it over with—you'll get used to it soon enough.

Stay on Bradley Creek Trail for its entire length. It eventually cuts a corner over to South Mills River by crossing through Pea Gap. Cross South Mills River, turn upstream, and very soon you're where the trail comes down from Turkeypen Gap

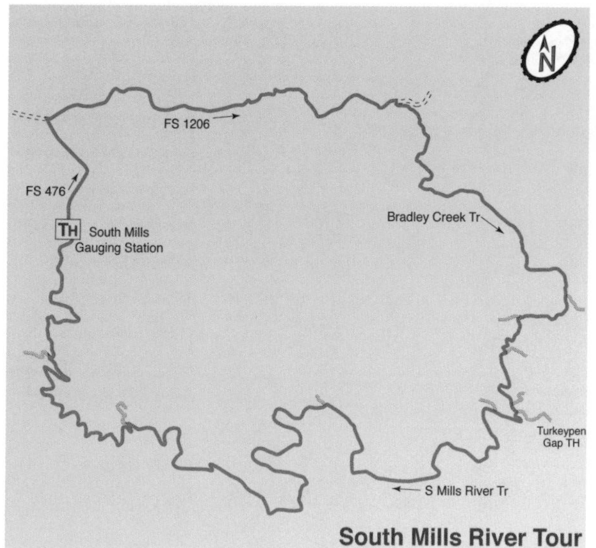

South Mills River Tour

trailhead. At this point, continue up along South Mills River on the South Mills River Trail. Be grateful you now get to cross the river on swinging bridges for a while; there are three of them between here and the Old Cantrell Creek Lodge site.

It's pretty simple from here on out. Just stay on South Mills River Trail all the way back to the gauging station. There's even one more swinging bridge way up where Squirrel Gap Trail spurs off, and a regular old bridge nearer to the trailhead.

Sixteen-Gap Third-of-a-Century

Distance 30 miles
Difficulty Extreme
Surface Single track, forest roads
Trailhead Turkeypen Gap

Okay, this one may be a bit much. Sixteen gaps in one day? Well, why not? You'll be exhausted, but you'll also see some amazing scenery and have at least one great story when it's over. Be sure to get an early start.

Begin this one at Turkeypen Gap Trailhead—it counts as gap #1 and you've yet to leave the parking lot. Ride down to the South Mills River and turn right on Bradley Creek Trail. Just down the trail is your first river crossing. Now you get to do the whole ride with wet feet! After this crossing you'll make a short climb up through Pea Gap (gap #2) and descend again to Bradley Creek. Cross the creek four more times and then look for the far end of FS 5015 in a clearing. It probably won't be marked here. Turn right on it and ride up the gradual climb to Yellow Gap (gap #3). Here you'll turn left, ride briefly on FS 1206, and then turn right on Laurel Mountain Trail.

Once on Laurel Mountain Trail, you'll climb for the next 6.5 miles up to Turkey Spring Gap (gap #8), passing through Rich, Johnson, Sassafras, and Good Enough Gaps (#4 through #7) on the way up. Turkey Spring is a beautiful gap in a fern glade at around 4,800 feet elevation. From here you turn left onto Laurel Mountain Connector Trail, cut over to Pilot Rock Trail, and then descend the mountain via a set of gnarly switchbacks. Don't get in such a hurry that you forget

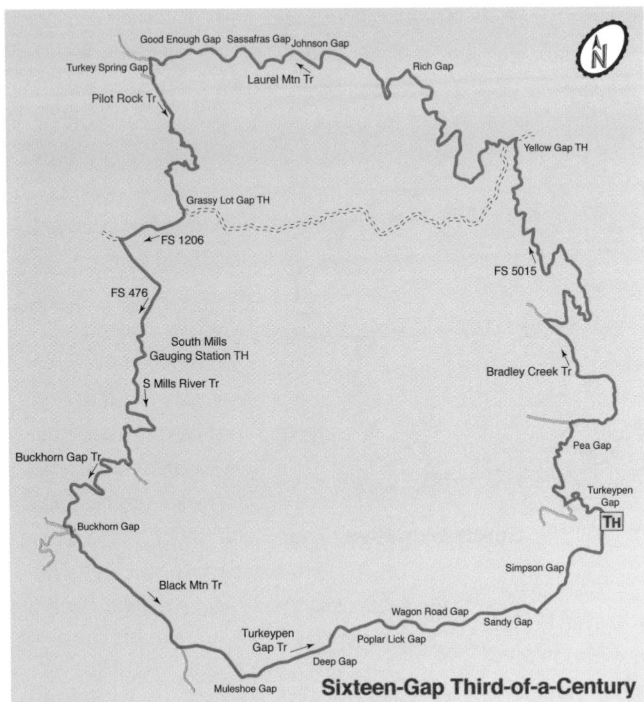

to stop and enjoy the view from atop Pilot Rock. It's a great lunch spot and about halfway around the big loop.

Pilot Rock Trail bottoms out on FS 1206 at Grassy Lot Gap (gap #9). Turn right on FS 1206 and then left on FS 476, making your way down to the South Mills Gauging Station trailhead. Here, you'll continue onto South Mills River Trail. It follows the river a ways before crossing (on a bridge!) and then climbing up the side of the gorge. Partway up when the trail splits, bear right onto Buckhorn Gap Trail. Continue on up to Buckhorn Gap (gap #10).

At Buckhorn Gap, turn left on Black Mountain Trail and ride/hike on up over Clawhammer and Black Mountains. There are good views here as well. Not long after you begin your descent of Black Mountain be on the lookout for the junction with Turkeypen Gap Trail. It's not far down the steep hill and comes up fast. Turn left here and head for Turkeypen Gap where you began. But don't get too excited, you still have 5.5 miles and six gaps to go. Ahead of you are Muleshoe, Deep, Poplar Lick, Wagon Road, Sandy, and Simpson Gaps (#11 through #16). There's a lot of up and down in between.

Laurel Mountain–Big Creek

Distance 23 miles
Difficulty Strenuous
Surface Single track, forest/paved road
Trailhead Trace Ridge

This one is a classic, with much of the route following single track trails. You'll climb from 2,500 feet at Trace Ridge trailhead to 5,000 feet on the Blue Ridge Parkway, just east of the Pisgah Inn. The climb is spread out over 17 miles, and then you lose it all in less than 5 miles. That's quite a drop—and much of it happens over the course of 2 miles where you fall 2,000 feet. And yes, the word "fall" was used intentionally. Just try to stay on your bike.

Begin at the Trace Ridge Trailhead and ride out onto lower Trace Ridge Trail. It will take you down to the North Mills River where you'll turn right on North Mills River Trail. After crossing the river a few times, you'll turn left on Yellow Gap Trail and climb up away from the river. This trail follows the route on an old logging road and eventually dead-ends into FS 5050 where you'll turn left and descend to FS 1206. Turn right on FS 1206 and climb up and over Yellow Gap to turn right on Laurel Mountain Trail.

Laurel Mountain Trail climbs forever. Stay on it all the way to the Blue Ridge Parkway. Most of it is ridable, but there are a few short, very steep uphills that require a hike-a-bike. Just before reaching the Parkway at Buck Spring Gap Overlook, you'll cross over onto national park land where bike riding on trails is not allowed. The U.S. Forest Service recommends you carry or push your bike the short distance to the paved road.

Once on the Parkway, turn right and descend 0.6 mile to Little Pisgah Ridge Tunnel. Turn right here on a service road that ends in a rock dump. Pick your way through this and onto Big Creek Trail, where again you'll need to walk the short distance to reach USFS land again.

Now the fun begins. The trail drops like crazy all the way down to Big Creek, 2,000 feet and 2 miles below. Be careful and have fun. Once you reach Big Creek you'll continue to descend, just much more sanely. This is an old logging railgrade and you might occasionally see what remains of the ties and workings. The trail crosses the creek a number of times, so if your feet have dried out they'll get wet again here. The downhill ends when you reach tiny Hendersonville Reservoir. Circle around it and onto FS 142 for the short climb back up to Trace Ridge Trailhead.

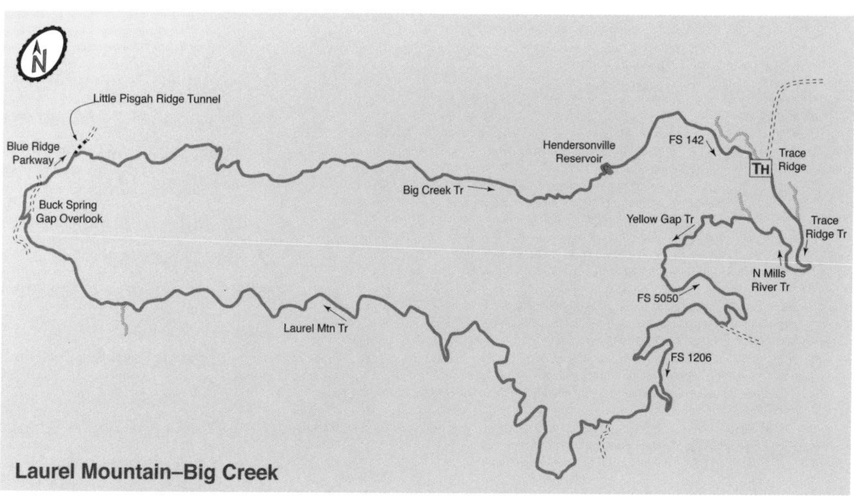

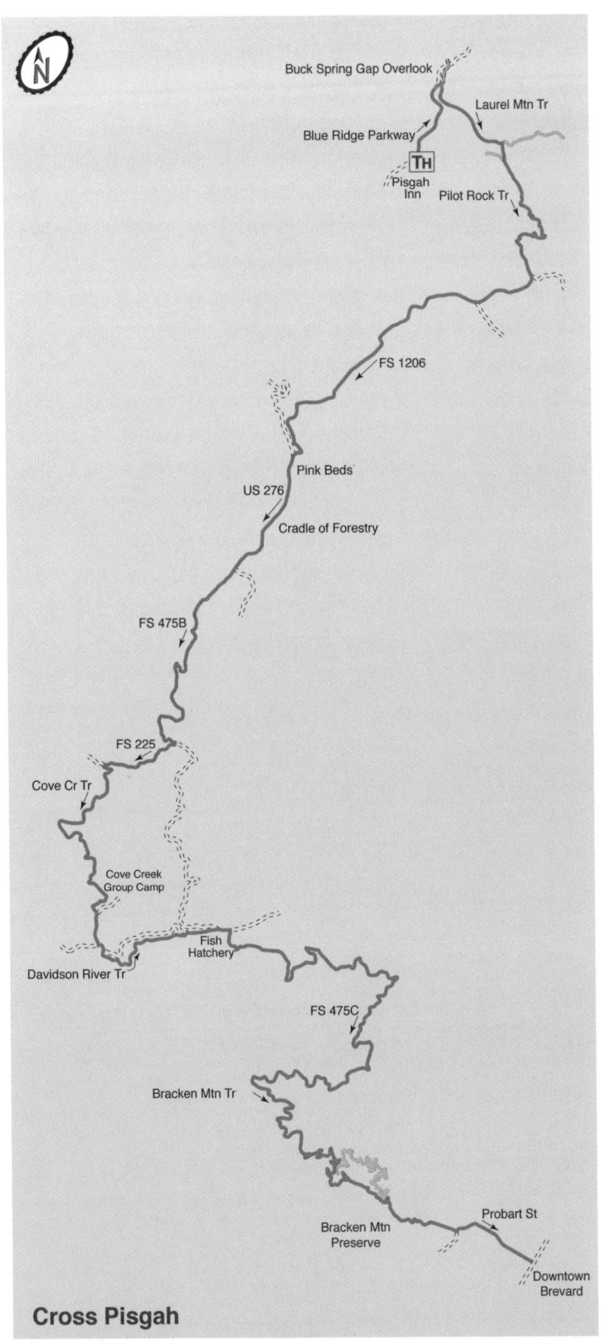

Cross Pisgah

Distance 32 miles
Difficulty Strenuous
Surface Single track, forest roads, short stretch of Blue Ridge Parkway
Trailhead Pisgah Inn

If you are creative enough you can dream up most anything. This ride starts at the Pisgah Inn on the Blue Ridge Parkway and finishes in downtown Brevard. Here's the idea. Get up early and drive up to the Pisgah Inn for breakfast. Afterwards, hop on your bike and ride north on the Parkway to Buck Spring Gap Overlook. At the south end of the lot are some rock steps. Take these and walk your bike past the Buck Spring Lodge site. In about 100 yards you'll come to Laurel Mountain Trail. Parkway rules do not allow riding bikes on trails within the Park. Once you are on USFS land, you can ride your bike again.

Take Laurel Mountain Trail over to Turkey Spring Gap, then turn right on the Laurel

Mountain Connector and head up to the Pilot Rock Trail. Turn left on Pilot Rock Trail and begin your descent. There are great views and some wicked switchbacks ahead.

Pilot Rock Trail takes you all the way down to FS 1206. Turn right on FS 1206 and ride it all the way to US 276. Here, take a left and cruise the short way down to FS 475B where you'll take a right. Take FS 475B to FS 225, the first non-gated road on your right. Turn right and continue over the small rise and down the hill to a gated road on your left, FS 225B. Take this left; just past the gate you should see a sign for the Cove Creek Trail.

You'll now take Cove Creek Trail all the way down, past the Cove Creek Group Camp, to FS 475 where you'll cross over onto the Davidson River Trail. Follow the Davidson River Trail downstream, jump back up on FS 475, and continue to the fish hatchery.

At the fish hatchery, ride out past the wildlife center and around the gate onto FS 475C. Settle in for a long climb. Ride FS 475C up and over the ridge where Art Loeb Trail crosses to begin a crazy long downhill run to Brevard.

FS 475C ends where the Bracken Mountain Trail begins. Continue onto Bracken Mountain Trail as it whoops and swoops, twists and turns its way down to the Bracken Mountain Trailhead. Once there, just continue down the paved road past the Brevard Music Center and then go left on Probart Street, which takes you downtown. Relax. Rest. Eat lots of pizza. Have a beer.

Okay. Now what do you do? You've still got a car up at the Pisgah Inn; you could just shuttle back up and pick up the car. *Or, you could make it a double epic.* Get a good night's rest. In the morning, grab your road bike and head up NC 215 to the Parkway at Beech Gap. Turn right and ride up past Devil's Courthouse, past Graveyard Fields, past views of Looking Glass Rock, and onward and upward: back to the Pisgah Inn for dinner.

DuPont Epics

Best of DuPont

Distance 15 miles
Difficulty Moderate/Difficult
Surface Single track, forest roads
Trailhead Corn Mill Shoals

This ride will give you a good taste of what DuPont is all about. You'll ride over bare rock mountains, careen down steep trails with major rock drops, go over some giant whoops, ride past two lakes, make three river crossings, and see one waterfall. It might not take you all day, but you'll be out long enough that you'll want to bring a lunch. If it's warm, allow time for a swim at Fawn Lake. There's a nice dock there to take a break.

Begin at Corn Mill Shoals Trailhead. Cross the road and go around the gate onto Corn Mill Shoals Trail; it's double track trail here. Stay on Corn Mill Shoals Trail until you reach the second junction with Burnt Mountain Trail. Turn right here and head into a major whoop-te-doo section. This trail takes you up the flank of Burnt Mountain and then loops back down. Take care on the descent, there's a major rock drop part way down that has claimed more than one collarbone.

Once you get back down to Corn Mill Shoals Trail, turn right and cover the same section you did a little earlier. This time stay on Corn Mill Shoals Trail to where it crosses the Little River at Corn Mill Shoals. This is a very slippery crossing. Take off your shoes, but leave your socks on and you'll get the best traction as you wade across. On the other side, continue a little farther on Corn Mill Shoals, and then turn right on Shoals Trail. This takes you up to a junction with Laurel Ridge Trail. Turn right on Laurel Ridge and ride along a fun stretch with plenty of rolling grade dips.

The next junction is with Mine Mountain Trail. Turn right on it and head up Mine Mountain. It's not too big a climb. At the top, turn left to stay on Mine Mountain Trail and ride back down to Fawn Lake Road. Once at the road, if you want to take a break at Fawn Lake, take a left and it's just a short distance down to the swim dock. Otherwise, turn right to ride out past the Fawn Lake trailhead. Continue past the trailhead to Conservation Road.

At Conservation Road hop onto Reasonover Creek Trail, which takes you across the creek and then up and over Reasonover Ridge. It's a good climb followed by a fast descent. You'll then cross Reasonover Creek again, this time on a bridge. Don't make the mistake of crossing at the horse ford; it's pretty deep.

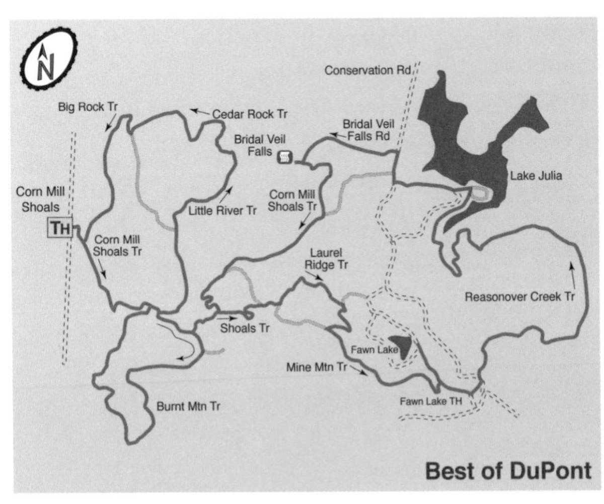

Soon you'll come to the shores of Lake Julia. There's another small dock here if you want to take a break. Turn left onto Lake Julia Road which takes you to Conservation Road, where you'll take a right. Ride briefly down Conservation Road and turn left on Bridal Veil Falls Road.

Bridal Veil Falls Road takes you past a horse barn and out to—you guessed it—Bridal Veil Falls. This is an awesome spot. Park your bike at the bike stand and explore around. You can even walk up beside the falls on the bare rock to the "bridal veil" above.

When you've had enough of the falls, backtrack from the bike stand up to Corn Mill Shoals Trail. It's just to the right of the road you came in on. Take Corn Mill Shoals Trail all the way back to Corn Mill Shoals to cross the river again and then up to the second intersection. Here you'll turn right on Little River Trail. Follow it until it ends, then turn left on Cedar Rock Trail.

Cedar Rock Trail is a grunt of a climb but the traction is great; it's mostly on bare rock the entire way. At the top there's a big cairn and a trail sign; there's also a good view. Turn right here onto Big Rock Trail. This will take you all the way back down to Corn Mill Shoals Trail again. Turn right at the bottom and ride the short distance back to the trailhead.

All of DuPont

Distance 27 miles
Difficulty Strenuous
Surface Single track, forest roads
Trailhead Lake Imaging

Okay, this is not all the trails of DuPont—that would be nuts. But this does hit all but one of the waterfalls, all the lakes, and most of the major stream crossings. It climbs over Cedar Rock, includes some little-used trails, and finishes with a bang of a downhill on Ridgeline.

Begin at the Lake Imaging trailhead and ride out past Lake Imaging on Lake Imaging Road. Climb the steep hill and head down the other side. Just before bottoming out, be on the lookout for Grassy Creek Falls Trail on your right. Zip over and have a look at the falls.

Now, continue down to Buck Forest Road and turn right to cross Little River at the covered bridge. Just beyond the bridge turn right on Covered Bridge Trail. Ride up the hill and turn right on High Falls Trail. Soon you'll get a great view of High Falls. Continue down to the junction with Triple Falls Trail. You can walk down the steps to Triple Falls or view it from up top near the picnic shelter. Circle back to Buck Forest Road on Triple Falls Trail. Turn right and ride down past the visitor center and across the road onto Sheep Mountain Trail.

Ride around Sheep Mountain and after crossing under the powerlines, be on the lookout for the junction of Cascade Trail and Pine Tree Trail. Turn left on Pine Tree and cross Staton Road to remain on Pine Tree Trail. Pine Tree twists and turns through the woods and eventually reaches Longside Trail. Turn left on Longside and ride toward the Corn Mill Shoals trailhead.

Upon reaching Corn Mill Shoals Trail, turn left and then left again on Big Rock Trail to go up and cross over the top of Cedar Rock. At the top, turn left on Cedar Rock Trail and ride back down the other side of the mountain. At the bottom, turn right on Little River Trail.

Little River Trail will take you back to a junction with Corn Mill Shoals Trail. Turn left and ride down to cross the river at Corn Mill Shoals. Stay on Corn

Leave Lake Julia and ride up Camp Summit Road to the airstrip. Cross over the airstrip onto Fawn Lake Road. Now ride down this road to Fawn Lake where you'll find another dock and a great swim spot. Continue on the road all the way to the Fawn Lake trailhead.

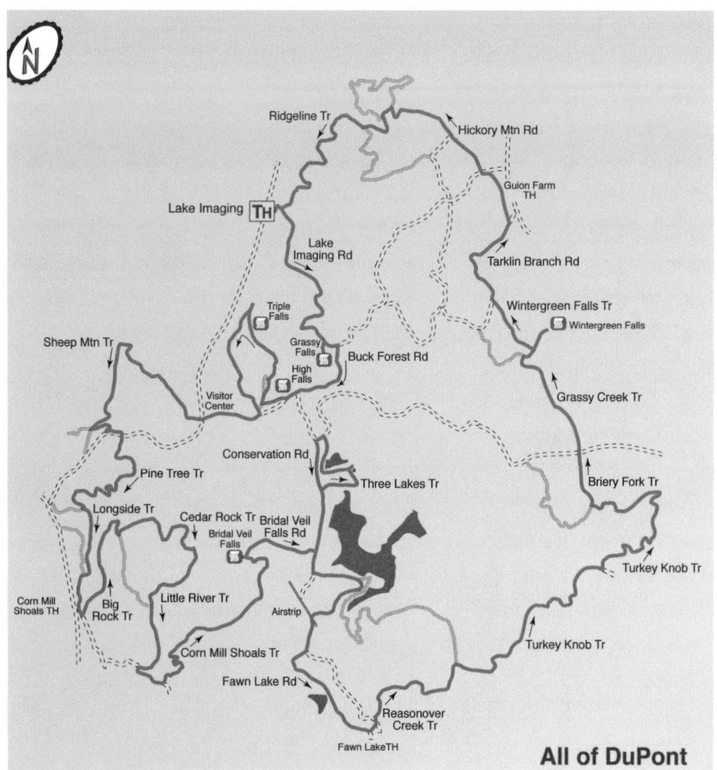

Mill Shoals Trail all the way to Bridal Veil Falls.

Once you've had a look at Bridal Veil, ride back out on Bridal Veil Falls Road to where it intersects with Conservation Road. Take a left here to jog down and have a look at Lake Dense and tiny Lake Alford. You'll do this by circling around on Three Lakes Trail, which begins just beyond the spillway river crossing below the Lake Julia dam. After viewing the lakes ride back on Conservation Road, past Bridal Veil Falls Road, and turn left on Lake Julia Road. You can now ride down to a pretty dock on Lake Julia. It's a nice spot.

Pass the trailhead and continue on down to Conservation Road where you'll cross onto Reasonover Creek Trail. Roll down and cross over the stones at Reasonover Creek and continue up the hill to the Turkey Knob Trail junction. Turn right on the trail and ride it all the way to the gate where it ends.

Just before the gate, turn left to remain on Turkey Knob Trail. On this trail you'll skirt the head of a tributary to Briery Fork Creek and eventually come to Briery Fork Trail. Turn right and ride down the hill to cross Briery Fork Creek and then up to Joanna Road.

Roll over Joanna Road onto Grassy Creek Trail and begin a long downhill run to Grassy Creek. It's a real jaw rattler. Cross the creek and bear right on Sandy Trail. It's just a hop up to Wintergreen Falls Trail where you can have a look at that scenic little waterfall. There's a nice quiet swimming hole at the base of this falls.

To continue, ride up the hill on Wintergreen Falls Trail and continue to climb after it merges with Tarklin Branch Road. Soon you'll find yourself at the Guion Farm Trailhead. If you're still feeling feisty you can burn off some energy on the Kids Bike Loop. The log rides, teeter-totters, and balance beams are always fun.

Leave Guion Farm on Hickory Mountain Road, which leads to the base of Hickory Mountain and the beginning of Ridgeline Trail. You are almost done. Take Ridgeline out the ridge and then enjoy the best downhill in DuPont to end up back where you started.

Appendix B: Easy Rides

Throughout the text, the easy rides are listed for the various areas. However, if you're just getting started on a mountain bike and you want to know where to begin, the following list should help you out.

Appendix C: Elevation Profiles

Asheville Area North

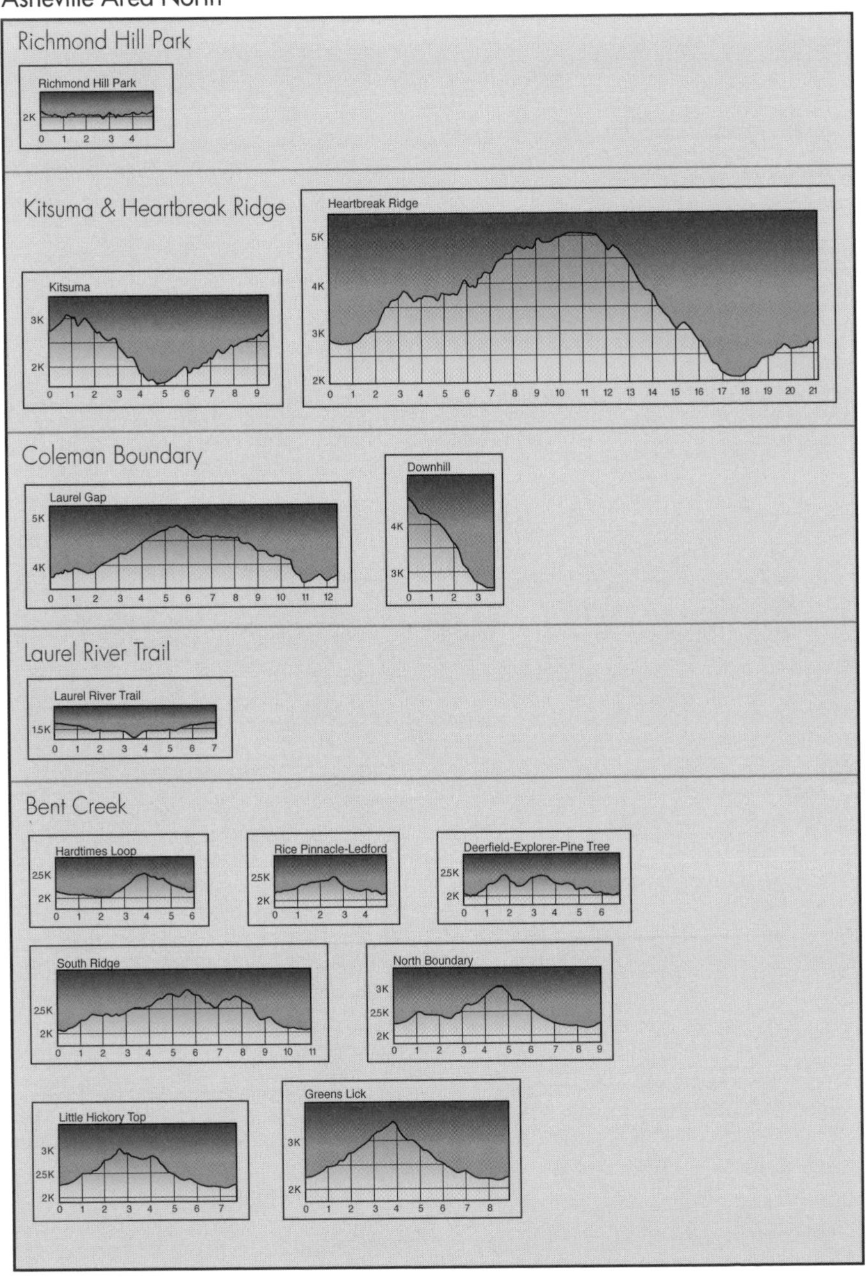

Pisgah District

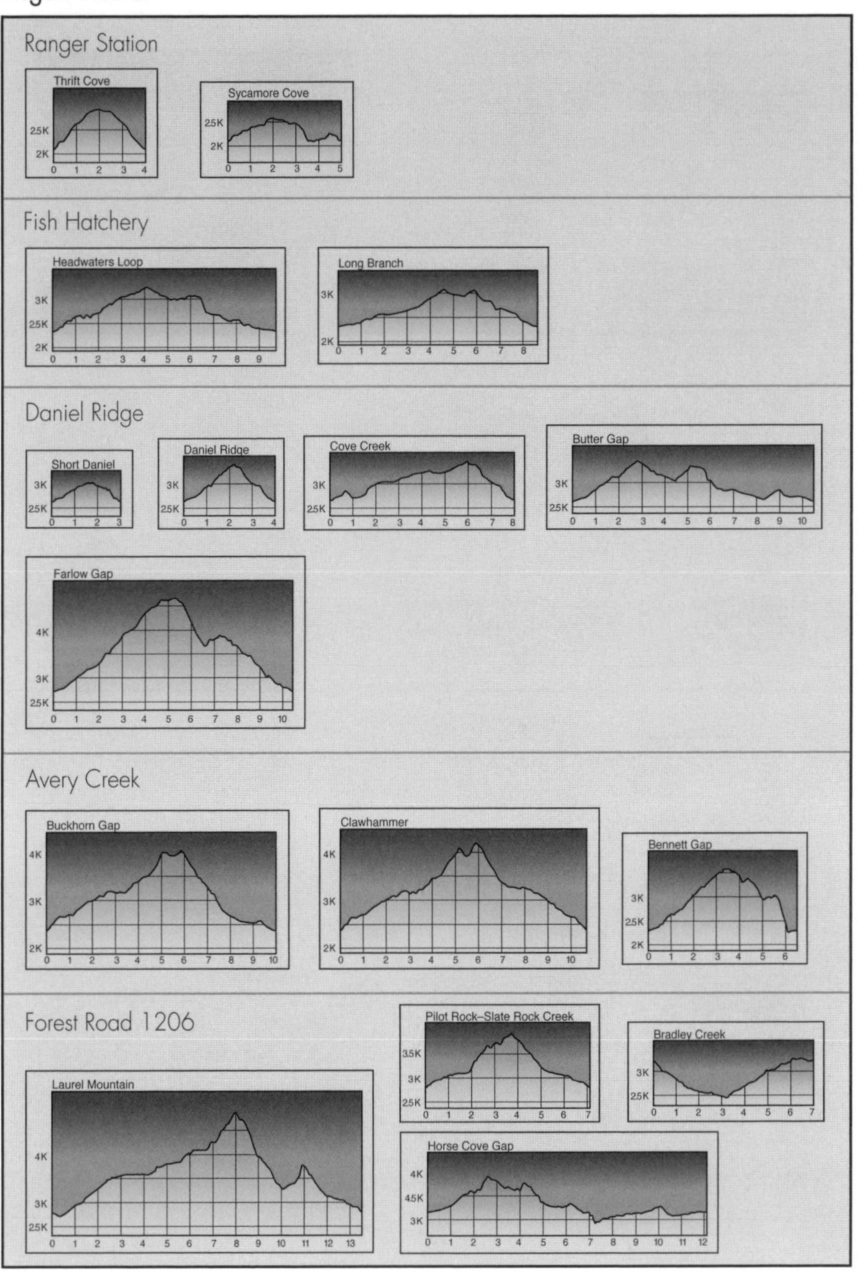

Pisgah District (continued)

Turkeypen Gap

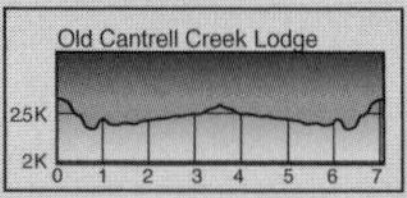

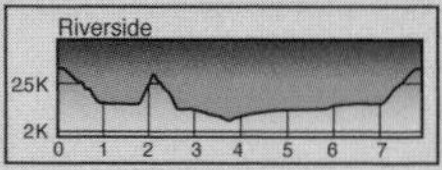

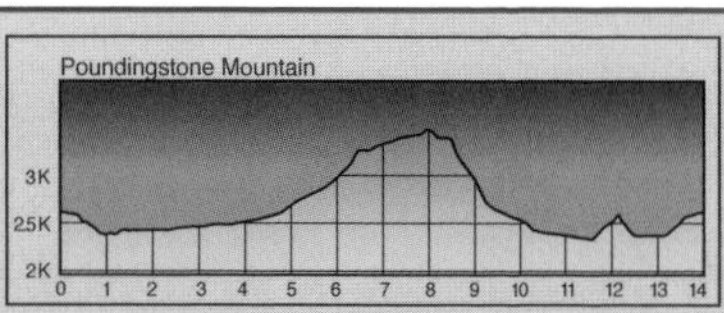

Old Cantrell Creek Lodge

Riverside

Poundingstone Mountain

Trace Ridge

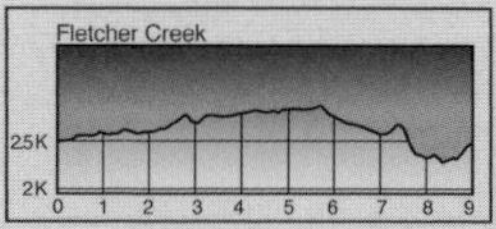

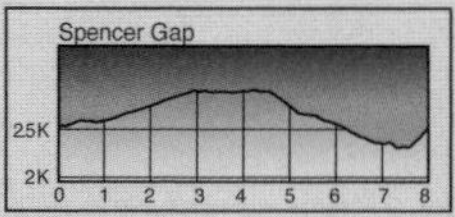

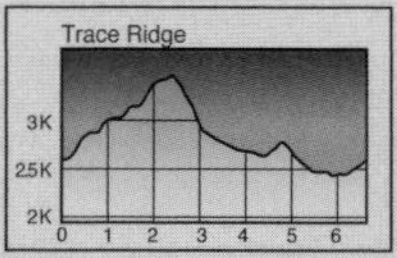

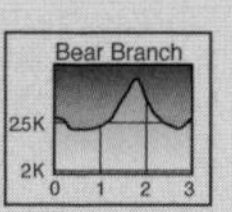

Fletcher Creek

Spencer Gap

Trace Ridge

Bear Branch

Black Balsam

Ivestor Gap

Flat Laurel Creek

Bracken Mountain

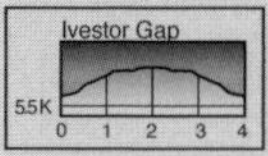

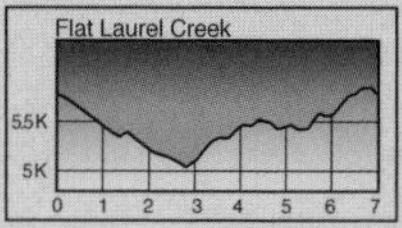

Bracken Mountain

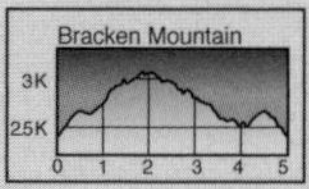

DuPont State Forest

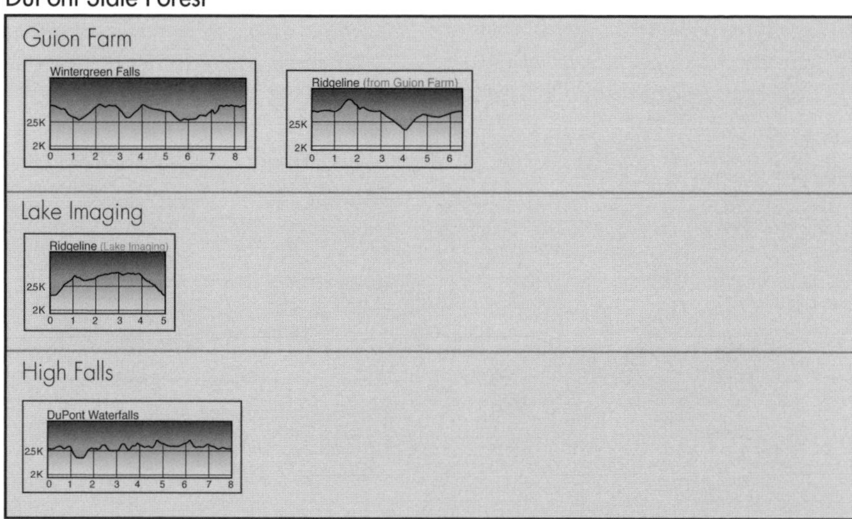

DuPont State Forest (continued)

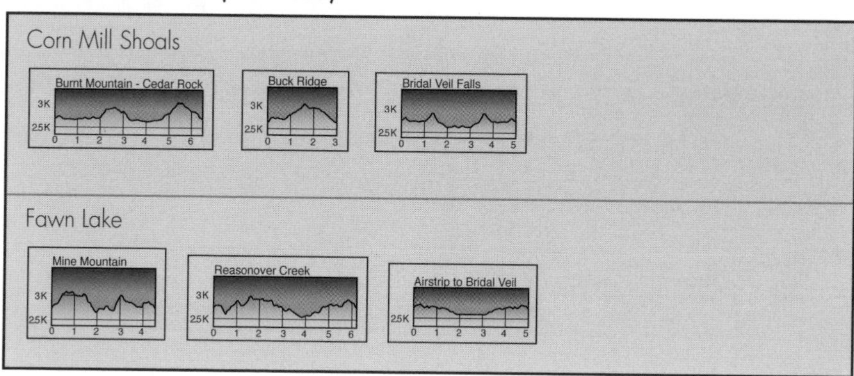

Nantahala & The Far West

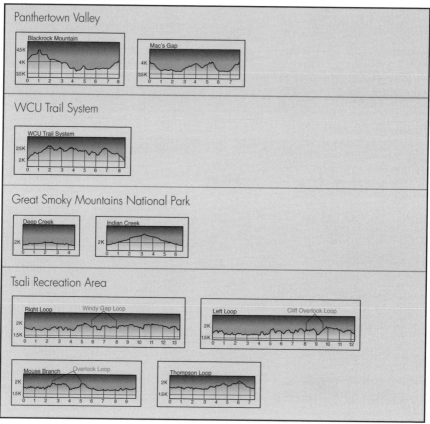

Panthertown Valley

Blackrock Mountain

Mac's Gap

WCU Trail System

WCU Trail System

Great Smoky Mountains National Park

Deep Creek

Indian Creek

Tsali Recreation Area

Right Loop — Windy Gap Loop

Left Loop — Cliff Overlook Loop

Mouse Branch — Overlook Loop

Thompson Loop

Nantahala & The Far West (continued)

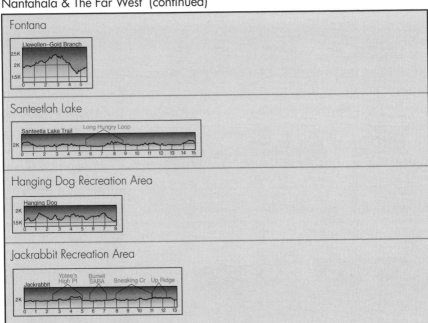

Fontana

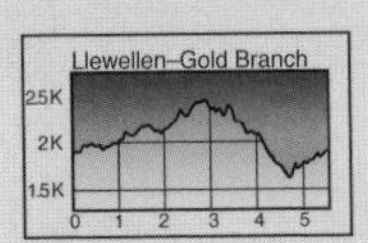

Llewellen–Gold Branch
2.5K
2K
1.5K
0 1 2 3 4 5

Santeetlah Lake

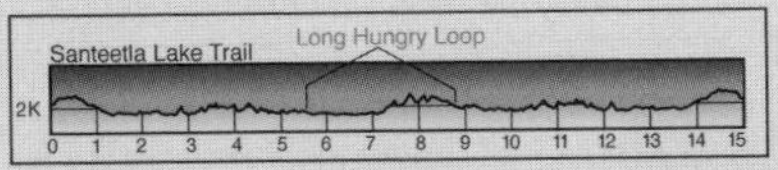

Santeetla Lake Trail
Long Hungry Loop
2K
0 1 2 3 4 5 6 7 8 9 10 11 12 13 14 15

Hanging Dog Recreation Area

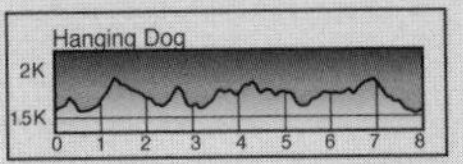

Hanging Dog
2K
1.5K
0 1 2 3 4 5 6 7 8

Jackrabbit Recreation Area

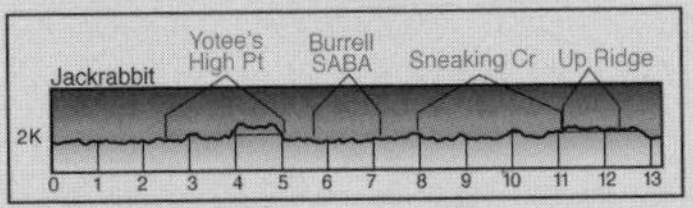

Jackrabbit
Yotee's High Pt
Burrell SABA
Sneaking Cr
Up Ridge
2K
0 1 2 3 4 5 6 7 8 9 10 11 12 13

Greenville–Spartanburg

Croft State Park

Southside
0.5K
0 1 2 3 4 5 6 7 8 9

Short Loop
0.5K
0 1 2 3 4 5

Duncan Park

Duncan Park
0.5K
0 1 2 3 4 5

Lake Conestee Nature Park

Lake Conestee
0.5K
0 1 2 3 4 5

Paris Mountain State Park

Mountaintop
1.5K
0 1 2 3

North Lake
1.5K
1K
0 1 2 3 4 5

Downhill
1.5K
1K
0 1 2

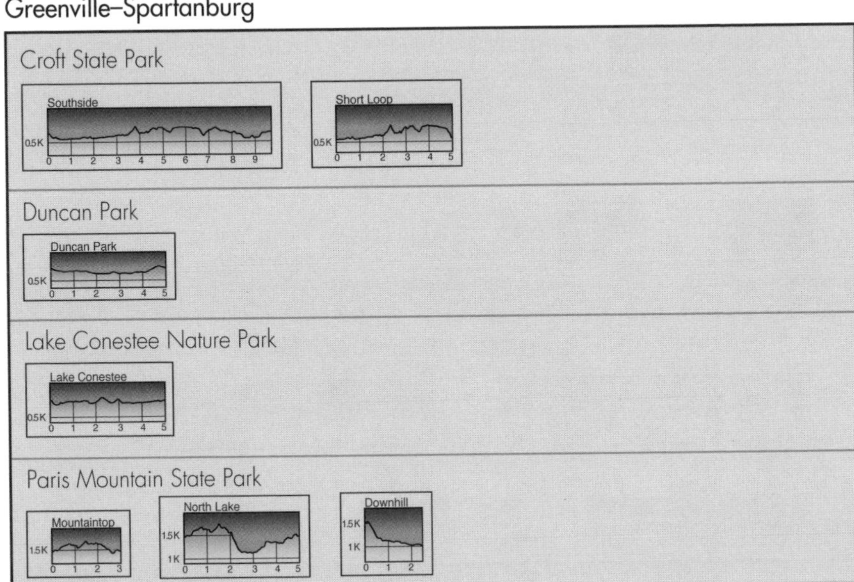

Greenville–Spartanburg (continued)

The Western Upstate

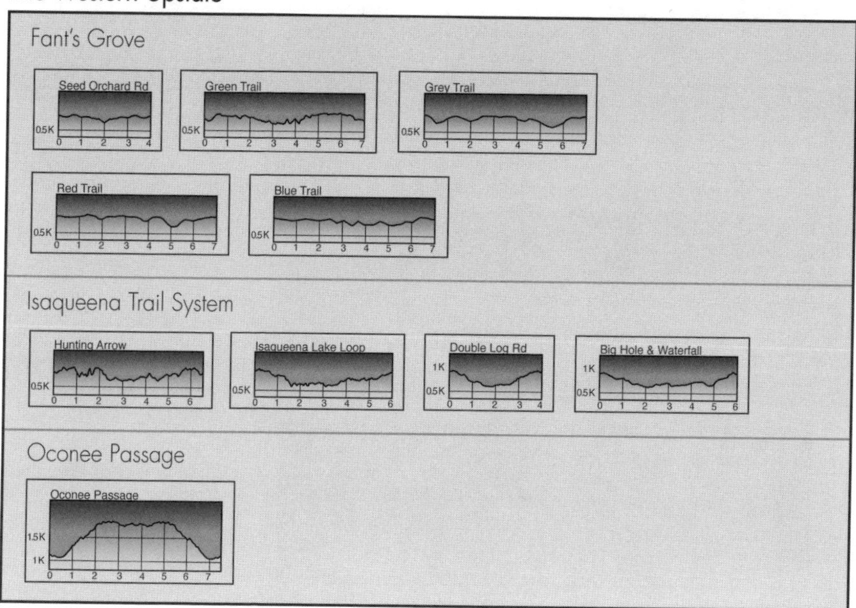

Epic Rides

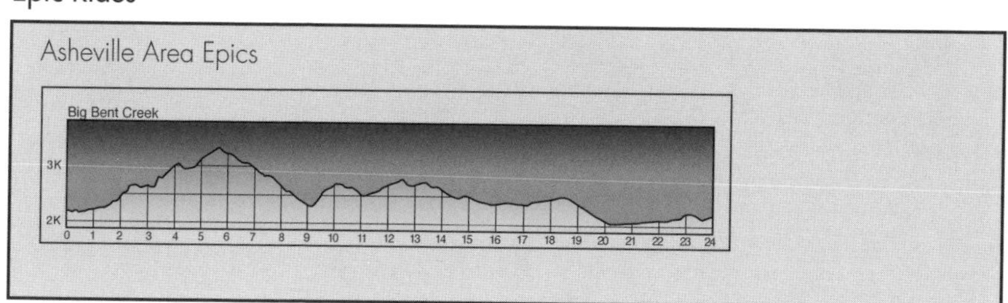

Epic Rides (continued)

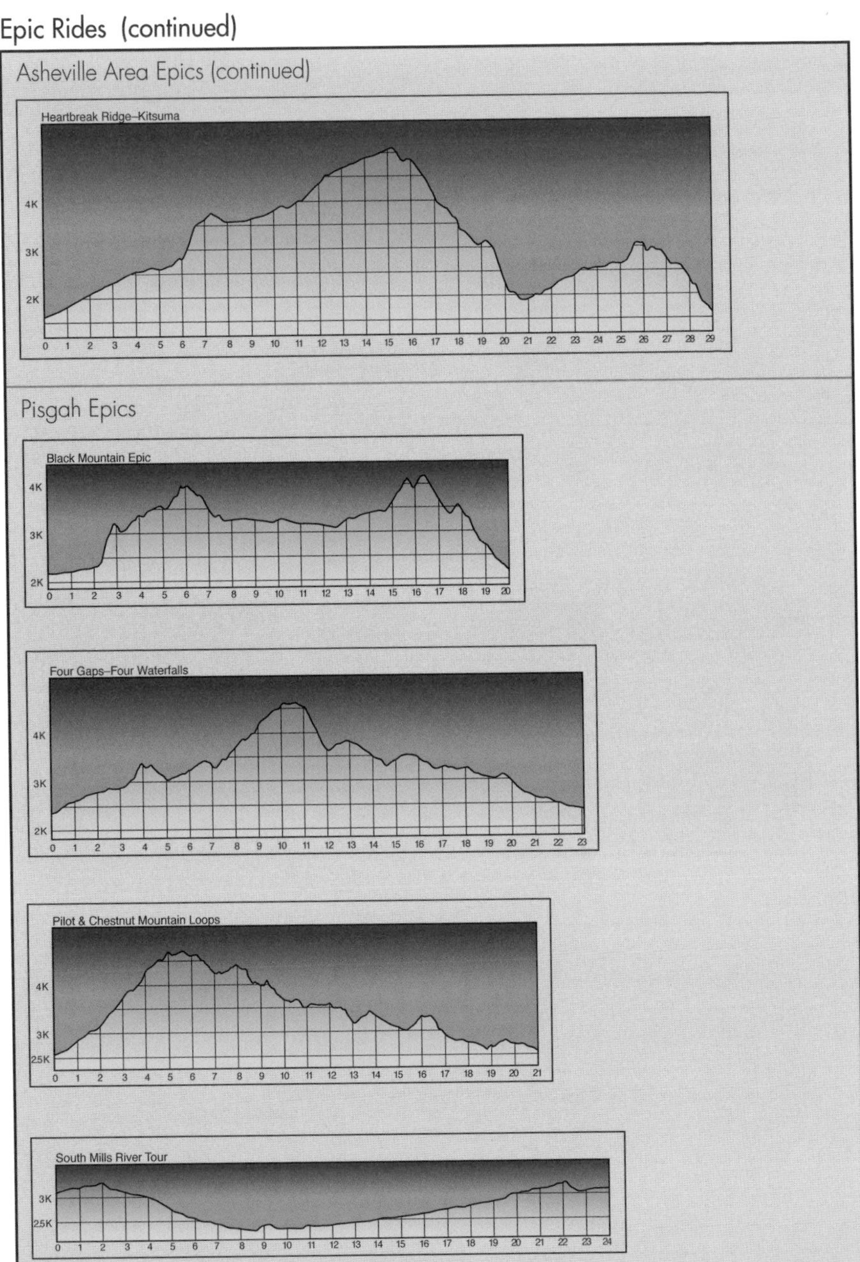

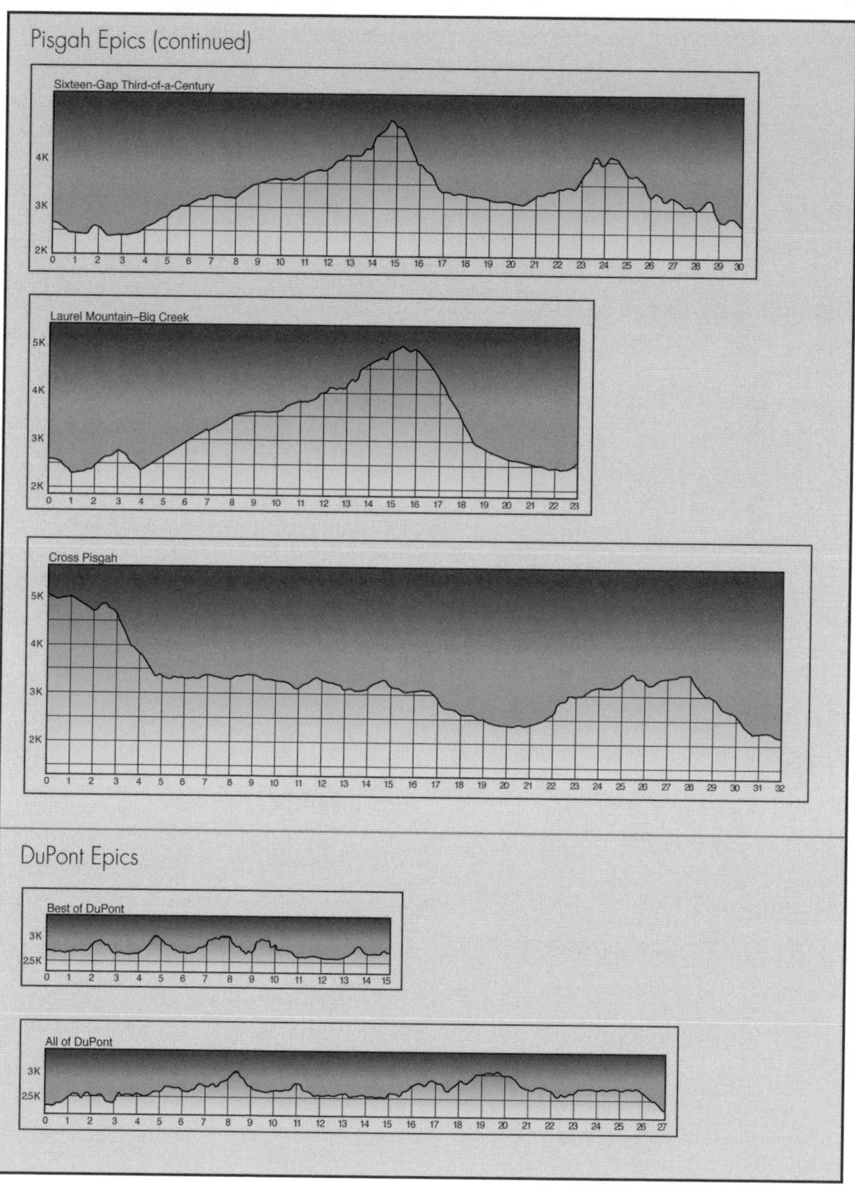
Pisgah Epics (continued)
Sixteen-Gap Third-of-a-Century
Laurel Mountain–Big Creek
Cross Pisgah
DuPont Epics
Best of DuPont
All of DuPont

Appendix D: Local Bike Shops

Finding a bike shop when on vacation or newly moved to town should be on every cyclist's priority list. Local shop staff typically know the trails like the backs of their hands. Show up on their doorstep and they can give you up-to-date trail information and all sorts of other advice. They're also the folks to go to for a bike repair or tuneup, not to mention a new bike or gear if you need it. Some shops are in the rental business as well; if you left your bike at home or you just want to try that latest "got to have" model, give them a ring.

Asheville Area North

Asheville

Asheville Bicycle Company
1000 Merrimon Ave
Asheville, NC 28804
828-254-2771
ashevillebikecompany.com

Beer City Bicycles
144 Biltmore Ave
Asheville, NC 28801
828-575-2453
www.beercitybicycles.com

Billy Goat Bicycles
5 Regent Park Blvd #106
Asheville, NC 28806
828-575-2460
www.billygoatbikes.com

Carolina Fatz
1240 Brevard Rd #3
Asheville, NC 28806
828-665-7744
carolinafatzmountainbicycle.com

Epic Cycles
800 Haywood Rd
Asheville, NC 28806
828-505-4455
epiccyclesnc.com

Hearn Cycling & Fitness
28 Asheland Ave
Asheville, NC 28801
828-253-4800

Liberty Bicycles
1378 Hendersonville Rd
Asheville, NC 28803
828-274-2453
libertybikes.com

Motion Makers Bicycle Shop
878 Brevard Rd
Asheville, NC 28806
828-633-2227
motionmakers.com

Youngblood Bicycles
233 Merrimon Ave
Asheville, NC 28801
828-251-4686
youngbloodbikes.com

Black Mountain

Epic Cycles
102 Sutton Ave
Black Mountain, NC 28711
828-669-5969
epiccyclesnc.com

Marshall

Mossy Mountain Bikeworks
133 South Main Street #104
Marshall, NC 28753
828-649-2554

Pisgah District & DuPont Forest

Pisgah Forest/Brevard

Sycamore Cycles
112 New Hendersonville Hwy
Pisgah Forest, NC 28768
828-877-5790
sycamorecycles.com

The Hub
49 Pisgah Hwy
Pisgah Forest, NC 28768
828-884-8670
thehubpisgah.com

Hendersonville

The Bicycle Company
779 N Church St # A
Hendersonville, NC 28792
828-696-1500
thebikecompany.net

Sycamore Cycles
146 Third Ave E
Hendersonville, NC 28792
828-693-1776
sycamorecycles.com

Nantahala & The Far West

Bryson City

Bryson City Bicycles
157 Everett St
Bryson City, NC 28713
828-488-1988
brysoncitybicycles.com

NOC Bike Shop
13077 W Hwy 19
Bryson City, NC 28713
(800) 232-7238
noc.com/trips/mountain-biking

Tsali Cycles
35 Slope St
Bryson City, NC 28713
828-488-9010
tsalicycles.com

Franklin

Smoky Mountain Bicycles
31 E Main St
Franklin, NC 28734
828-369-2881
madone6.wix.com/smbi

Murphy

Appalachian Outfitters
104C Tennessee St
Murphy, NC 28906
828-837-4165
appalachianoutfittersnc.com

Sylva

Motion Makers Bicycle Shop
36 Allen St
Sylva, NC 28779
828-586-6925
motionmakers.com

Waynesville
RollsRite Bicycles
1362 Asheville Rd
Waynesville, NC 28786
828-276-6080
rollsritebicycles.com

Greenville–Spartanburg

Greenville
Carolina Triathlon
928 S Main St
Greenville, SC 29601
864- 331-8483
carolinatriathlon.com

Freehub Bicycles
25 Peden St
Greenville, SC 29601
864- 520-5099
freehubbicycles.com

Sunshine Cycle Shop
1826 N Pleasantburg Dr
Greenville, SC 29609
864- 244-2925
sunshinecycle.com

Trek Store Greenville
1426 Laurens Rd
Greenville, SC 29607
864- 235-8320
trekbikessouthcarolina.com

Spartanburg
Bike Worx of Spartanburg
1321 Union St
Spartanburg, SC 29302
864- 542-2453
bikeworx.net

Trek Store Spartanburg
105 Franklin Ave
Spartanburg, SC 29301
864- 574-5273
trekbikessouthcarolina.com

Travelers Rest
Sunrift Adventures
1 Center St
Travelers Rest, SC 29690
864- 834-3019
sunrift.com

Western Upstate

Anderson
Trek Store Anderson
2714 N Main St
Anderson, SC 29621
864- 226-4579
trekbikessouthcarolina.com

Clemson
Southpaw Cycles
103 Canoy Ln #113
Clemson, SC 29631
864-653-4485
southpawcycles.com

Pickens
Southern Appalachian Outdoors
506 W Main St
Pickens, SC 29671
864-507-2195

Appendix E: Local Bike Clubs

SORBA (Southern Off Road Bicycle Association) pretty much rules the South when it comes to mountain bike clubs, with various chapters throughout the Southeast. These are the go-to clubs for trail advocacy and maintenance. The local chapters are listed here. Also listed is SABA, which maintains the Jackrabbit trail system.

Pisgah Area SORBA
PO Box 61
Skyland, NC 28776
pisgahareasorba.org

Nantahala Area SORBA
www.facebook.com/NantahalaAreaSORBA

Upstate SORBA
PO Box 9461
Greenville, SC 29604
upstatesorba.com

Southern Appalachian Bicycle Association (SABA)
PO Box 542
Hayesville, NC 28904
sabacycling.com

Appendix F: Land Managers

When you want to know fast what the current trail conditions are, the first, best place to check is with the land manager. Typically these guys will list trail closings and the like on their websites. And of course, you can always give them a call if you want to speak to a ranger or someone in charge of the trails.

Asheville Area North

Richmond Hill Park
City of Asheville Parks
70 Court Plaza
PO Box 7148
Asheville, NC 28802
828-251-1122
ashevillenc.gov

Kitsuma, Heartbreak Ridge
Pisgah National Forest
Grandfather Ranger District
109 Lawing Dr
Nebo, NC 28761
828-652-2144
fs.usda.gov/nfsnc

Montreat Conference Center
401 Assembly Dr
Montreat, NC 28757
800-572-225
montreat.org

Ridgecrest Conference Center
1 Ridgecrest Dr
Black Mountain, NC 28770
828-669-8022
ridgecrestconferencecenter.org

Coleman Boundary, Laurel River
Pisgah National Forest
Appalachian Ranger District
632 Manor Rd
Mars Hill, NC 28754
828-689-9694
fs.usda.gov/nfsnc

Bent Creek
Pisgah National Forest
Pisgah Ranger District
1600 Pisgah Hwy
Pisgah Forest, NC 28768
828-877-3265
fs.usda.gov/nfsnc

Pisgah District

All National Forest Trails
Pisgah National Forest
Pisgah Ranger District
1600 Pisgah Hwy
Pisgah Forest, NC 28768
828-877-3265
fs.usda.gov/nfsnc

Bracken Mountain Preserve
City of Brevard
95 West Main St
Brevard, NC 28712
828-885-5630
cityofbrevard.com

DuPont State Forest

All DuPont Forest Trails
DuPont State Recreational Forest
PO Box 300
Cedar Mountain, NC 28718
828-877-6527

Hendersonville Bike Park
Henderson County Parks
708 South Grove St
Hendersonville, NC 28792
828-697-4884
hendersoncountync.org

Nantahala & The Far West

Panthertown Valley
Nantahala National Forest
Nantahala Ranger District
90 Sloan Rd
Franklin, NC 28734
828-524-6441
fs.usda.gov/nfsnc

WCU Trail System
Western Carolina University
Base Camp Cullowhee
Campus Recreation Center
Cullowhee, NC 28723
828-227.7069
wcu.edu

Deep Creek
Great Smoky Mountains
National Park
107 Park Headquarters Rd
Gatlinburg, TN 37738
865- 436-1200
nps.gov/grsm

Tsali, Fontana, Santeetlah
Nantahala National Forest
Cheoah Ranger District
1070 Massey Branch Rd
Robbinsville, NC 28771
828-479-6431
fs.usda.gov/nfsnc

Hanging Dog, Jackrabbit
Nantahala National Forest
Tusquitee Ranger District
123 Woodland Dr
Murphy, NC 28906
828-837-5152
fs.usda.gov/nfsnc

Greenville–Spartanburg

Croft State Park
450 Croft State Park Rd
Spartanburg, SC 29302
864- 585-1283
southcarolinaparks.com/croft

Duncan Park
City of Spartanburg Parks
145 W Broad St
Spartanburg, SC 29306
864- 596-2026
cityofspartanburg.org

Lake Conestee Nature Park
Greenville County Recreation
601 Fork Shoals Rd
Greenville, SC 29605
864- 277-2004
lakeconesteenaturepark.com

Paris Mountain State Park
2401 State Park Rd
Greenville, SC 29609
864- 244-5565
southcarolinaparks.com/
parismountain

Gateway Mountain Bike Park
Pleasant Ridge Park
Greenville County Parks
4806 Old Spartanburg Rd
Taylors, SC 29687
864- 288-6470
greenvillerec.com

The Western Upstate

Fant's Grove & Issaqueena Lake
Clemson University
Clemson Experimental Forest
Box 340334
Clemson, SC 29634
864- 656-4826
clemson.edu/cef

Oconee Passage
Sumter National Forest
Andrew Pickens Ranger District
112 Andrew Pickens Cir
Mountain Rest, SC 29664
fs.usda.gov/scnfs

Oconee State Park
624 State Park Rd
Mountain Rest, SC 29664
864- 638-5353
southcarolinaparks.com/oconee

About the Author

Since publishing his first mountain bike guide in1992, Jim Parham has written more than a dozen adventure guidebooks for hiking, backpacking, mountain biking and road biking in the Southeast, and drawn his signature trail maps for numerous guides by other authors. A native North Carolinian who grew up in north Georgia and lived for years in east Tennessee, he now resides on the North Carolina side of the Great Smoky Mountains.

Milestone Press

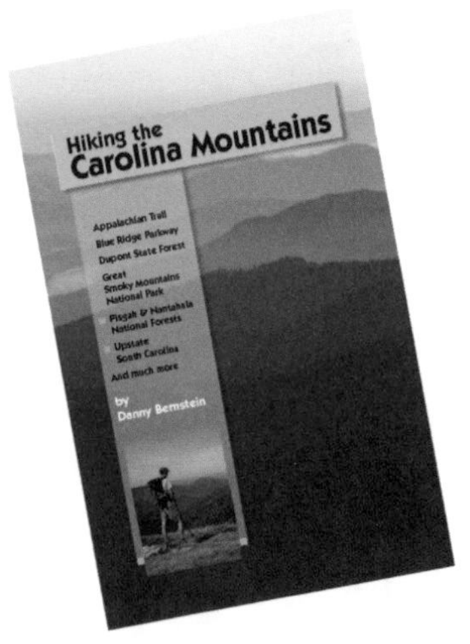

Hiking

- *Hiking the Carolina Mountains*
  by Danny Bernstein
- *Hiking North Carolina's Blue Ridge Mountains*
  by Danny Bernstein
- *Day Hiking the North Georgia Mountains*
  by Jim Parham
- *Waterfalls Hikes of Upstate South Carolina*
  by Thomas E. King
- *Waterfalls Hikes of North Georgia*
  by Jim Parham
- *Backpacking Overnights: NC Mountains • SC Upstate*
  by Jim Parham

Motorcycle Adventure Series

by Hawk Hagebak

- *1–Southern Appalachians: North GA, East TN, Western NC*
- *2–Southern Appalachians: Asheville NC, Blue Ridge Parkway, NC High Country*
- *3–Central Appalachians: Virginia's Blue Ridge, Shenandoah Valley, West Virginia Highlands*

Mountain Bike Guides

by Jim Parham

- *Mountain Bike Trails: NC Mountains • SC Upstate*
- *Mountain Bike Trails: North GA • Southeast TN*

Milestone Press

Road Bike Guide Series

- *Road Bike Asheville, NC: Favorite Rides of the Blue Ridge Bicycle Club*
  by The Blue Ridge Bicycle Club

- *Road Bike North Georgia: 25 Great Rides in the Mountains and Valleys of North Georgia*
  by Jim Parham

- *Road Bike the Smokies*
  by Jim Parham

Family Adventure

- *Natural Adventures in the Mountains of North Georgia*
  by Mary Ellen Hammond & Jim Parham

- *Family Hikes in Upstate South Carolina*
  by Scott Lynch

Pocket Guides

- *Hiking South Carolina's Foothills Trail*
  by Scott Lynch

- *Hiking & Mountain Biking DuPont State Forest*
  by Scott Lynch

- *Hiking & Mountain Biking Pisgah Forest*
  by Jim Parham

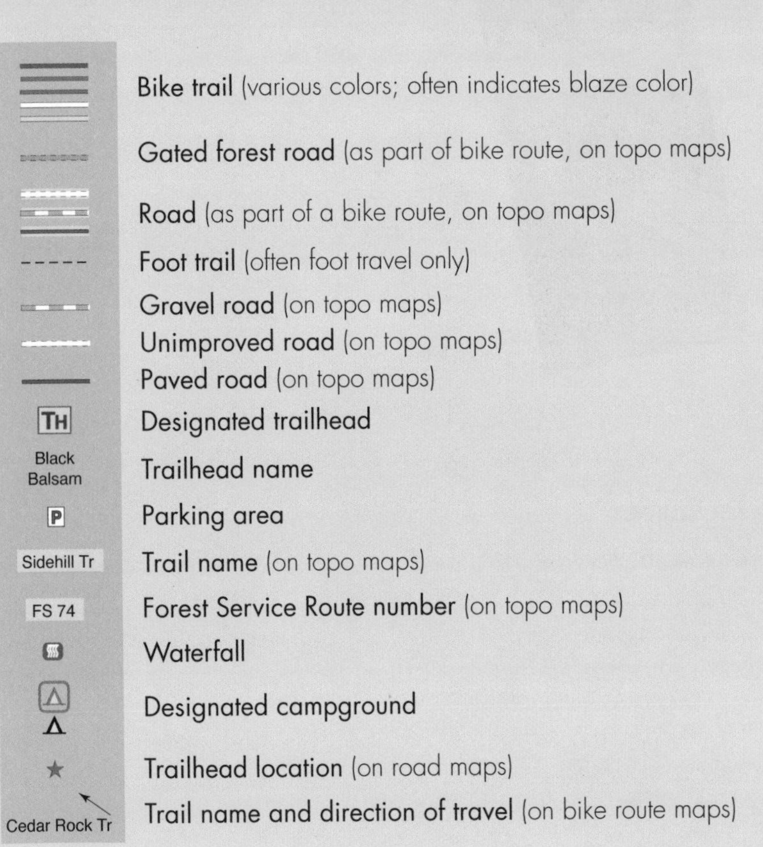
Maps Legend
Bike trail (various colors; often indicates blaze color)
Gated forest road (as part of bike route, on topo maps)
Road (as part of a bike route, on topo maps)
Foot trail (often foot travel only)
Gravel road (on topo maps)
Unimproved road (on topo maps)
Paved road (on topo maps)
TH
Designated trailhead
Black Balsam
Trailhead name
P
Parking area
Sidehill Tr
Trail name (on topo maps)
FS 74
Forest Service Route number (on topo maps)
Waterfall
Designated campground
Trailhead location (on road maps)
Cedar Rock Tr
Trail name and direction of travel (on bike route maps)